# OVERCOMING WORRY

*A self-help guide using
Cognitive Behavioral Techniques*

## KEVIN MEARES
### AND
## MARK FREESTON

D0101541

ROBINSON
London

Constable & Robinson Ltd
3 The Lanchesters
162 Fulham Palace Road
London W6 9ER
www.constablerobinson.com

First published in the UK by Robinson,
an imprint of Constable & Robinson Ltd 2008

**Important Note**

This book is not intended as a substitute for medical advice or treatment.
Any person with a condition requiring medical attention should consult
a qualified medical practitioner or suitable therapist.

ISBN 978-1-84529-636-0

Printed and bound in the EU

3 5 7 9 10 8 6 4 2

# Table of contents

# Acknowledgments

*Dedicated to the memory of Josée Charbonneau 1960–2007*

We owe an incalculable debt of gratitude to the individuals we encountered in our clinical work who suffered with excessive worry; their collective experience is the principal source for this book. As this is a self-help book we have limited the number of references to research but acknowledge that the information is based on the silent yet generous contribution of many. We would like to thank all of those who have contributed to the pool of knowledge from which we have drawn. With this in mind we would like to thank all those who contributed to the program of research at l'Université Laval, leading to the development of the model of Generalized Anxiety Disorder that forms the foundation for this book. We would especially like to thank Robert Ladouceur, Michel Dugas and Eliane Léger.

We thank all our colleagues at the Newcastle Cognitive and Behavioural Therapy Centre for their good humour, support and friendship, with special thanks to Dr Stephen Barton, for his generosity with both his time and his ideas particularly related to the chapter on the heart of worry and on goal-setting. Many thanks also to Dr Andrew Wilkinson, Dr Tracy Thorne, Dr Douglas Maisey, Jenny Shannon, Emma Thomas, Carol Thackery, and Dr Jen Lane for their helpful feedback on early drafts. Thanks to Peter Armstrong for many helpful discussions.

Thanks to Peter Cooper, Fritha Saunders, Hannah Boursnell and Elizabeth Stone for their expert guidance. Many thanks to Ricky, Debi and Ian at Ellipsis Books for their hard work and commitment. Thanks to Karen Lysakowska, Anita Allinson, Jo Thomas and Jon Chapman for their contributions. In addition, we thank the numerous supervisors, supervisees, trainees and students who have contributed along the way.

Finally we thank our families and friends for putting up with the absences, both physical and mental, the long hours, the late nights and the inevitable worry, both real and hypothetical.

# Preface

## Is this book for me?

There are an overwhelming number of self-help books about all sorts of problems, so the first point that needs to be addressed is whether this book will be of use to you. Here are some simple questions that may help you answer this:

**Have you always been a worrier?**
Yes ☐　No ☐

**If there is nothing to worry about, do you still find yourself worrying?**
Yes ☐　No ☐

**Do minor everyday things spiral into major concerns?**
Yes ☐　No ☐

**Once it starts, is your worry hard to stop?**
Yes ☐　No ☐

**Does worry stop you enjoying life?**
Yes ☐　No ☐

If the answer to at least two of these questions is yes, and if your worry is having a significant impact on how you function at work, at home or in social settings or is causing you distress, then this is probably the book for you.

## How can this book help me?

This book will help you to build your understanding of worry step by step. If we can help you to understand what leads you to worry and what keeps you worrying, then we are good step closer to helping you overcome it. With each step we will introduce new ideas that add to the picture of worry, and with these ideas you will find questionnaires, exercises and tasks to help you understand and then challenge unhelpful habits and beliefs that keep you worrying.

The 18 Chapters roughly divide into three parts. Chapters 1–3 set the scene: they introduce everyday and problem worry using some case stories, give some facts and figures about worry and offer advice about how best to use this book. Chapters 4–7 look at how cognitive-behavioural therapy can help us to understand worry and start the process of building up the picture of worry. They teach us to become aware of our worry in a new way, standing outside, rather than living within. With this new awareness, you will then learn to think about what you would like to achieve and set yourself realistic goals. Chapters 8–17 explain the areas you will need to focus on to overcome your worry, namely, learning to tolerate uncertainty (Chapters 8–10), learning about ideas that lead us to worry (Chapters 11–13), how to solve problems (Chapters 14–16) and how to face ideas or thoughts that we would much rather avoid (Chapter 17). Don't be concerned if these are unfamiliar – we take time to make sure that we explain each area thoroughly. Finally, we tie up the loose ends in Chapter 18.

We sincerely hope that you find this book useful. Good luck and do let us know how you get on (see page 446).

# Introduction

## Why a cognitive behavioral approach?

The approach this book takes in attempting to help you help you overcome your problems with worrying is a 'cognitive-behavioral' one. A brief account of the history of this form of intervention might be useful and encouraging. In the 1950s and 1960s a set of therapeutic techniques was developed, collectively termed 'behavior therapy'. These techniques shared two basic features. First, they aimed to remove symptoms (such as anxiety) by dealing with those symptoms themselves, rather than their deep-seated underlying historical causes (traditionally the focus of psychoanalysis, the approach developed by Sigmund Freud and his associates). Second, they were scientifically based, in the sense that they used techniques derived from what laboratory psychologists were finding out about the mechanisms of learning, and they put these techniques to scientific test. The area where behavior therapy initially proved to be of most value was in the treatment of anxiety disorders, especially specific phobias (such as extreme fear of animals or heights) and agoraphobia, both notoriously difficult to treat using conventional psychotherapies.

After an initial flush of enthusiasm, discontent with behavior therapy grew. There were a number of reasons for this. An important concern was the fact that behavior therapy did not deal with the internal thoughts which were so obviously central to the distress that many patients were experiencing. In particular, behavior therapy proved inadequate when it came to the treatment of depression. In the late 1960s and early 1970s a treatment for depression was developed called 'cognitive therapy'. The pioneer in this enterprise was an American psychiatrist, Professor Aaron T. Beck. He developed a theory of depression which emphasized the importance of people's depressed styles of thinking, and, on the basis of this theory, he specified a new form of therapy. It would not be an exaggeration to say that Beck's work has changed the nature of psychotherapy, not just for depression but for a range of psychological problems.

The techniques introduced by Beck have been merged with the techniques developed earlier by the behavior therapists to produce a therapeutic approach which has come to be known as 'cognitive behavioral therapy' (or CBT). This therapy has been subjected to the strictest scientific testing and has been found to be highly successful for a significant proportion of cases of depression. It has now become clear that specific patterns of disturbed thinking are associated with a wide range of psychological problems, not just depression, and that the treatments which deal with these are highly effective. So, effective cognitive behavioral treatments have been developed for a range of anxiety disorders, such as panic disorder, generalized anxiety disorder, specific phobias, social phobia, obsessive compulsive disorders, and hypochondriasis (health anxiety), as well as for other conditions such as drug addictions, and eating disorders like bulimia nervosa. Indeed, cognitive behavioral techniques have been found to have an application beyond the narrow categories of psychological disorders. They have been applied effectively, for example, to helping people with low self-esteem, those with weight problems, couples with marital difficulties, as well as those who wish to give up smoking or deal with drinking problems. In relation to the current self-help manual, over several years effective CBT techniques have been developed for helping people overcome their problems with distressing and disabling worrying.

The starting-point for CBT is the realization that the way we think, feel and behave are all intimately linked, and changing the way we think about ourselves, our experiences, and the world around us changes the way we feel and what we are able to do. So, for example, by helping a depressed person identify and challenge their automatic depressive thoughts, a route out of the cycle of depressive thoughts and feelings can be found. Similarly, habitual behavioral responses are driven by a complex set of thoughts and feelings, and CBT, as you will discover from this book, by providing a means for the behavior, thoughts and feelings to be brought under control, enables these responses to be undermined and a different kind of life to be possible.

Although effective CBT treatments have been developed for a wide range of disorders and problems, these treatments are not widely available; and, when people try on their own to help themselves, they often, inadvertently, do things which make matters worse. In recent years the community of cognitive behavioral therapists has responded to this situation. What they have done is to take the principles and techniques of specific cognitive behavioral therapies for particular problems and present them in manuals which people can read and apply themselves. These manuals specify a systematic program of treatment which the person works through to overcome their difficulties. In this way, cognitive behavioral therapeutic techniques of proven value are being made available on the widest possible basis.

The use of self-help manuals is never going to replace the need for therapists. Many people with emotional and behavioral problems will need the help of a qualified therapist. It is also the case that, despite the widespread success of cognitive behavioral therapy, some people will not respond to it and will need one of the other treatments available. Nevertheless, although research on the use of these self-help manuals is at an early stage, the work done to date indicates that for a great many people such a manual is sufficient for them to overcome their problems without professional help. Sadly, many people suffer on their own for years. Sometimes they feel reluctant to seek help without first making a serious effort to manage on their own. Sometimes they feel too awkward or even ashamed to ask for help. Sometimes appropriate help is not forthcoming despite their efforts to find it. For many of these people the cognitive behavioral self-help manual will provide a lifeline to a better future.

Peter J Cooper
The University of Reading, 2007

# The experience of worry

## What is worry?

Worry is often experienced as a chain of negative thoughts, images and doubts about things that might happen in the future. In essence, worriers tend to be concerned by what's 'around the corner' rather than what's here right now. So, for the most part, worry is not about things where the outcome is *certain*, it's about things where the outcome is *uncertain*. Worrying about one thing often tends to lead quickly and easily to worrying about something quite different. As a result, worriers can get caught up in a whirlwind of thoughts about bad things that *might* happen. These are often either highly unlikely or are about very distant possibilities, but, when caught up in a chain or spiral of worry, they seem very real.

Once people are caught in this whirlwind, they often feel as if they can't stop worrying. The worry seems uncontrollable, and attempts to stop or divert it may not appear effective or may even seem to make it worse. People often report feeling tense, nervous or panicky, or they describe feeling overwhelmed, helpless or paralysed with uncertainty. Worriers tend to have an overriding sense they cannot cope with the problems and situations the world throws at them. They may feel inferior, with low confidence and self-esteem. During the whirlwind, the predominant feeling is anxiety, but once the storm eases off, worriers often feel demoralized and exhausted.

People caught up in this whirlwind often show various other signs of anxiety. These signs or symptoms appear as a product of excessive worry. Those experienced most often are muscle tension, restlessness (being unable to relax), tiredness, irritability, difficulty in getting to sleep or staying asleep and difficulty in concentrating or focusing one's attention. As well as these main symptoms, other types of experiences can also develop, such as palpitations, butterflies, a knot in the stomach, digestive upset or headaches. Once these intense physical sensations appear they can trigger more worry and set up a vicious cycle by reminding the worrier about the very things they were trying to avoid thinking about.

The whirlwind can be so much part of the way we think that we may not even notice it is happening. It may also circulate at the back of our minds, coming into sharper focus every now and again. When this happens, the often repetitive and usually dreadful content of our worry can force us to try to submerge it deeper in our minds. So worry can be a vague, hazy experience punctuated by sharp, distressing thoughts that emerge from the fog of our minds, only for us to try to push them back again. By doing so, we may lose them for a moment; but, like a horrible presence, not knowing where or what it is feels much worse than knowing. This leads us to worry all the more. Just like a whirlwind, worry moves fast, and we can quickly get lost in its labyrinth. It can be a confusing experience where reality and worry merge. The speed of thought gives us the impression that our thoughts are chaotic and lack any pattern or order. This sense of chaos yet further adds to the idea that our thoughts are out of control, causing us to worry all the more.

To use another metaphor, worry is a little like the fun-fair game where a player has to hit with a mallet the heads of plastic puppets, usually rats or moles, which pop out of holes. Each time they hit one, another appears somewhere else on the board, and when they hit that one, another appears, and so it goes on and on. The 'game' is impossible to win: the rats and moles always win. If you have ever watched people play this game you may have noticed how frustrated and tense they become.

We tend to keep worry to ourselves, as a private experience – even close friends may be unaware of our worrying. Often we worry late at night or in the small hours of the morning, or at other times when we are 'alone with our thoughts'. This very personal experience has a profound impact on how we relate to others. For instance, our worry may motivate us to be over-protective: we may continually check on our loved ones, who may interpret this as intrusive or nagging. We may avoid situations or people that we know will set off worry. Sometimes worry drives us to seek reassurance from those around us, 'checking out' our fears with others in subtle or obvious ways. If we share our worries, it may only be because they are getting too much for us, and even then we may worry about burdening or bothering others. More usually, we worry about what people will think of us, concerned that others might see us as odd, weird, weak, stupid or even crazy.

Worriers also tend to focus on what may happen and so 'live' in the future. For example, while meeting friends their focus might be on whether they will be able to make time next week to meet up; or, at a football match, rather than enjoying the game, they think about whether they will be able to get their bus home. Living in this way has a profound effect on the capacity to simply live and enjoy life in the moment. Whatever the circumstances, their worry transports them away to a tense, often bleak and anxiety-provoking future.

Again, worry can be likened to a mirage in the desert. Classically, in the 'comic book' image, a man is crawling across the desert in search of water when he observes what appears to be an oasis close by. Convinced that what he is seeing is real, he believes that salvation is at hand. He may start to feel euphoric, and even more thirsty at the thought of water. He may, for a moment, suspect that what he is seeing can't be true, but because his life depends on it he pushes this idea away. Thinking that the oasis is within reach, he runs and throws himself into the water. Alas, the oasis is hundreds of miles away; the mirage disappears and all he grasps is sand.

So what are the parallels to worry? Both mirages and worry are real: mirages are not imaginary, they're actually there – we can photograph them, but they're distorted and 'bend' reality. In the same way, when worry develops it is distorted and takes on the *illusion of being true*. Our worries seem *very real* and *convincing*. Even if we doubt them to some extent, they twist and turn around important personal issues such as the loss or death of a loved one, or what is important to you, or a sense of inadequacy. Like the thirsty survivor who starts to run on seeing a mirage of an oasis, worriers have a tendency to believe their worries and then act on them. For example, José (who appears in the case stories below) worried about how his children would manage his new relationship after his divorce. His worry seemed so convincing that he felt sure they would not cope and would end up rejecting him. He tried to win his children's affection by buying them gifts, even though he had no evidence that they thought badly of him. Like the mirage, his worries seemed real and they loomed menacingly over his future relationship with his children. This motivated him to try to stop them coming true, but his actions were based not on facts but on worries, for which he had no evidence to support.

Once the worry has passed, the worrier is often left feeling exhausted and demoralized. Having braved and fought the experience, we then take stock. Often it is only then that we start to feel tired and drained, and only then do we reflect on how the whirlwind has impacted on our lives. This exhaustion is both emotional and physical. The brain uses up about 20 per cent of the body's total energy supply, so if you're wondering why worrying is so exhausting then reflect on this: during a bout of worry you burn more energy than usual, since mental activity demands energy too. Imagine you are running within a giant hamster wheel for all the time you spend worrying – how exhausting would that be? The sense of demoralization is also influenced by our thinking about worry. Worriers often 'beat themselves up' mentally after the whirlwind has passed; or, if their worry has got in the way of solving a problem or stopped them from doing something important, this can leave them feeling useless and down.

## Understanding worry – a traffic metaphor

One of the important steps towards overcoming worry is getting a better understanding of what worry is and how it sticks around as a problem. When teaching health professionals about worry, we have found that thinking of worry as a stream of traffic is helpful. We will refer to this traffic metaphor throughout the book.

Learning to manage worry is like trying to manage the flow of traffic at rush hour. Imagine that you have been asked to solve the traffic problems of a major city. How would you go about doing this? Would you head out at each rush hour to direct the traffic? Would you focus your attention on each car or driver and ask them to do things differently? Would you try to understand the things that cause traffic congestion or that make congestion worse? Would you try to introduce new laws or rules to help people behave differently? You may want to start by getting a good idea of what the problem is, so it would make sense to monitor the traffic and understand when, where and what causes the major problems. You could also find out whether particular problems were caused by particular types of vehicles.

As we have said, worry is a chain of thoughts or images that quickly spirals out of control. Trying to stop the flow of worry and to pick on an individual worry is difficult, because once you have worked one worry through another appears hard on its tail. Imagine trying to solve traffic problems by stopping each car and talking over the problem with each driver. What might happen? Would it solve the problem or would it actually make the problem worse? Given that there are thousands of cars, buses and trucks, it is doubtful that this strategy would work.

To understand and improve traffic flow, it appears we have to begin to recognize that we cannot do this by focusing our attention on each car, bus or truck. Instead, we have to think about what influences the flow of traffic, such as types of vehicles (buses or cars), drivers' strongly held beliefs (e.g. that driving is much less hassle than public transport) and other factors such as the school run, the influence of 9–5 working hours, the weather, road works, holidays and so forth. By doing this we can begin to understand the ebb and flow of traffic. The crucial message is that we cannot solve traffic problems by focusing our attention on each car. This is also true of worry. Like traffic flow, in order to overcome worry we must attend to the flow of worry and the factors that influence this, rather than focusing on each individual worry (each individual car).

## Influences on traffic flow

**Living with uncertainty.** Uncertainty is an inherant element in travelling, including unforeseen delays, breakdowns, accidents, slow moving traffic, punctures, debris on the road and so forth. When the flow of traffic is very heavy or if conditions are bad, as in heavy rain, these other factors act together to increase the level of uncertainty, making journey times even more unpredictable. Living with the uncertainty that driving creates is something we have to learn to tolerate in our modern world if we are to get to our destinations without blowing a gasket. Despite having satellite navigation and radio broadcasts telling us where the traffic problems are, we are still in the lap of the gods when driving from A to B. The bottom line is that we have to learn to learn to tolerate the uncertainty.

**Driving rules.** Other factors that influence traffic flow are the general rules that govern driver's actions. For example, *If I keep up with the flow of traffic I am less likely to have an accident*; this idea might mean that drivers keep up with the flow of traffic, even when conditions are such that they'd be safer slowing down. *I should never be late*; this idea might result in drivers trying to make up time by speeding when they have been delayed by road works. You may believe that *no one should get by me* or that *no one should cut in front of me*; this belief might make you an irritable driver. General rules seem to influence the flow of traffic just as much as weather or road works. So, to manage traffic problems we would need to work out which rules were problematic and try to change them.

**Types of vehicle:** in trying to manage traffic, it also helps to think about the vehicle categories. Each type of vehicle may require different traffic management solutions – the introduction of bus lanes, lower speeds for trucks or crawler lanes on long slow hills, for example.

**Unhelpful attitudes to traffic problems and avoidance:** finally, when trying to approach the problem of traffic management we may be resigned to the idea that traffic problems will never be solved; we may be pessimistic about any solution and intimidated by the size of the problem. This unhelpful stance towards the problem of managing traffic might leave us feeling frustrated or depressed, meaning that we avoid trying to do something about the problem. We might simply *avoid thinking about it* or avoid things that remind us that there is a problem: we may just *bury our head in the sand*.

## So how does this help us understand worry?

**The nature of worry:** first, just as with traffic flow, in order to overcome worry we must attend to the flow of worry and the factors that influence this rather than focusing on each individual worry. Traffic jams and congestion call for our attention, but to solve them we must concentrate our efforts elsewhere, rather than focusing solely on the traffic itself. In worry this is also true: some of the products of worry might seem to be the things to focus on – for instance, irritability, sleep problems, concentration problems and more – but our attention should be on the things that influence and 'tell' us to worry.

Worries, like traffic problems, do not just appear from nowhere, although they often feel like they do. To overcome your worry you need to be more aware of when and how your worry develops into a whirlwind of worry.

If traffic is blocked on one lane, it finds another way of moving, by changing lanes, using rat runs and short cuts, which also tend to suffer from more and more traffic. Often these rat runs develop on roads that are completely unsuitable, or take us miles out of our way. So, like traffic, worry also has a tendency to spread, change topic and shift transporting us away from the idea or problem that triggered it in the first place. You will learn to understand more about what triggers your worry and how it develops in Chapters 4 and 5.

**Living with uncertainty.** There is inherent uncertainty in driving that we have to learn to cope with. Many worriers find uncertain situations intolerable and tend to avoid uncertainty if they can. They often have a series of ideas that suggest to them that uncertainty is a stressful and hazardous experience and should be avoided if possible. We end up deploying worry as a strategy for dealing with all of life's uncertainties, even when worry might be an unsuitable solution to the problems or events we face. In order to overcome your worry you will have to learn to deal more effectively with uncertain situations, by finding other things to do instead of worrying. We will turn to the issue of uncertainty in Chapters 8–10.

**Worry rules.** Just as there are rules and assumptions that influence drivers and thus the flow of traffic, worriers often have particular rules and ideas that influence their tendency to worry. For example, *If I worry about my family, then it shows I care*, or, *If I worry I will be able to spot problems before they happen*. These rules or beliefs support and maintain your worry, and in order to overcome this you will need to experiment with breaking these rules. We will turn our attention to these rules and assumptions in Chapters 11–13.

In trying to fix traffic problems we may frequently do things that seem to improve the situation in the short term, but tend to make the problem worse in the longer term: for example, road widening works for a while, but when the number of cars increases the advantage is lost. Or, if you take a shortcut to avoid a busy junction, you may be caught in a jam along with all the other drivers who did exactly the same. With worry, we often try to manage our worry using sensible strategies. Unfortunately, these have a tendency to backfire and make the worry worse. So we have to help you to recognize how you manage your worry and then ask if this is one of those things that make it worse. We have outlined these unhelpful strategies throughout the book.

**Different types of worry:** just as different types of vehicle, these require different management strategies. In general, there are two categories of worry to consider, worries about events that have happened (*Real Event Worry*) and worries about things that have not happened yet (*Hypothetical Event Worry*). Again, this reminds us that to overcome our worry we must become much more curious about what types of worry make up the flow. Are we worrying about real events that have happened, or about things in the future that have not happened yet? We will return to this distinction later, when we turn our attention to recognizing the types of worry in Chapter 5, but just keep this in mind for now.

**Unhelpful attitudes to problems and avoidance:** in order to begin to solve the problem of traffic flow, we have to engage with the problem. Worriers tend to have an unhelpful attitude towards problems. Typically, they see problems as threatening; they doubt their ability to cope with them and, even if they do try to engage in problem-solving, they are pessimistic about the outcome. So in order for us to help you overcome worry, you will need to adjust your view of problems and remind yourself that you have the capacity to solve them successfully. You will learn more about problem-solving in Chapters 14–16.

Worriers tend to avoid situations that might trigger worry or try to block the worry out of their minds. Like many other things, if worry is not dealt with it will keep coming back, since unfinished business has a tendency to keep popping up into our minds. We will turn our attention to facing your fears in Chapter 17.

**Measuring change:** we need to monitor what happens when we try to change things. Throughout this book there are questionnaires and ideas to help you do just this.

**Summary:** ultimately, to solve the problem of traffic flow, we will need to reduce the number of vehicles using a particular lane or road. So the problem needs to be solved in a different way rather than by using short-term strategies. It is the same with worry: we need to stop the worries 'getting on the road' by finding new and better ways of working with them.

## Stories of worry

The following stories describe how excessive worry can impact on people's lives. They illustrate the way worriers tend to think, some of the consequences of their worry, and some underlying themes. It might be worth making some notes and asking yourself some of the following questions as you go through them; Exercise 1.1 may help you do this (see page 16–17).

- Is there an aspect of this person's story that reminds me of myself? If so, what is it?
- Which story feels closest to home and why?
- What has been going through my mind as I read these accounts?
- What links these stories together?

These stories are based on the worriers we have worked with in our careers. They are not modelled on any one person but have been put together to describe the typical patterns we see in our clinics.

### ALISON

Alison is in her late forties. Her three children are still living at home. She feels tense the whole time and worries about her blood pressure. She loves her job, but finds it very stressful and from time to time too much to cope with. She has recently been promoted to a senior administrative role, and heads up a small but talented team. She finds it hard to delegate and does too much of the work herself. It's not that she doubts the quality of her colleagues' work but she knows that *even good people can make mistakes.* She checks her own work repeatedly and never sends an email without reading it several times. She worries especially on a Friday night and will often drop in to work at the weekend to check things over.

Recently she wanted to buy a new digital camera to take pictures at her son's 21st birthday, but she couldn't decide which one to choose. She visited nearly every shop and got conflicting advice. She worried: *What if I make a bad decision? If I do, I may not understand the instructions, and if I take the photos I could annoy everyone by being intrusive.* Her worries went on and on. Paralysed by them, in the end she gave up on buying the camera. She regretted this and felt ashamed that her worry had got the better of her. She always phones her husband to check he is on his way home, and worries if her husband or children are late. Often she builds horror stories in her mind as her worries take hold. She is a lovely woman and is loved by her family and friends; but they get annoyed with her because she's very protective of them and she often needs reassuring that they are OK. When she gets worn out with worry her concern turns out the wrong way; her kids feel she is intrusive, her husband feels he is alternately nagged and asked to be a rock of security.

## JOSÉ

José is a divorcee with two children, aged 10 and 12. He has a new relationship with a younger woman called Jane, who wants to have a family with him. His job is secure, but he gets very tense and agitated when he hears rumours about how things might change. Since his divorce he has lost confidence and worries about his ability to cope with his busy job, his children and his new relationship. Jane is great with his kids, but he is concerned that she will leave him in the same way his wife did. He feels tense and notices that he is snappy with the kids. He finds himself daydreaming about his future, when all he can see is catastrophe after catastrophe: *What if the kids don't manage the divorce? They may start to fail at school, and then they'll start to take drugs; they'll wind up in jail; they'll hate me and never want to speak to me again. And then Jane will leave me and I'll lose my job* . . . His worries whirl on and on and leave him anxious and upset. Although José knows that these are 'just' worries, he sometimes feels they are real, which makes him anxious that he is losing his mind. He is confused because he thinks if he didn't worry about his children he'd be a poor father. He knows he is starting to spoil his children by giving them too much, but he can't help himself. He never used to worry; before the divorce his life was planned out and he knew where he was going. His divorce really unsettled him, and at the moment he doesn't think he can really rely on anything. He hates his life being so uncertain.

## ALEX

Alex is 23. He's full of nervous energy and rarely sits still for long. He makes impulsive decisions that sometimes work out for him but usually end up badly. As a consequence, he has debt problems: he bought warranties he didn't need, and he is locked into an expensive mobile phone contract. When faced with a decision, he would rather act than live with the overwhelming sense of uncertainty. He is good at his job. He is never late for work, but all the way there he thinks about what will happen if he is late: *What if I'm late? I'll miss that meeting and lose my job.* His anxiety triggers more worries and he starts to worry that he will miss his stop. He listens to music on his MP3 player, but pulls the headphones off to make sure he hasn't missed anything. He checks his ticket for the number of the bus, even though he knows he's on the right one. By the time he gets to work he's exhausted. His worry follows him throughout the day, into the office, into meetings, into telephone conversations, at lunchtime and breaktime. He has avoided promotion at work because he doesn't think he could cope with the new challenges this would bring. He recently started to worry more about terrorist attacks and put off going on holiday with his friends, not sure if he'd be safe at the airport. Nor did he think he could cope with being severely injured or burnt. He hates himself for worrying so much, but also thinks that his worry helps him to spot dangers, keeps him safe and solves problems.

## MAYA

Maya is 15 and lives at home with her mum and younger brother. She is bright and could do well at school but worries about her work and about fitting in. She describes herself as a perfectionist and works really hard to make sure that her worries don't come true. She's makes a great friend and helps others when she can. She tells her friends about her worries, but, at the same time, fears that her friends won't want to know her if she keeps bothering them. She feels confused and alone. Worrying helps her to plan and prepare for exams; she says it keeps her motivated. However, worrying also makes her much less efficient because she worries much more than she actually works, though her friends say she spends too much time working. She doesn't want to stand out and so she never goes out without texting her friends, to make sure she is wearing the 'right' clothes. When she is out, she worries about lots of things, including whether she is in the right place to meet her friends, about her studies, about what her friends might think of her and about finding her way home. All these worries make it impossible for her to enjoy being with her friends.

PAUL

Paul recently turned 60 and retired from work. He was a successful engineer and is in a supportive, solid marriage. He planned wisely for his retirement and has sound invest- ments and a good pension. Despite being financially secure, he worries about whether he has chosen the best invest- ments and has recently taken to continually comparing his investments with others on the Internet. His children are grown up and he has several grandchildren; some he sees regularly, the others live too far away. He is fit and well but since his retirement his mind has started to focus on his health. He has also been thinking more about his family and how he should make more effort to hold them together. At night he spends hours worrying about them, his health, his financial situation and about being a burden to his children. He recently took out more insurance to cover the gaps that his other insurance policies didn't cover. He worries about whether his kids will look after one another, and about the health of his grandchildren. Although his children are in good relationships, he has doubts about how long their rela- tionships will last. His worries go round like a carousel, one after the other, and lead him to some very dark places; to him they seem out of his control and he drinks in order to sleep. He keeps his worries to himself, because he fears burdening his wife for fear of making her ill.

## Getting better

We know from research that roughly two-thirds of worriers get much better when they follow the treatment programs that use the type of approach found in this book; the other third will also get some form of relief. Furthermore, the gains made can be long lasting and, with careful follow-up plans, worry can become a thing of the past rather than a current problem. While we recognize that one-to-one therapy is different from a self-help approach, in our experience as therapists nearly all the people we see report some benefit from taking a closer look at the things that start them worrying and keep them worrying. So keep this mind. Is this something that you would want to have a go at? The book will draw your attention to worry, which may feel uncomfortable, but by understanding worry you will be better placed to overcome it.

Exercise 1.1 is the first step in bringing your mind to think about your worry. As you read the stories above you may have recognized aspects of the stories that hit home for you. Table 1.1 will help you to think about this further and about what life might be like if you worried less.

## EXERCISE 1.1: REFLECTIONS

Use a notebook to write down your answers to these questions.

My reflections on the case stories

Which story feels closest to home? Why is this? Which aspects of the stories remind you of your own experiences?

Do these stories tell you anything about your worry? If so, what?

What has been going through your mind as you read these stories?

Are there things that tie these case stories together? What themes or commonalities stand out for you?

Thinking about what you have written so far, do you have any ideas about what might you want to try to change?

If you did change the things mentioned in the question above, what difference would that make to your life? Is that something you want to invest time in?

If worry was less of a problem for me then . . .

It would mean . . .

I could . . .

I would be able to . . .

I might be able to . . .

I want to . . .

We asked a number of non-therapists to read these stories and give us feedback on what they thought tied them together. We thought you might like to see their responses. They appear more or less as they were given to us, edited only to make them clearer. Responses that seemed to us particularly important are in italic. Do these responses add to your understanding? What have they picked up on? Do any of the features feel like something close to home? You may want to revisit your own responses and add to them. Have your goals changed as a result?

---

**TABLE 1.1 RESPONSES TO THE CASE STORIES**

**Response 1:**

All want to be in control, but can't quite manage it.

Low personal confidence.

Their focus seems to be on what they can't control rather than what they can.

No direction for the future (no positive goal to aim for).

Personal insecurity (not having the courage of their convictions).

Social expectations - how to meet them? (Alex was a salesman's dream, Paul and Alison had to provide for extended family, Maya wants to be perfect, etc.).

Obsession.

Expanding range of worries (i.e. one building on top on another).

Rather than addressing the root concern, focusing on ways to manage (e.g. drinks in order to sleep, looking for issues that don't exist).

None is happy or content.

Loss: they each stand to lose (family, friends, job) if their worry comes true.

**Response 2:**

Worries /concerns about decisions seem to be the manifestation of the problem (whether it be investments, what to wear, what to buy, or what bus they're on . . .).

So, probably associated with a lack of confidence in their own decisions, and maybe even low self-esteem or the belief that they are not valued.

That nothing will ever be OK, no matter what one does.

Sometime this is associated with major changes (e.g. José's divorce, Paul's retirement), sometimes just with the stresses of everyday life (Maya, Alison, José).

So much is triggered by major or minor life changes (or the fear of them), which shows that life is not stable or predictable. Their response to this is to try to cover all possibilities to ensure nothing bad happens, which no one can ever do.

Trying to control outcomes to minimize risk (e.g. crosschecking everything, not sharing responsibility with others).

All rob the individual of the ability to live in the moment even if something is not going wrong at the time; their worries are about what might be.

They all start out as good or reasonable values (e.g. Paul's care and responsibility for the family, Alison's care of friends, family and high standards at work, Maya's 'motivation' to do well, José's concern for his children, his wanting to do his job well) but they end up being motivated by fear, not positive outcomes, and their worries become generalized and spiral out of control.

| Response 3: | Response 4: |
|---|---|
| Seeking reassurance. | Uncontrollable nature of worry. |
| Extremely high personal standards. | Worry is event-related and its content is related to experience and future-orientated. |
| Difficulty in making decisions. | |
| | There are positive and negative aspects of worry. |
| Looking for info from lots of sources. | Individuals' perceptions of worry and how this feeds worry. |
| Critical of self for being like this. | |

Low expectations of others.

Chain of thoughts leading to catastrophizing.

Something about uncertainty.

*Living in the future not in the here and now.*

Chained reasoning *what ifs*.

Dislike of vagueness.

Feels a burden.

**Response 5:**

Their worries prevent them from living and enjoying their lives.

Most of the worries are very unlikely.

The *what ifs* have the potential to become self-fulfilling prophecies

## The silent burden of worry

As can be seen from the above, worry can have extensive and often devastating effects on people's lives. Worry is a burden. It is like living each day as if carrying the weight of one's own world on our shoulders. Worry saps our energy and leaves us feeling tense. It interferes with our lives: we have to plan for it, we give in to it, we accommodate it, and it pushes us to avoid situations where we know it will get worse. For some, it stops career plans, it interferes with relationships, and life goals are suspended as a consequence. Often we are so used to carrying the burden of worry that we forget how much it is impacting on our lives – it has become a damaging habit that we no longer even notice.

A critical step in overcoming our worry is to begin to be more aware of how far worry may be impacting on our lives.

## Pit stops

Throughout this book you will find pit stops. These are to encourage you to get into the habit of stopping and reviewing what you have read. Do this as often as you need to. The pit stops will prompt you, but if you are confused, then stop and think about what you understand and what you don't understand. Write it down and return to it once you have read further. In order to get things clear in your mind, take your time and reread passages if necessary.

Here is an example for you to look at:

---

### PIT STOP

Let's stop and think about what you have just been reading. Can you summarize the key ideas you have taken on board? What is sticking in your mind? Maybe write them down. If you have any questions, jot these down too. You can return to them once you have had a chance to digest the information.

What is sticking in my mind from my reading so far?

1.

2.

3.

## 2

# Using this book

## How can I be sure the advice given is good?

The National Institute for Health and Clinical Excellence (NICE) is an independent organization responsible for providing national guidance on the promotion of good health and the prevention and treatment of ill health in the UK. In 2004 NICE published their guidance on anxiety, and recommended that high levels of worry, or Generalized Anxiety Disorder (GAD), its medical name, should be treated by using a psychological therapy called cognitive behavioral therapy (CBT). You will find more information about CBT in Chapter 4. NICE also recommended using self-help approaches based on CBT principles; this self-help book on worry is based on CBT principles. The way that worry is described in this book, and the ideas the book suggests to help you overcome it are also based on up to date research and the best psychological understanding of GAD or worry. *Overcoming Worry* is the product of several different groups of researchers from around the world who have worked on worry, some of them for nearly thirty years.

Worry is very common among the general population and so not everyone who worries will have all of the symptoms of GAD (you will find more about the diagnosis of GAD and facts about worry in Chapter 3). This book aims to help both people who suffer from this clinical disorder and those who feel that they are worrying more than they would like to.

## How to use this book

1. Getting this book is a good first step to overcoming your worry. However, reading and then applying the ideas it contains are crucial. This may well sound obvious, but from our personal experience it is very easy to feel as if we are *doing* something about our problems by *thinking* about them. So the first piece of advice is this: once you have a copy, make sure you read this book and then follow the advice it contains.

   Reflecting and thinking is, of course, an important phase of new learning; but, as David A. Kolb, a professor at Case Western Reserve University in Ohio, has suggested, this is only one aspect of learning. Professor Kolb developed the Kolbian learning cycle.

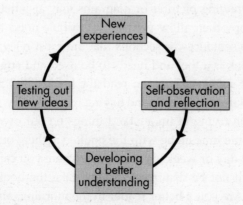

Figure 2.1. Kolbian learning cycle

He believed that in order to learn we should go through four types of experience. These include engaging in new experiences, learning to observe our own experience, creating ideas to explain what we are seeing, and finally testing out these ideas by making new decisions or solving problems, leading back to new experiences, and so on. This book will help you with each of these stages; to engage in new experiences to overcome your worry; to learn to be curious about your worry and observe it; to develop a better understanding of your worry; and to do things differently to overcome your worry. The crucial step is putting new ideas into practice, doing things differently and reacting in new ways to your worry.

2. Don't try to read this book all at once – pick a chapter or a few pages and focus on these. If you are worrying a lot this often makes concentration very difficult. If your worry makes you hop from one thought or subject to the next, then having a small goal is better than trying to read a whole chapter at once. You may find it helpful to ask yourself, *What was I doing* (e.g. reading) *before I started to worry?* And then return to doing it.

3. Make notes: have a pen and a notebook with you as you read. Drawing pictures or diagrams may also help. If this is your copy then allow yourself to scribble notes and underline the sentences or sections that are most relevant to you. This book is a tool and needs to be used and engaged with.

4. Is there someone you can read the book with? Some of us find talking about ideas and having conversations more effective than trying to understand things on our own.

5. Plan some time alone with the book. Are there quieter times in your day or week? Is there somewhere you can go where you will not be disturbed? Maybe take the book out for a coffee! Are you a better reader in the morning, afternoon, or evening?

6. Is now the best time for you to try to overcome your worry? If there are difficult life events such as births, marriages, new jobs, promotions, or moving house, then it might be better to wait until you have some stability in your life before attempting change. However, our lives are full of challenges and big events, and waiting for a quiet moment may be ill-advised, so be aware of the tendency to avoid facing your problems. Ask yourself these questions: *Am I putting off starting because I am worried about the outcome? Am I putting 'imaginary problems or issues' in the way of trying something new?* What would you advise a friend to do, if they were considering trying to overcome their worry now?

7. Write down the advantages and disadvantages of overcoming your worry. When you consider what you have written, where does the balance lie?

## Can I use this book if I am taking medication?

GPs often prescribe medication to help with anxiety and worry. Many people we meet in our clinical work have taken or are currently taking medication to help with their psychological problems. We would generally offer them psychological treatment even when they are on a prescribed medication, and the effect of this drug is taken into consideration when developing the treatment plan. So, in short, you can still use this book even if you're taking medication. If you're concerned, then have a conversation with your GP or other health professional; it might be helpful to take this book with you to show them. Together you can decide on what is the best course of action.

If you are already on medication, then it's probably better to continue with it and work on your worry until it starts to improve. Once this has happened, then might be the time to visit your family doctor to review your medication. On the other hand, if you have just started taking medication, this may not be the best time to begin working on your worry. Stability is the link here; it is better to hold one thing constant while you change the other than to try changing everything at once. Or, put another way, it is best not to widen the roads, put in traffic lights, start a bus lane, introduce congestion-charging and a new one-way system all at the same time. One step at a time, one problem at a time.

You may also want to visit the website of the National Institute for Health and Clinical Excellence (NICE), where you will find more information about GAD and drug treatments (see also Appendix 5).

If you are really not coping, please visit your doctor.

## Your approach to this book

This book is about learning to do things in a different way. When we are learning new skills or tasks, it is not unusual to feel unsettled or nervous. Anxiety or nervousness can close down our mind by drawing our attention to worrisome thoughts, which in turn makes learning much harder. So, *keeping your mind open to new ideas is important*. As Sir James Dewar, a Scottish chemist and physicist said, 'Minds are like parachutes, they work best when open'. Keeping your mind open means being prepared to listen to new ideas or trying new skills even if they make you feel anxious. Another way of keeping your mind open is to become more aware of your worry and to pay attention to it rather than just being 'in' it; this is like stepping out of traffic flow and sitting on a bridge to observe. Self-observation, as Kolb's learning cycle suggests, enables the development of new perspectives, which in turn will help you to understand your worry and overcome it. In following this book you will become better at self-observation and consequently become more aware of your worry. We will help you develop a better understanding of worry and will then suggest exercises, ideas and practical advice for overcoming worry.

This book does not offer a miraculous cure. Remember – worry is normal and we all worry from time to time. So trying to rid your life of a normal, everyday mental activity is impossible. What we can try to do, however, is 'turn down the worry dial', so that you worry less. This book is about helping you deal with your worry in an effective way. As a rule of thumb, the more you apply yourself to the ideas found in this book, the more you will get out of it. The journey you are about to embark on will require hard work, but if you apply yourself then the least that will happen is that you will understand more about worry, and at best you may learn to worry less. Is this something you would value?

## The approach of this book

CBT provides the framework and foundation for this book. It is a form of psychotherapy that was developed as a treatment for depression by Professor Aaron T. Beck while working at the University of Pennsylvania in the early 1960s. Over the next decade Beck's ideas revolutionized the way we thought about and treated depression. In the following thirty years, CBT came to be the most dominant and widespread way of understanding psychological and emotional distress. Since Beck's innovation, academic and clinical research have continued to improve and to develop cognitive behavioral treatments. CBT is now offered as a successful and evidence-based treatment for a variety of psychological problems including worry, panic attacks, shyness, obsessive problems and post-traumatic stress. You may wish to explore the other titles that are published in this series to get a sense of the kind of problems that CBT can help with: please see page ii or visit www.overcoming.co.uk.

## Pinning our colours to the mast

*Well, we all would worry about that, so what's the problem?*
*He's just a worrier – he's always like that, ignore him.*

Does this sound familiar? Worry is normal. We all worry. But we believe that excessive worry should not be accepted as a normal response to all life events, nor should it be accepted as part of someone's personality. Excessive worry is not something that just happens. We can understand it and we can outline the factors that start us worrying and those that keep us worrying. For individuals who suffer with excessive worry these processes have usually become automatic. So, in order to modify the normal way of reacting (i.e. worrying), individuals need to be willing to try out new things, to learn to focus their attention on what keeps worry alive, to reflect on the experience of worrying and then, once they understand how it works, adopt a new way of reacting: then to *practise* these processes over and over until new more helpful patterns are firmly established.

## The consequences of worrying less

In our clinical work we find that some people, when they start to get better and their worry becomes less of a problem, begin to look back on their lives and feel sad for the time they have lost through worrying. It's almost as if they are grieving for a life that could have been, a life without worry. Worry has such a pervasive and eroding affect that, once it is less of a problem, we see more clearly how our lives have been affected. This phase will pass as you learn to accept your past and embrace your future. This is something to bear in mind particularly if you have worried and tended to avoid change; it is not a sign of things getting worse, but a natural consequence of moving on.

## PIT STOP

Let's stop and think about what you have just been reading. Can you summarize the key ideas you have taken on board? What is sticking in your mind? Maybe write them down. If you have any questions, jot these down too. You can return to them once you have had a chance to digest the information.

What is sticking in my mind from my reading so far?

1.

2.

3.

# 3

# Everyday and problem worry – introducing Generalized Anxiety Disorder

## Worry is a normal process

All of us worry. Worry is a normal process. Research suggests that whether you worry a lot or a little we all worry more or less about the same kinds of things. From time to time we may worry about our families, relationships, our working or school lives, health or finances. For people who worry excessively though, the problem is not so much what things they worry about – these are common to us all – but more the ease with which they fall into worrying. There are some subtle differences between people who worry excessively and others. For example, people who worry excessively worry much more about minor things – missing the bus, car repairs, forgetting groceries, buying the right sandwich for their colleagues – and these minor experiences can quickly telescope into major worries of disastrous proportions. A Swedish proverb captures well this idea: it tells us that 'worry gives small things a big shadow'. Worriers also tend to worry more about remote or unlikely events: for example, a father worrying about how he would cope with his grandchildren, even though his own children were still in nappies; or a woman worrying about the possibility of rain ruining her daughter's wedding even though the wedding was still seven months away; or someone worrying about the possibility of a flight being cancelled, while sitting at home booking a summer holiday in January. Sometimes worriers can worry about the future with no specific threat in mind, just a sense of impending doom.

## 'Big occasion' worry

Chronic or habitual worriers need to learn to keep worry for the 'big occasion', when it can be of some use. With big events, worry may help to anticipate danger, solve problems, motivate to action, protect, or show caring. With these types of events, the downside of worrying – namely the high degree of preoccupation with it and the inability to turn it off, the muscle tension, the inability to sleep, the uncomfortable feelings of anxiety – may be an acceptable price. This type of worry means that we are engaged in trying to deal with a situation that really is there and can't be dealt with by ignoring it or running away. It normally means that something important to us is being threatened in some way. It may be possible to meet big occasion problems with calmness and detachment, but most people, even those who are not worriers, will worry in these situations. The muscle tension means that we are ready to act, the preoccupation means that we are engaged in thinking about the situation, and the disturbed sleep tells us that this is top priority stuff. We find concentrating on other tasks difficult: the big occasion worry demands our attention, and since we are in a state of alertness so we feel restless. Being on guard and ready for action means that we are prepared to act, but also means that we are overly alert and sensitive, which often translates into irritability.

The problem for worriers is that they use worry as a way of reacting to everyday life events as well as these big occasions. In these everyday incidents using worry can be thought of as using a sledgehammer to crack a nut. Worry is therefore a mismatch for events that are highly unlikely, or that are so far in the future that we can't do anything about them, or for things that are not really here right now or only just around the corner.

Most people will automatically worry when it really matters, but the worried mind is unfortunately hyperactive, unfocused, repetitive and undermining. To get the better of worry we have to learn to save it for the big occasions and not use it as a *one size fits all* approach to everything in life. The goal of over-coming worry is to get to this point where worry is no longer an omnipresent, costly and exhausting approach to life, but a state of mind that is active, focused, creative and commanding when the situation truly demands it. We want to enable you to apply worry in short bursts for the big occasions at the right time, rather than for long periods at the wrong time.

## Differences between excessive worry and everyday worry

In general, the difference between excessive and everyday worry is a matter of degree rather than outright difference. Unsurprisingly, chronic worriers tend to worry more often and for longer periods of time than people with everyday worry, and they tend to believe that their worry is more out of control. However, worry is a common, everyday experience, and from time to time each of us might feel we worry too much, or that worry has taken over. This suggests that everyday worry and excessive worry run on more or less on the same tracks. We can begin to think of worry as existing on a continuum or dimension, and whether you worry a little or a lot, the same underlying processes are at work. This idea is also a central principle of cognitive behavioral therapy or CBT, which suggests that psychological problems are exaggerated or extreme versions of everyday experiences. In Figure 3.1, worry is demonstrated on a worry gauge. This diagram illustrates that worry exists on a scale or dimension from 'no worry' to 'severe worry'. At times we all can experience the severe end of worry, and our worry gauges are constantly fluctuating in response to life events and how we think about them. For example, most people suffer a bout of severe worry (spiking into the 'red') before an important exam, job interview or tough meeting; they may also have a fitful night of sleep beforehand. In these cases, severe bouts of worry tend to appear before and during major life events. Those who suffer with excessive worry not only worry in response to these major events but also about minor events. Such minor events are usually much more frequent, and as a result their worry gauge is often in the 'red'. If they notice that their worry gauge is not in the red (i.e. that they are not worrying), further worry may also be triggered, yet again pushing their gauge up into the red. It is not surprising that worriers suffer with other signs of anxiety as well, such as restlessness, irritability, difficulty in sleeping, fatigue, muscle tension and concentration problems.

When worry tends to stray and stay in the red, and when worry feels more out of control and couples with other signs of anxiety, the individual may be given a diagnosis of Generalized Anxiety Disorder, or GAD for short; the symptoms of GAD are listed below (pages 35–7).

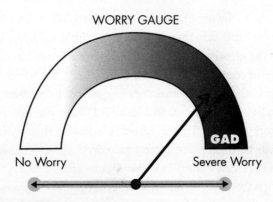

**Figure 3.1. Worry gauge**

- Where would you put your average worry on this gauge? Put a line there.
- Where would you like it to be (remembering that worry is normal)? Put a second line there.

Please remember that worry is normal and that this book will not eliminate worry completely. But it can help you to turn down the worry dial.

## The diagnosis of Generalized Anxiety Disorder (GAD)

Classifying a problem like worry with a psychiatric label (a diagnosis) can be considered either helpful or frankly unhelpful, depending on your viewpoint. There is much controversy and debate about the usefulness of diagnosis. However, in our clinical experience we have found that, for the most part, the people we have worked with have been relieved or found it helpful to find a label or name for their problem – often because their problem had been previously missed or, worse, dismissed. For the clinician, a diagnostic label may also be a guide to the right kind of treatment. On balance we think it's worthwhile spending time in helping you to understand what GAD is. In the shaded box below you will read an extract from the fourth edition of the *Diagnostic and Statistical Manual of Mental Disorders* (DSM-IV, 1994, APA). This is a handbook for mental health professionals: it lists different categories of psychological problems and the criteria for diagnosing them. The American Psychiatric Association published the latest version in 1994; it is updated as our understanding improves and as we get better at describing psychological problems more accurately.

In brief, and as we have stated above, the key features of GAD are excessive and uncontrollable worry about a number of different subjects, together with other symptoms of anxiety. Take a moment to read through the criteria. Which statements apply to you?

## DIAGNOSTIC CRITERIA FOR GENERALIZED ANXIETY DISORDER

- Excessive anxiety and worry (apprehensive expectation), occurring more days than not for at least six months, about a number of events of activities (such as work or school performance).
- The person finds it difficult to control the worry.
- The anxiety and worry are associated with at least three of the following six symptoms (with at least some symptoms present for more days than not for the past six months).
  - Restlessness or feeling keyed up or on edge
  - Being easily fatigued
  - Difficulty concentrating or mind going blank
  - Irritability

- Muscle tension
- Sleep disturbance (difficulty falling or staying asleep, or restless unsatisfying sleep).
- The focus of the anxiety and worry is not *confined* to another clinical problem like having a panic attack (as in panic disorder) or being embarrassed in public (as in social phobias) etc.
- The anxiety, worry, or physical symptoms cause clinically significant distress or impairment in social, occupational or other important areas of functioning.
- The disturbance is not due to the direct physiological effects of a substance (e.g. a drug of abuse, a medication) or general medical condition (e.g. hyperthyroidism) and does not occur exclusively during a bout of depression, for instance.

Source: reprinted with permission from the *Diagnostic and Statistical Manual of Mental Disorders*, 4th edn text revision (© 2000) American Psychiatric Association, 1994.

Of course, you may not have full-blown GAD, but you may still worry a lot. For example, research has shown that not everyone who suffers with excessive worry will have three out of the six required symptoms for the required time. In fact, research using questionnaire data and informal observations of people who attend for treatment suggests that a significant proportion of worriers can have the typical psychological profile (such as excessive worry and a belief that their worry is out of control) but do not suffer the associated physical symptoms. Some people tell us that they worry infrequently, say once a month, but when they do worry they do so severely, sometimes worrying for days at a time. Furthermore, the profile of worry can shift and change over time; so, one week or month a particular symptom such as sleeplessness is dominant, the next week or month another comes to the fore, such as irritability.

Of the associated symptoms found in chronic worriers, muscle tension seems to be more specific to GAD than any other and may be the best current unique predictor of excessive worry. However, muscular tension may not improve in everyone when worry decreases; so it's not a foolproof marker for everyone who worries. A wide range of other physical symptoms have been reported in worriers; these appear in the lists below. Although these are linked to GAD and can be common, they are not symptoms that contribute towards the diagnosis.

### Other common physical symptoms linked to GAD

- Upset stomach
- Headaches
- Dry mouth
- Peeing more often
- Being very jumpy
- Feeling shaky
- Nausea
- Diarrhoea
- Heart flutters
- Sweating
- Difficulty swallowing
- Tremor

### Other common experiences linked to GAD

- Feeling tuned out
- Unable to focus
- Nail biting
- Feeling isolated
- Feeling jittery
- Sense of impending doom
- Feeling alone
- Alcohol problems
- Pacing the floor

Although the formal diagnostic criteria are helpful, they are essentially a guide – many people with disabling and distressing experiences of worry fall outside the diagnostic framework.

**SUMMARY BOX**

**GAD** = **G**eneralized **A**nxiety **D**isorder

**GAD** = EXCESSIVE, UNCONTROLLABLE WORRY ABOUT SEVERAL SITUATIONS OR EVENTS

## Worry and other psychological problems

Anxiety problems tend to hunt in packs, and the vast majority of individuals with GAD will have at least one other coexistent psychological problem. 'Pure' GAD is therefore rare. Like salt, probably the most common ingredient in recipes, worry appears as the most common extra ingredient in other psychological problems. The most common problems that coexist with worry are depressive disorders, and about 70 per cent of people with GAD will report depressive problems at different times. Many people with GAD may also suffer from another anxiety problem such as social phobia, panic attacks or health anxiety.

## Other anxiety problems that coexist with GAD

There are three main types of coexistence. The first is where the GAD is the main or primary problem and the other anxiety problems are secondary. The second is the other way round, when GAD is secondary to other primary anxiety problems. The third is when it is hard to tell which problem is the primary or secondary problem and the problems appear as equals. It is worth bearing this in mind while reflecting on your difficulties, because knowing whether your worry is primary or secondary will help you to know which problems to work on first. We will explain this further below.

Let's take the first of these. For many people, mode severe GAD may be accompanied by other mild to moderate anxiety problems such as social phobia (fear of what others think of you) or specific phobias (fear of spiders, dogs, heights). These secondary problems are more likely to get better on their own during successful GAD treatment. So the simple message is this: if GAD is the main problem, then work on this and the other problems will, in all likelihood, disappear. However, for some worriers these secondary problems may require attention in their own right.

The second way that GAD coexists is as a secondary problem. In this case it makes sense to focus on the more problematic difficulty first. For example, in situations where someone is suffering with moderate to severe obsessive-compulsive disorder, post-traumatic stress disorder, panic, agoraphobia, or social phobia, with secondary GAD, we should treat these primary problems first. (There are self-help books written for each of these problems in the overcoming series.) It is worth mentioning that often, as these primary problems are treated, the person with GAD may feel that their worry problem is getting worse. However, this is a case of being able to see more of an object as the tide recedes; the object was always a certain size, but as you see more of it, it looks bigger. So, in these cases, worry *feels* as if it's getting worse but is not *actually* getting worse. Of course, once the first problem has been addressed then we would expect to turn our attention to the GAD.

The third coexistence pattern is when neither problem appears to be the main problem. In these cases, the problems have equal weight and we have to try to make a decision about which one to tackle first. We may decide to work on the one that will shift more easily or address one problem and see how this affects the second.

## nd GAD

symptoms are normal in moderate to severe GAD. Wh... ...pression appears as a secondary problem it is often typi-fied by exhaustion and demoralization rather than clinical depression. Worry is an extremely tiring activity; just remember the last time you worried about and then attended an interview. While the interview may have lasted only 20 to 30 minutes, afterwards you may have felt exhausted. Without the focus, drive or energy of the worry, you may also have felt deflated. When we are trying to separate the typical type of depression that comes with GAD from clinical depression we have to look closely at some of the specific symptoms of depression that may not fit with GAD. For example, individuals suffering from clinical depression may experience sadness or weeping, a generalized loss of interest, loss or gain in weight, a noticeable and significant change in their appetite, overactivity or underactivity, poor self-worth, excessive guilt and suicidal thoughts.

Another feature of depression, which is very similar to worry, is rumination. When cows chew the cud, they are essentially rechewing grass they ate earlier. (They are called ruminates, and this is where the word comes from.) Put simply, rumination is going over and over *past* events or negative experiences, whereas worry is more often about *future* events or things that have not happened yet, but seem as if they could or will. Rumination is mostly associated with low mood or depression and worry with anxiety. It appears that people who worry will also probably ruminate on past events. It might be that we flip-flop between worry and rumination, moving from thinking about past events to then thinking about how these events might influence our future. As we move from one to the other, the signature emotion may change from depression to anxiety and back again. Both rumination and worry are like our thoughts going round and round in a washing machine, and both can be intensified or 'put into a spin cycle' by other thoughts, such as *I'm losing my mind*, or *I'll feel like this forever*: see the diagram below.

**Figure 3.2. The relationship between rumination and worry**

If you're feeling depressed and you're not sure whether it's because of your worry or whether it's a problem in its own right, then we would suggest you visit your family doctor and discuss these ideas further.

Irrespective of where your worry sits on the worry gauge, we hope this book will have something in it to help you. In short, the diagnosis is not needed for you to get something from this book. When we talk about chronic worriers or people with severe worry, we are referring to people whose worry is interfering with their lives, irrespective of whether they have been given a diagnosis of GAD.

The DSM-IV criteria are used to formally diagnose GAD. On page 44 is a questionnaire based on the DSM-IV. This has been developed to make it easier to spot if worry is a significant problem. Please spend a few moments completing it. We will discuss what it reveals in due course.

## Problems with spotting GAD

One of the main difficulties in spotting problematic worry is that health professionals may not ask the right questions at the right time. This happens for many reasons, but a principal cause is that people with chronic worry tend to worry more when stressful life events happen (e.g. a daughter's wedding, job deadlines, exams). At these stressful times, worriers suffer with more worry, which produces anxiety symptoms (e.g. muscular tension, sleep disturbance, or concentration problems). The increase in these symptoms eventually leads them to visit their family doctor or other professional. Unfortunately, the worry is commonly seen as normal because the health professional assumes that everyone worries about such stressful events. As a result, clinically significant worry is often overlooked. If worry as the central problem is overlooked, the person's problems go unrecognized and they fail to find the help they need to target their problem. The person may begin to think that this is something they have to just live with. Alternatively, they may blame themselves for worrying, or they may begin to view their excessive worry as normal or as part of their personality. It's almost as if the belief that *I am a worrier* is the only answer. As we have mentioned, worry is often a 'silent problem', like carrying a heavy weight; worriers may simply just get used to carrying the burden, but the impact on the lives of worriers is immense.

## Getting better at spotting worry as a problem

Remember the questions posed at the beginning of this book. These are the critical questions we ask in our clinical assessments to help us work out if someone is suffering with excessive worry or full-blown GAD. These need to be taken together with the diagnostic criteria to reach a formal diagnosis, but they are helpful, straightforward questions that will help you to assess whether worry is a significant problem in your life. Please review them.

You may need to help your doctor or other health professional to understand more about your experience of worry. On the next page is a questionnaire developed by a group of researchers in Canada. It is designed as a quick way of spotting excessive worry and helping to diagnose GAD. If you want help to work on your worry, you may want to take it along with you to show your doctor or health professional.

It is worth bearing in mind that mental health professionals are often anxious about accepting the idea that we have a particular problem without investigating the problem for themselves. They may be a little sceptical, but that is probably helpful. They will help you stand back and think carefully about what is going on for you and consider all the things that are having an influence on your problems. Don't be put off by this: overall health professionals think it is better to be careful and thorough than obliging and potentially careless.

## WORRY AND ANXIETY QUESTIONNAIRE

*For numbers 2 to 4 and 6, circle the numbers most relevant to you.*

1. What subjects do you worry about most often?

   a)                              d)

   b)                              e)

   c)                              f)

2. Do your worries seem excessive or exaggerated?

| 0 | 1 | 2 | 3 | 4 | 5 | 6 | 7 | 8 |
|---|---|---|---|---|---|---|---|---|
| Not at all excessive | | | | Moderately excessive | | | | Totally excessive |

3. Over the past six months, how many days have you been bothered by excessive worry?

| 0 | 1 | 2 | 3 | 4 | 5 | 6 | 7 | 8 |
|---|---|---|---|---|---|---|---|---|
| Never | | | | 1 day out of 2 | | | | Everyday |

4. Do you have difficulty controlling your worries? For example, when you start worrying about something, do you have difficulty stopping?

| 0 | 1 | 2 | 3 | 4 | 5 | 6 | 7 | 8 |
|---|---|---|---|---|---|---|---|---|
| No difficulty | | | | Moderate difficulty | | | | Total difficulty |

5. Over the past six months, to what extent have you been disturbed by the following sensations when you were worried or anxious?

Rate *each* sensation with the following scale:

| 0 | 1 | 2 | 3 | 4 | 5 | 6 | 7 | 8 |
|---|---|---|---|---|---|---|---|---|
| Not at all | | | | Moderately | | | | Very severely |

\_\_\_\_   Restlessness or feeling keyed up or on edge

\_\_\_\_   Being easily fatigued

_____ Difficulty concentrating or mind going blank

_____ Irritability

_____ Muscle tension

_____ Sleep disturbance (difficulty falling or staying asleep, or restless unsatisfying sleep)

**6. To what extent does worry or anxiety interfere with your life, for example, your work, social activities, family life, etc.?**

| 0 | 1 | 2 | 3 | 4 | 5 | 6 | 7 | 8 |
|---|---|---|---|---|---|---|---|---|
| Not at all | | | | Moderately | | | Very severely | |

## How to review the Worry and Anxiety Questionnaire

This questionnaire has been used extensively in research and has been found to be a good way of working out whether someone has a problem with worry or not. You will notice that all the questions on the Worry and Anxiety Questionnaire are scored on a 0–8 scale. If you have scored 4 or more on most of the items, then this suggests that excessive worry is a problem that you may need to face up to. If you score between 2 and 3 on most items, then it still may be helpful for you to learn more about how to turn down your worry dial.

What questions did you score most highly on?

Which symptoms of anxiety do you experience most severely?

## Getting a snapshot of the level of your worry

Below is one of the most widely used questionnaires for assessing worry; it is called the Penn State Worry Questionnaire. Professor Tom Borkovec and his colleagues at Pennsylvania State University developed this questionnaire in the late 1980s and early 1990s. It measures an individual's tendency to worry and enables comparisons to be made with other people who worry excessively. You may wish to fill it in at regular intervals to track your progress (once every two weeks perhaps: see Appendix 3 for a form to help you with this).

Please see below for the instructions – in particular the importance in reversing score items 1, 3, 8, 10 and 11. Take a notebook and write down your responses. What is your total score? What thoughts were going through your mind as you completed this questionnaire? Note these down too.

Your score can be anywhere between 16 and 80; higher scores indicate higher levels of worry. People with GAD tend to score over 57, so our target is to help you get your score below this, but getting a lower score that this is even more encouraging. Of course, some people may score less than this but still have a problem with worry.

Note that some items are reverse scored **(R)**. On these items, if you scored 5 (i.e. very typical) then your score changes to 1, 4 changes to 2, 3 remains the same, 2 changes to 4 and 1 changes to 5. Once you have 'reversed' the scores, write in the new number and cross out the old one. To find your score, add all the numbers you have put on the lines below the ↓ above.

## THE PENN STATE WORRY QUESTIONNAIRE

Enter the number that best describes how typical or characteristic each item is of you, putting the number next to each item.

| 1 | 2 | 3 | 4 | 5 |
|---|---|---|---|---|
| Not at all typical | | Somewhat typical | | Very typical |

1. ___ If I don't have enough time to do everything, I don't worry about it (R).
2. ___ My worries overwhelm me.
3. ___ I don't tend to worry about things (R).
4. ___ Many situations make me worry.
5. ___ I know I shouldn't worry about things but I just can't help it.
6. ___ When I'm under pressure, I worry a lot.
7. ___ I'm always worrying about something.
8. ___ I find it easy to dismiss worrisome thoughts (R).
9. ___ As soon as I finish one task, I start to worry about everything else I have to do.
10. ___ I never worry about anything (R).
11. ___ When there is nothing more that I can do about a concern, I don't worry about it anymore (R).
12. ___ I've been a worrier all my life.
13. ___ I notice that I have been worrying about things.
14. ___ Once I start worrying, I can't stop.
15. ___ I worry all the time.
16. ___ I worry about projects until they are all done.

Source: T. J. Meyer, M. L. Miller, R. L. Metzger and T. D. Borkovec, 'Development and validation of the Penn State Worry Questionnaire', *Behavior Research and Therapy*, 28 (1990). With permission from Elsevier.

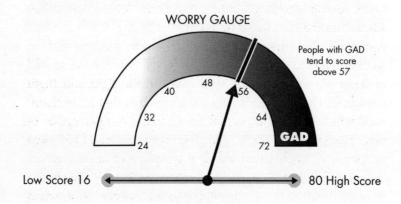

## Fear and worry – an evolutionary perspective

Fear and worry help us deal with danger, either real and immediate danger in the case of fear, or anticipated or future danger
in the case of worry. Short bursts of fear and its accompanying
anxiety occur in response to physical danger, and they help us
to deal with that danger through three main mechanisms, namely,
fight, flight or freeze. These responses are 'hard-wired' and are
linked to the parts of brain that developed relatively early in
an evolutionary sense (the reptilian part or limbic system). When
an event is perceived to be life threatening, the body's systems
react incredibly quickly, often without our awareness. Through
million of years of evolution our bodies have been 'hard-wired'
to react to and deal with threat, preserving what is most important, ourselves and our group. At these moments of threat, the
more primitive part of our brain takes over to protect us. What
we end up doing depends to large extent on interaction between
the event and the chemical processes in our brains. In simple
terms, the adrenal gland (found just above the kidneys) will, in
dangerous situations and under instruction from part of the

brain, pump chemicals into your body. These are called adrenaline and noradrenaline and they work together to prepare your body for either 'getting the hell out of there' (flight) or 'getting ready to rumble' (fight). The freeze reaction is less well understood, but has many similarities to the fight and flight responses. This reaction is also influenced by other brain chemicals, which have an impact on memory and our perception of time, place and what's real. The freeze response might be linked to a sense of dissociation; this is a symptom of anxiety where the person might feel 'spaced out' or 'not really here'. The freeze response might 'take us out of a situation', almost as if, when things get to too much, our mind decides to shut down from our body. We can't really predict which of the fight, flight or freeze reactions will happen to us in any given situation; they can all have adaptive or evolutionary value and can help us to survive.

For example, in North America, in the very rare event of being attacked by a Brown bear – a medium sized omnivore – if you have exhausted all the options available to you, the advice is to fight and fight for your life. A well-aimed blow to the nose with a stick might just do the trick and save you. However, if confronted by the much larger Grizzly bear, then the best chance of survival is not just freezing, but playing dead. This tactic doesn't guarantee your survival, but there's little hope in doing anything else, like fighting or running. Indeed, there are survivor accounts where this is exactly what people have done and lived to tell the tale. If you are reading this book while hiking in North America, then the other thing you need to know is that both types of bear are quick – so don't run. Nor would we advise you to throw this book at them, partly because bears can't read, but partly because there's no evidence that they worry, and such an action may make them angrier!

## Why do we anticipate danger and why do we worry?

If fear is a way of responding to immediate danger, worry is a way of dealing with possible danger at some point in the future. In other words, worrying is planning to make sure that you don't meet the bear, or that, if you do meet one, it won't attack you, or if it does, then you know how to get away, and if all else fails, you know what to do, depending on whether the bear is black or brown!

Some anthropologists have argued that the emergence of language, coupled with living in complex social groups, were two of the main influences on how our modern brains developed, particularly the frontal lobes. Looking after our social group and our position within the group thus became a critical element for survival. At the same time, humans were evolving problem-solving skills and developing the capacity to think and plan ahead. As planning ahead became more important, they also learnt to live with uncertainty. It was important that at least some people were looking ahead: *We've had a poor harvest. What if we don't have enough grain to get us through winter? Maybe we could trade some cattle for grain with our neighbours*? Worry might be considered useful in this context, as it allowed our ancestors to think ahead and run through in imagination what might happen next, with multiple endings and possibilities. So, when we worry, our frontal lobes are thinking through the possibilities and looking for solutions to manage and prevent real or likely threats from happening. It is no accident then, given that we are largely social animals, that within the general population roughly one-third of all worry is focused on the breakdown of social relationships. And, through adaptive problem-solving, we try to ensure that the social groups we live in, such as our families, friendships or social networks, survive or stay together.

Brain research has shown changes in blood flow in different parts of the brain when people worry. An American team has shown that during worry by people who do not worry excessively there is increased blood flow that indicates increased brain activity in the fronto-orbital regions, the parts of the brain associated with language and attempts to integrate information and look for solutions. There is also less activity in the limbic system, parts of the brain associated with more primitive fear responses. So it would seem that, although related, fear and worry have two different functions and have developed at different times in human evolution. The fear response system evolved very early and is shared with many animals, even quite primitive species with tiny brains. The worry system evolved much later and required the large forebrain that evolved with language, problem-solving and planning. Its basis is probably shared only with higher mammals or the most advanced primates, and even then it is likely to be far more evolved in humans. When the worry system is more active, the fear system is less active, and rather than reacting with flight, fright or freeze, the brain goes into *What if?* and *What could I do then*? mode. We all need some of this ability; the question is how much do we need?

So to worry is to be human. But to worry excessively is to try to be superhuman – that is, to be able to anticipate, prevent, deal with, make better or pick up the pieces after anything and everything that could possibly go wrong at anytime and anywhere. What kind of superhero would we need to be able to do this? What special powers might they need? Do you have them?

## How many people worry?

If to worry is to be human, how many of us worry excessively or have a diagnosable problem with worry? Between March and September 2000, trained psychologists working for the National

Psychiatric Morbidity Survey randomly interviewed over 8,000 adults living in the UK. This survey aimed to find out how widespread psychological problems were in the UK population. The survey found that in every 1,000 adults, forty-four reached a diagnosis for GAD. GAD was second only to mixed anxiety and depression in terms of how commonly it occurred; indeed, GAD was found to be more common than depression. Furthermore, research in many different countries has suggested that roughly somewhere between 2 and 4 per cent of a population will have enough symptoms to get a diagnosis of GAD in one year, and 4 to 7 per cent of people will develop GAD at some point in their lives. Between 2 and 4 per cent may not sound very many, but with the use of these figures, of the 60 million people who live in the UK, this equates to between 1.2 and 2.4 million people with diagnosable GAD, that is, 1.2 to 2.4 million people who suffer with excessive worry. If you included people who worry a lot but who do not have enough symptoms to reach a diagnosis of GAD, the numbers will be even greater. Playing it safe, that's roughly about one person in every twenty-five. Next time you are sitting in a café watching the world go by, think about this statistic. So you are not alone!

Worry seems to have been around for as long as modern man. It appears that even in the first century AD worry had a dramatic impact. The Roman poet Ovid (43 BC–17 AD) told us that 'happy is the man who has broken the chains which hurt the mind, and has given up worrying once and for all'.

## When does GAD usually begin?

Worry can occur at any time, and this is also true for GAD. If there is life stress, or if our lives have changed in a major way, or if we have increased responsibilities, then we will be more susceptible to worry. Consider the example opposite.

Abby was fifteen weeks pregnant. Prior to her pregnancy she would not have considered herself a worrier. However, her pregnancy and the uncertain future of her baby triggered worry about her partner and her baby. She worried about her partner having a car crash and her baby not having a father; she started checking on him to make sure he arrived at work. She tried to make sure that he spent as little time in the car as possible, offering to do trips so that he did not drive as much. She did this to control uncertainty as far as possible, so rather than not knowing where he was, she could keep tabs on him. She became irritated when he ate unhealthy food since she was convinced that this would lead to ill health and sudden death. She felt keyed up and couldn't sit still. In an effort to manage the uncertain situation she found herself in, she searched the Internet for information about pregnancy. She found more and more information, some of which contradicted other information. This fuelled her sense of uncertainty and thus generated more worries. She worried about whether her child would be born early and whether it would develop normally. She worried that if it did develop and grow to be as smart as she hoped for, whether she would be able to help with the homework at secondary school. When she wasn't worrying about the child taking a wrong turn in life and ending up dropping out of school, she was worrying that the child would go to university, succeed and leave her behind. These worries triggered more *what if* statements, leading to more worry and so on.

Research tells us that roughly two-thirds of clinically significant worry tend to appear early in a person's lifespan, between the ages of eleven and our early twenties. This phase of our lives is important, when we are laying the foundations for the years to come. It is a time fraught with uncertainty as we try to find our feet and establish the sense of who we are, and the fact we tend to have relatively little control makes these transitions much harder. Worry appears at these early moments as a result of many subtle influences, and tends not to be triggered by a major life event or trauma. It might be linked to some of the developmental hurdles we have to cross, such as adolescence and having more and more responsibility.

The other time that worry tends to appear is much later in the life span, during middle age. This is the time of life that is often typified by stability in a number of areas of our lives. We might be more certain of who we are, and where we fit in the world. We may have an established career and home life. So why would worry tend to appear at this time? When worry appears later on it is usually linked to some significant change, such as bereavement, trauma or disaster, or a major shift in the way we live our lives, such as retirement. This might challenge the status quo and generate doubt and uncertainty, fuelling worry.

Hence worry is *more likely* to appear at these times, that is, either during our early development to adulthood or later, in middle age. But it is important to remember that worry can appear at any point in a person's life, given the right circumstances, just as Abby's experience above demonstrates.

## What causes GAD?

First of all, worry is a normal and helpful process when we are faced with real situations where the outcome is uncertain. But why do some people come to worry excessively or why is their worry gauge turned up so high so much of the time?

A precise cause of GAD is not known. There are several factors involved in its development, including biological influences, such as our genes, or the levels of certain brain chemicals. The biological view of GAD suggests that we can treat it by using medicine to alter the levels of brain chemicals. While there is always merit in considering other approaches, this book is written from a psychological perspective and as a result we will focus next on some of the psychological pathways to excessive worry.

According to our clinical experience there are many pathways to worry, but our early experiences seem to be important. Why this should be so is a very complex question. There is no set pattern and an infinite number of influences. Below are some themes that might be important; they are not in any particular order and there will be others we have not listed.

1. Growing up with a parent who worried, and learning to worry from them.
2. Growing up in a very unstable or uncertain household, where someone in the household was affected by illness, or unemployment or some other stress, without being able to do very much about it.
3. Being told by someone important that there was no way that you could cope with life, and believing them.
4. Being given too much or too little responsibility at a very early age, or being overprotected and never learning to deal with life's uncertainties.
5. Living in a household where no one worried, but someone had to.
6. Being left alone to cope.
7. Trying to make sense of a situation that you could not make sense of.
8. Experiencing a traumatic event as a child or teenager.
9. Losing a parent.
10. Refereeing the arguments between your parents.
11. Being bullied.
12. Having an abusive, aggressive, drunk or violent parent or carer.

Any of these experiences can leave people with a sense of threat and uncertainty. This is often associated with a lack of confidence in their ability to cope or deal with everyday problems, coupled with a sense that they should do so – although most worriers in fact deal very well with problems when they arrive.

Sometime worriers build on past experience to build a sense of future threat. An example of this is seen in José's story (see pages 12–13). His previous relationship did not work out and there was a set of circumstances that influenced the break-up of his relationship. José's worry is about whether something similar could happen again. This worry makes him more aware of events or issues within his new relationships that match those within his failed marriage. In psychological terms, he is hypervigilant, or on the look out for any matching features between his failed marriage and his new relationship. This would encourage him to imagine that the same thing could happen in his current relationship; he would see his new partner and his ex as one and the same, ignoring any information that suggested otherwise.

There are many different ways worry can appear, and no fixed set of circumstances that will definitely lead to worry. In CBT, however, we are often interested in understanding how our early and later experiences influence the development of our ideas about worry. For example, growing up in an unstable household might lead us to think, *If I work out what might go wrong, then I will be able to stop it from happening*, or *If I am certain, then nothing bad will happen*; *If I tie up the loose ends, everything will be Ok*; or, *Worry helps me deal with uncertainty*. These ideas guide us and influence how we act. We discuss this further in Chapter 7. However, although it is interesting to find out where this way of thinking comes from, in CBT we are much more interested in seeing how it keeps worry going; and our greatest interest is in finding out how we might change things.

## What is a normal amount of worry?

This is very difficult to answer – it's like answering the question *What is normal weight* or *What is normal height?* In just the same way, a 'normal amount of worry' will vary for each individual. This does not mean that hours and hours of uncontrollable worry should be normal for anyone and that even people who have a greater natural tendency to worry cannot learn to turn down the worry gauge to more everyday levels. However, some research gives us an idea of the range of normal worry. In a questionnaire study on 128 students in the early 1990s, Frank Tallis and his colleagues at the Institute of Psychiatry in London found that nearly all the students said that they worried. About 40 per cent of them worried at least once a day, 20 per cent worried every two to three days, and about 15 per cent worried about once a month. In terms of how long a worry episode lasted, they found that about a quarter said their worries were fleeting, about 40 per cent said it lasted between 1 and 10 minutes, 18 per cent said their worry lasted 10 to 60 minutes and 20 per cent said that their worry lasted over one hour. The students who reported the most worry would probably have been diagnosed with GAD. In this number of people (128), it is likely that five or more of them would have GAD and ten or more would have shared many of the other features. The students also said that they worried more in the late evening or in the small hours of the morning. Of course, people who have GAD tend to worry more than those without it; one study found that people with GAD worried for about 60 per cent of the day. Some people with GAD report worrying in every waking moment and some that they worry even while sleeping, with worry themes appearing in dreams. On the other hand, others report that their worry is on the 'back burner', simmering away and it will 'come to the boil' rapidly when something sparks it off.

Another way of thinking about normal levels of worry is to reflect on the average scores on the Penn State Worry Questionnaire. You might expect the average to be very low, somewhere around 20–25, but this is a long way from the truth. The average score on this questionnaire is around 40 (including adults, older adults, students and others). This reminds us that worry is normal and that everyone worries.

## What do people worry about?

People with GAD tend to worry about the same kinds of things as people without GAD – they just worry more. Because of the hundreds of worries that race through our minds when we worry, and because we rarely stop to observe or step out of the stream of worry, it can often seem that there is no pattern or order to our anxiety. However, research on people who worry and those who worry less suggests that worries tend to cluster around particular themes. These include social-, financial-, work-, illness- or death-related themes, and even worrying about worrying. This last theme is exactly what you imagine it to be, namely that as a consequence of worrying so much, worriers tend to start to worry about the consequences of their worry. Typically, worriers might think that their worry will drive them out of their minds, or that not worrying is a bad sign.

Roughly one-third of all worry is focused on the family and interpersonal relationships. This type of worry is usually focused on the breakdown of the family circle, friendship or other important relationships. It usually revolves around real or imagined events such as illness, death or other life events such as children leaving home, friends moving away or anything that could potentially disrupt social relationships. Financial worries tend to revolve around what might happen if bills aren't met, or if money becomes tight, or not being able to meet changes in interest rates, and so on. The implications of financial difficulties are often social, since the worrier is concerned by what their friends or others will think of them. They may worry about how to tell their children they can't afford the school trip and then how to face the school and other parents. Their worry also projects them into the future, and they may see themselves losing their home, needing to downsize or even ending up on the streets. With illness- and death-related worries, the worrier often thinks about how they might fail to cope with the pain or discomfort of a crippling, usually life-threatening illness, and, even more likely, about how close friends or family might suffer or fail to cope following their death, or who will look after their loved ones.

Worry themes are typically related to the stage of life we find ourselves in. For instance, as teenagers we worry most about our peers and fitting in. Some recent research has suggested that as we approach adulthood we begin to think about and worry more about the distant future. The students in the studies mentioned above worried about school performance and peer relationships. In middle age we are concerned about the onset of old age. As older adults we worry about our health and death. Interestingly, some research shows that with adults over 75 worry tends to decrease (there may be much to be learned about life from the over 75s). One of the problems with the link between life stage and worry themes is that our worry is often seen as normal for the relevant life stage. For instance, what teenager doesn't worry about fitting in? Another problem is that the worry seems all the more believable and likely to happen, since it fits neatly to the life stage, making it harder to spot and to challenge.

So although worry feels like a whirlwind with an unpredictable course, there are patterns and rhythms to it because it tends to circle around a number of themes that reflect the things that are important in a person's life.

## Types of worry

Broadly speaking there are at least two different types of worry. Some of the problems we worry about already exist; these are called *Real Event Worry*. And there is worry about problems that *could potentially* exist at some point in the future (although there is no evidence now that this is the case), otherwise known as *Hypothetical Event Worry*. This second type of worry may never exist in the sense that it is imagined, but it can have the feel of a nightmarish daydream. This type of worry is often set in the distant future and is usually very unlikely to ever happen.

For example, if I worry about a piece of work I am working on, then this problem exists and my worry is *Real Event Worry*. However, if I worry about the idea that I may develop cancer although there are no signs that I am unwell, then this worry does not yet exist and is therefore *Hypothetical Event Worry*. Let's consider another example: my wife has been in a car wreck and I am worried about how she will cope with her pain; this is *Real Event Worry*. On the other hand, I may worry that my wife *could be* involved in a car accident; this is *Hypothetical Event Worry*, the second type of worry. We will return to this distinction later.

## PIT STOP

Let's stop and think about what you have just been reading. Can you summarize the key ideas you have taken on board? What is sticking in your mind? Maybe write them down. If you have any questions, jot these down too. You can return to them once you have had a chance to digest the information.

What is sticking in my mind from my reading so far?

1.

2.

3.

# 4

# What is CBT?

The 'C' in CBT refers to *cognitive*. Cognition essentially refers to what we think and how we think. It includes all the different things our minds can do, like planning, problem-solving, decision-making and drawing conclusions. Cognitive behavioral therapists, however, are usually most interested in the thoughts (or cognitions) that pass through the mind – literally, what a person is thinking. The 'B' in CBT refers to *behavior* and includes our actions, what we do and what we avoid doing. It includes subtle actions like where we look or how we stand and more obvious actions like which places we tend to avoid. A central idea of CBT is that the perspective or view we take of an event or situation has a profound influence on how we feel and act. In other words, how we think about an event is vital in helping us understand why we feel and act in particular ways. Dave Westbrook, a consultant clinical psychologist working in Oxford, has found a very clear way of explaining this principle. The diagrams below are an adaptation of his ideas. Let's consider the 'common sense' model. Here events lead directly to feelings. For example, if someone lost their job, you might expect them to feel down.

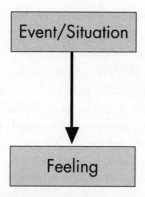

Figure 4.1. The 'common sense' model.

However, we also know that the same event can have different emotional consequences for different people. For example, losing a job could leave people feeling anxious, angry or even relieved (see below). So, how can we explain this and what does it tell us about the common sense model shown above?

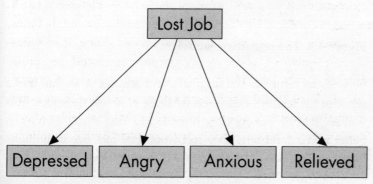

Figure 4.2. The 'common sense' model expanded.

First, it tells us that we cannot assume to know what people feel when something happens to them. Second, it shows that in order to better understand how they feel, we must pay close attention to what they are thinking. We could ask, *When you felt this way, what went through your mind?* Below is a diagram showing the cognitive model. Here the thinking or cognitive element is added. Does this make sense to you? It may be helpful to pause to reflect on this fundamental point by thinking of a time when you noticed strong feelings (such as anger, anxiety, guilt or depression) and then ask yourself, *What was going through my mind just before I started to feel this way?* or, *What was I thinking that might have led me to feel like this?*

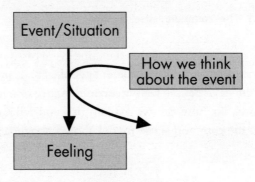

**Figure 4.3. The cognitive model.**

Now let us return to the original event and see if we can make sense of the feelings expressed by those who lost their jobs. You will see that by paying close attention to their thoughts we can better understand why they feel what they feel. See if the links between each person's thoughts and feelings make sense to you.

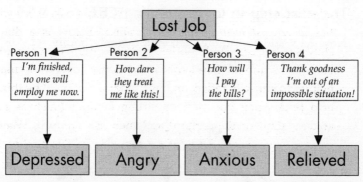

**Figure 4.4. Adding thoughts into the 'common sense' model.**

In summary, a central idea of CBT is that the perspective or view we take of an event or situation has a profound influence on how we feel and act.

---

**PIT STOP**

Let's stop and think about what you have just been reading. Can you summarize the key ideas you have taken on board? What is sticking in your mind? Maybe write them down. If you have any questions, jot these down too. You can return to them once you have had a chance to digest the information.

What is sticking in my mind from my reading so far?

1.

2.

3.

## The next step in understanding CBT

Now let's add two more elements, namely bodily sensations and actions or behaviors.

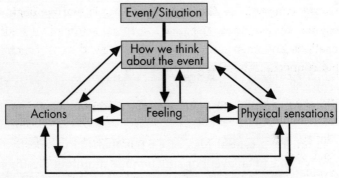

Figure 4.5. Adding sensations and actions in the model.

Let's take the actions first. In the CBT approach there is a strong relationship between our thoughts, feelings and actions. For example, when we feel frightened because we see danger, our feelings motivate us to act – perhaps keeping us away from the danger. Or, when we feel annoyed, possibly because someone has offended us, this may prompt us to ignore them. In CBT the interaction between our thoughts, feelings and actions is seen as central in keeping our problems going. Finally, our thoughts, actions and emotions also have an effect on how our body feels.

On the following page we take each of the examples above a little further to include actions and bodily sensations. There are many ways that our thoughts, feelings, actions and bodily sensation interact, and the pattern of interaction may be subtly different for each individual. Try to track the patterns in the following examples both on the diagram and in the text below.

## How to read the diagrams

The arrows are there for good reasons. See if you can work out what the arrows mean for each person. Sometimes they mean *leads to*, sometimes they mean *influence*, and sometimes they illustrate connections. The important thing is that we begin to recognize and separate thoughts, feelings, actions and bodily sensations and then get curious about how they fit together, what connects to what and how.

**Person 1** thought she was finished, washed up and useless and that no one would ever want to employ her again. Understandably, she felt down and depressed. She noticed that she was more tearful than usual, which meant she avoided her friends. She didn't feel hungry, so she stopped eating regularly. Her mood and her poor diet contributed towards her feeling physically tired. Because of how she felt, both emotionally and physically, she stayed in bed and avoided trying to do anything about getting a job. She was convinced that if she did try to find a job she would fail, which made it much harder to look. This unwittingly meant that she never found out if she was really washed up or whether it was just the way she was thinking. From this point of view, she couldn't see that her thoughts were not facts.

**Person 2** had given years to the company and couldn't believe that his employers had the nerve to sack him. He was furious. He found it much harder to sleep because he was so keyed up and he also suffered with tension headaches. The lack of sleep resulted in his feeling much more irritable, and to manage this he started taking a large nightcap before going to bed. While this helped him get to sleep, having alcohol meant that he did not get good, restful sleep, which left him even more tired and irritable. Drinking alcohol did little to help with the tension headaches. In addition to all this, his anger motivated him to call his union to see if there was something that could be done.

**Person 3** was concerned about how he would cope financially and started to feel very anxious and nervous about how he would pay the bills. He worried in response to this, which made him feel more anxious. He avoided opening bills, which would pile up on the kitchen table. Each day he saw the pile he was more convinced that he could not afford to pay them. Since he never opened the bills, he never found out if this was true or not, and continued to worry as a consequence. He felt tense and had that feeling of butterflies in the stomach. He used the physical sensations as proof that there was something to worry about.

**Person 4** was in the enviable position of being not that bothered about losing her job. She felt quite relaxed as a result and noticed that she had good energy levels; she felt as if a weight has been lifted from her. This helped her to take a positive step; she took the jobs section of the newspaper to the beach and started looking for a new job.

## Using the cognitive model

Let's take an example to illustrate the principles described overleaf. If you saw a friend in the street and they ignored you, what might go through your mind? How might you feel and what might you do as a consequence? Would you notice any physical sensations? You'll find a worked out example below, but, for a moment, just reflect on these questions and see if you can get a sense of how you might think, feel and act.

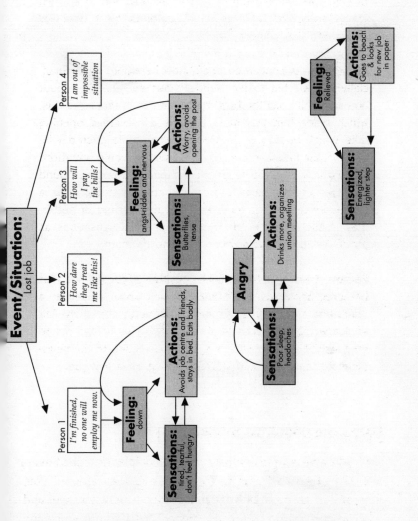

**Figure 4.6: How different views of an event influence feelings, actions and bodily sensations.**

## EXERCISE 4.1: STARTING TO USE CBT

**Event/Situation:** You see a friend in the street and they apparently ignore you

| Elements | Questions | Your Answers |
|---|---|---|
| Thoughts (Cognition) | What would go through your mind? | |
| Feelings | How might you feel? | |
| Actions (Behavior) | What might you do? | |
| Bodily Sensations | What bodily sensation might you notice? | |

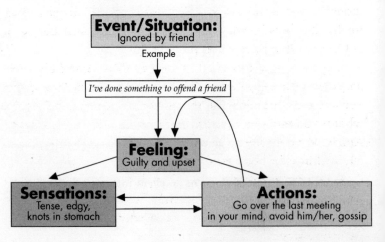

Figure 4.7: How this situation might play out.

In the example above, the person felt guilty and upset as well as physically tense and edgy – both the feelings and the physical sensations were motivated by their thoughts. They started to replay their last meeting, reviewing in their mind what they could have said to cause such a reaction. Their focus is entirely on what they may have done wrong and they fail to think of other explanations; this reinforces the idea that they have done something to offend their friend. Rather than approaching their friend to ask them, they are so convinced by their thoughts that they avoid them. In order to get their side of the story in first, they start to gossip to mutual friends about what has happened. This means that they continue to believe that they did something wrong and push themselves further away from simply contacting their friend and asking how they are.

A cognitive behavioral therapist will often ask, 'What was going through your mind when you saw your friend?' They may follow this question with, 'When this went through your mind, what did you do?' These two questions have made the thoughts explicit and made clear the relationship between thoughts and feelings and then linked them to actions. And, finally, they would ask you to reflect on what sensations you felt in your body when you thought this.

Supposing you thought this instead, *My friend looks really preoccupied, there must be something going on with him.* How might you feel and what might this thought motivate you to do? Again, what if you thought, *How dare he ignore me, after all these years!* And what would you do, and what would you feel both emotionally and in your body as a consequence?

As you can see, changing the thought has an impact on how we feel and act. So, in summary, how we think about an event is vital in helping us to understand why we feel and act in particular ways.

## In CBT we treat GAD differently from other anxiety problems

Cognitive therapy self-help books usually suggest spending time weighing up the evidence for a particular idea or thought. There are many reasons why this might be helpful. For example, it may open our field of view to consider things we had not thought of before; it may shift our perspective with the aim of enabling us to develop new ways of thinking, or it may aim to get us to reflect on what is at the heart of our concern by focusing in on underlying meaning. Another general aim is to help us realize that the likelihood of our fears coming true is very slim and even if they did we would probably be able to cope with the outcome. For example, a man was concerned that he would bump into a workplace bully in a local pub; that if his fear came true he would not be able to cope and would go to pieces. Furthermore, he felt sure that this was highly likely to happen even though the bully lived miles from his home. Understandably, he felt anxious and started to avoid his local pub. Using cognitive therapy, we first aimed to help him work on the likelihood that this man would walk into his pub. Secondly, we discussed what he would do if he did. He quickly realized that, because he was amongst his friends, he'd feel more confident, and began to see that, even if the bully turned up, he'd be able to cope. His anxiety reduced as a consequence. To help him we focused on guiding him to think through the following questions: *How likely is it that this will happen? And even if it did, would it be as bad as you think?* Helping him see that the probability of his fear materializing was very low, and that if it did, his worst fears of running out would not happen, enabled him to overcome his fear and return to the pub.

The problem we face with the whirlwind of worry is that this idea of looking at the evidence for and against this stream of thoughts may not work or will need to be repeated over and over again. This is for several reasons. First, worry is phrased in terms of *'what if'* statements, and we cannot reason out a question; we need a statement to do this. Second, worry is a chain of thoughts that shift and change, so once you work with one, another will take its place. Third, people who worry have sensitivity to uncertainty. As a result, worriers tend to need absolute certainty to feel better, which is impossible. Think of the man mentioned above: he could see that the chances of the bully's appearing were very low, and realizing this was enough for him to begin to feel better. If he were a worrier, then this would not be enough, because a *splinter of doubt* would trigger off worry – *What if he comes into my pub?* In order to deal with this sense of uncertainty, worriers will start to worry. To help them, rather than work with their worries themselves we should focus on other things, like enabling them to cope better with uncertainty, which removes one of the things that fuels worry.

People who worry seem to have a worry box. No matter how small or large their problems are, the box is always full. Worry seems to expand in the space and fill it, no matter how small the worry is to start with.

## What is the aim of CBT for worry?

The aim of CBT is to enable you to develop new ways of thinking about your worry and to help you to break out of the vicious cycles that keep you worrying. CBT can help you to make sense of your experiences by looking in detail at how you think, feel and act in situations that trigger worry. With the help of this book, you will explore how the interactions between your thoughts, feelings and actions can keep your problems going. CBT concentrates on the difficulties you are facing now, rather than focusing on the past, except when it helps to make sense of your current problems. You will be encouraged to develop skills that help you to feel better and keep you feeling better. These skills can also be applied to other difficulties that you may encounter in the future.

CBT techniques may be difficult to grasp at first, but most people can learn them with practice. *Practising the skills in this book is vital to improvement.* If you signed up for a Spanish course and attended every week but never spoke or practised outside of your lessons, how much progress would you expect to make? Compare this with practising an hour a week, or, even better, an hour a day. The same is true of CBT; without repeated practice, you will not notice or feel any improvement. Practising new skills feels unnatural, deliberate and conscious at first, almost like wearing someone else's shoes. This is especially true if you started worrying when you were very young and the 'worry shoes' are familiar, even if they have never been that comfortable. But as we internalize new ideas they become our own, and this instils confidence.

## Practise, practise, practise!

As far as possible we will offer you good explanations for the tasks we suggest in this book. It's essential that you understand why we're asking you to engage in particular tasks before trying them out. Our aim is to enable you to learn what you need to keep you feeling better.

We would also like to make clear a few key messages. First, excessive worry should not be accepted as a normal response or as part of one's personality. Second, excessive worry is not something that just happens: the process of worry can be understood. Third, people play an active role in initiating and maintaining their worry, but this role becomes automatic. Finally, once people understand the processes, they can modify their normal way of reacting so that they can 'turn down the worry dial'. This is why it's important you begin to step out of the flow of your worry and understand what keeps it going.

## Building on CBT to help us understand worry

As already mentioned, in CBT we are interested in how and what people think and how this influences their feelings, actions and bodily sensations. In the examples above, a situation triggered thoughts that led to strong emotions. In worry the same is true, although there are some minor differences. The following diagrams are the first steps in developing your understanding of worry; it's worth spending some time on them and reflecting. Let's take an example.

Tom has a really important meeting today and he's waiting for his train. The train is late and he wonders, *What if I'm late for work?* This thought opens up doubt and uncertainty, and he starts to worry. He thinks about the implications of being late for work, how this will impact on his job, his relationship and his life. His worry quickly turns into a nightmarish daydream. His worries feel very real, they arrive thick and fast, which generates more doubt and uncertainty, and he worries all the more. His worry feels out of control. He is barely aware of where he is as his worry carries him further away. He starts to *feel* anxious, tense and restless and he looks about nervously. He nearly misses his train because he's so lost in his worry.

He has been worrying much more recently and it's taking its toll. The negative tone of his worry starts to impact on his mood and his worry begins to drag him down. Going through these whirlwinds of worry is so often draining; he feels exhausted and demoralized as a consequence.

Track this example through on the diagram below: please note that you should read this diagram from the bottom up. Does it make sense to you? Does the order of the stages fit with your experience?

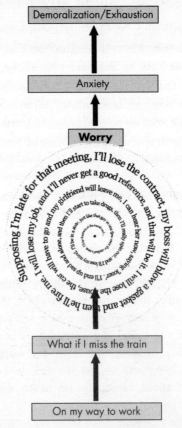

Figure 4.8. Developing the picture: Tom's example.

Read from the bottom upwards.

There are a number of points we'd like to make clear. Worry can be triggered by external, observable events, like a late train, or by internal events, such as a physical sensation – like palpitations – or a mental event – like a thought that pops into your mind. These situations tend to trigger *what if* questions or their equivalent (*supposing that, imagine if* and so forth). Worry has a particular quality and is often triggered by a particular kind of question; usually these are phrased as *what if* questions. The *what if* questions can be thought of as a signal or sign that some form of uncertainty or doubt has been 'spotted' by the worrier within the situation they face. In Tom's case, the uncertainty centred around the delay of his train. And each *what if* question leads to a chain of worry or further *what if* questions. As you can see, worry is a chain of thoughts that spirals out of control; one worry follows closely behind the others. In addition to *what if* statements there are other trigger thoughts including, *Wouldn't it be terrible if* or *Supposing this happened I wouldn't be able to cope and even if I did then . . .*, or *Imagine if it turned out like this* or, *Say, if this happened then . . .* Each of these statements function to open up doubt and uncertainty and lead to the spiral of worry.

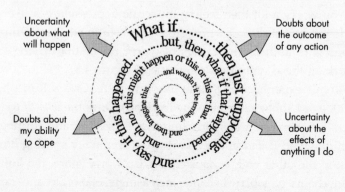

**Figure 4.9.** *What if*'s and worry generate uncertainty.

The *what if* questions open up uncertainty, which in turn sets off worry, which in turn 'ratchets up' uncertainty. Worry is comprised of a chain of thoughts and images whose sheer numbers and the rapidity with which they appear – combined with the fact that the topic of the worry can shift and change – mean that trying to reason with each worry is impossible. So, to overcome your worry, we have to focus not on each individual worry but on factors that provide conditions that stimulate worry. We have to learn how to spot different types of worry, as each type of worry needs a different solution. We have to treat the stream of worry like an action our mind performs; this puts worry into the family of actions or behavior rather than thoughts. Anxiety is the short-term or immediate emotional consequence of the stream of worry. Anxiety includes the physical experience of worry, like muscular tension and fatigue, and also the psychological experiences, like difficulty in concentrating or irritability. Anxiety and the other physical symptoms appear as the products of worry, so rather than trying to focus on the results of worry, we should focus on what causes worry to spiral and grow. Low mood, demoralization and exhaustion are the longer-term consequences of worry and, unfortunately, if you worry a lot then feeling moderate depression is a likely side-product of chronic worry. Again, the solution to these symptoms is to address the causes of worry rather than trying to work on these symptoms directly (see Figure 4.8).

Tom's experience is a little like riding the Cresta Run (the 1,200-yard Toboggan run in Switzerland). Once the *what if* triggers his worry, it transports him away, twisting and turning, building speed and anxiety as it goes, eventually spitting him out at the other end, exhausted. As we worry more, the links and chains of worry become increasingly elaborate and far-fetched, bringing with them even more uncertainty and chaos.

But even at these moments there is the potential of finding a new way of being, of accepting uncertainty and letting go of worry – and thus freeing us from our burden.

Now turn to the worry diagram below. Think back to the last time you worried. Can you track through your worry by using this diagram?

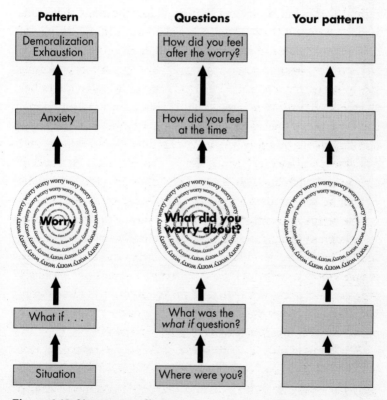

**Figure 4.10. Your worry diagram.**

Think of the last time you worried. Can you fill in the blank boxes in the right hand column?

## EXERCISE 4.2: QUESTIONS TO HELP DEVELOP YOUR WORRY DIAGRAM

| Situation | What ifs | What you were worrying about | How did you feel at the time? | How did you feel after you stopped worrying? |
|---|---|---|---|---|
| **Date and Time** Where were you? What were you doing? Who were you with? | What went through your mind just before you started to worry? Can you spot the 'what if' statements (or equivalents) that triggered your worry? | Briefly describe what you were worrying about. Could you spot other *what ifs* within this bout of worry; where did they take the worry? | What physical sensations did you experience? How did you feel while you were worrying? How strong was this feeling? (0 = not very strong, 100 = intense feelings) | How strong was this feeling? (0 = not very strong, 100 = intense feelings) Did you notice any other sensations? |
|  |  |  |  |  |
|  |  |  |  |  |

**PIT STOP**

Let's stop and think about what you have just been reading. Can you summarize the key ideas you have taken on board? What is sticking in your mind? Maybe write them down. If you have any questions, jot these down too. You can return to them once you have had a chance to digest the information.

What is sticking in my mind from my reading so far?
1.

2.

3.

# Chapter 5

# Becoming more aware of your worry

The last chapter outlined the situations or events that triggered *what if* statements (or equivalents), which then led to worry. As we have seen, worry is a chain of thoughts that shifts and twists as it develops; the whirlwind of worry then builds anxiety. Anxiety includes physical and emotional sensations such as butterflies in the stomach, muscular tension, being unable to relax, irritability, or a sense of impending doom. Furthermore, in the longer term we tend to feel exhausted by our worry, because it is simply an exhausting activity. Our worry often leaves us feeling demoralized, since we fail to act to solve problems that trigger our worries, or because we are 'cheesed off' with worrying so much. Below you'll find a quick summary.

**Trigger ⇨ What if . . . ⇨ Worry ⇨ Anxiety ⇨**
**Demoralization and Exhaustion**

This chapter will help you to stop and to become more aware of your worry. As we have said about the traffic metaphor earlier, one of the first things we have to do when trying to understand and improve traffic problems is to define the problem and work out a way of measuring it so that we can track change. You may also want to train yourself to separate out the different types of vehicle you come across, as each type may require different solutions (for example, bus lanes, car share, sending heavy goods vehicles around the city rather than through it) – and cars may need to be identified and separated from buses or lorries. In this chapter, we will turn our attention to helping you become more aware of your worry and enabling you to spot the different types of worry that come to mind.

It may sound a little odd for us to suggest that you turn your attention to your worry, as this is probably the last thing you want to think about. You may also feel that your worry already takes up far too much of your time, and turning your attention to it might seem to be doing the wrong thing. We have also suggested that to overcome your worry you have to attend to the things that keep it going rather than each individual worry, so you may be rightly thinking that this does not add up. We recognize that there is a slight contradiction in what we are saying, but we hope the value of doing what we suggest will become clear as we go through this chapter. In essence, we are asking you to begin to pay attention to your worry and begin to try to work out what type of worry it is. To become good at this you must focus on your worry. This is like stepping out of a stream and sitting on the bank and watching the worry flow past. This is important, as it allows you to reflect on worry rather than being in it; from the 'riverbank' you are in a better place to recognize the different types of worry that float past.

## *Real Event* and *Hypothetical Event Worry*

As you will have read earlier in this chapter, there are usually several themes that underpin worry – money worries, worries about children or family, or worry about friendships or work. So your first task is to get a feel for what you worry about. Second, you need to think about the type of worry that you experience on these themes. Remember that there are broadly speaking two different types of worry. There are real problems we worry about, which exist; these we have called *Real Event Worry*. In addition, there are worries about problems that *may* exist, which we have called *Hypothetical Event Worry*. This second type of worry may never actually exist except as imagined by an individual, but it can have the feel of a nightmarish daydream. It is often set in the distant future and is usually very unlikely to ever happen. For example, while many of us dream about winning the lottery, worriers would also worry about winning it – about what they'd buy, how they'd deal with all the requests, even what to do when all the money had gone! This is classical *Hypothetical Event Worry* – they may have not even bought a ticket yet, let alone having the life-changing jackpot win.

Here are another two everyday examples:

**Real Event Worry:** my central heating system is making a funny knocking noise, and I worry about when I can get the serviceman around.

**Hypothetical Event Worry:** *if* the central heating system is making a funny noise, I will get carbon monoxide poisoning, and it will then blow up and then the house will burn down (despite the heating system being serviced every year and only being a couple of years old).

**Real Event Worry:** my credit card bill *has arrived* and I'm worrying about whether to pay it all off this month and leave myself short on cash or pay some interest but have enough cash to take my mum out for dinner for her birthday.

**Hypothetical Event Worry:** my credit card bill is *due to* arrive and I am worrying about being able to afford the monthly instalments. If I can't pay my credit cards bill then I'll have to go to court, I'll have the bailiffs around and they'll kick in my door, they'll throw all my stuff into the street and everyone will see what a loser I am.

So what is there to be gained from thinking about worry in this way? In short, *Real Event Worry* you can do something about, by problem-solving the situation – even if you are not quite sure how to go about it, or not confident that you will succeed. In fact, worriers are rarely confident about their true abilities. *Hypothetical Event Worry* events, by definition, are not real and are both so unlikely and so far in the future that problem-solving will *never* work. So, with this kind of worry, we focus on the worry itself and study the underlying message that it contains. You will learn more about this later. But for now consider the following quote from *Shantideva*, an eighth-century Indian Buddhist scholar, who said,

If you *can* solve your problem, then what is the *need* of worrying? If you *cannot* solve it, then what is the *use* of worrying?

This quotation illustrates why it is important to become more curious about the type of worry you are experiencing. To recap, you can work on *Real Event Worry* by problem-solving rather than worrying, whereas with *Hypothetical Event Worry*, which is often far removed in time and highly unlikely to happen, there's no use in worrying. In this case we investigate and confront the 'awful truth' that we think lies at the heart of our worry. So, again, we must do something other than worry.

In the diagram below, the whirlwind of worry is made up of two shades, representing the two types of worry, namely *Hypothetical Event Worry* and *Real Event Worry*.

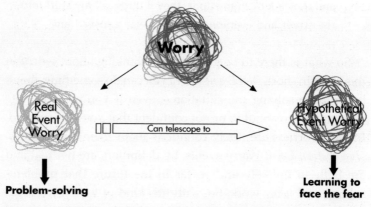

**Problem-solving**

**Learning to face the fear**

**Figure 5.1. Splitting *Real Event* from *Hypothetical Event Worry*.**

It might also help you to reflect on the Serenity Prayer, which asks for the

> serenity of mind to accept that which cannot be changed; the courage to change that which can be changed, and the wisdom to know the one from the other.

Of course, this is not always easy to do, especially when we have been caught up in worry and learned to respond to our worries in the same way. Also, *Real Event Worry* and *Hypothetical Event Worry* are often mixed in together and to separate them requires some effort. To complicate things further, worry can have both hypothetical and real aspects and so the distinction is not absolutely clear (see the exercise on page 92). We have to learn to live with the uncertainty that this might trigger in us. However, separating the two types of worry is important, as each type requires a different solution, just as solving the traffic flow problems requires different strategies for different modes of transport. In practice this means we need to become skilled at recognizing the different types of worry. The reason for being interested in this will become clearer later in the book (see Chapters 14–17).

Sometimes it's not possible to change *Real Event Worry*. For example, when someone is in deep poverty or living with serious illness, or working in a situation where there is real uncertainty, the solutions may lie elsewhere (such as in seeking practical help) – working with your worry alone may not be enough in cases like these.

## 'Telescoping' worry

In Table 5.1 below you will find examples of each type of worry and how they tend to overlap. Worry also has the tendency to telescope to the future, so that *Real Event Worry* will evolve into *Hypothetical Event Worry*. Let's take the first example. Here the person starts to worry following an argument with their partner.

> Although most of the time we get on well, I have just had an argument with my partner and we are not talking. I start to worry about the consequences of the argument. *What if* we stop talking completely, and then my partner finds someone else? And what if they have an affair and I never know, but then stumble across them together? And supposing I lose my rag and do something stupid, and then I'll have to leave and I'll lose the house. I'll go to pieces, I won't

cope and my life will go down the tubes. *Ending with,* the trial will go on for months and I'll end up in jail, and I'll be left with nothing. My partner will have it all and I'll never find anyone again. And if my wife takes out a court order and I break it because I want to see the kids, she'll have me arrested for harassment.

In this example the worrier is transported by worry away from the issue at hand to an imaginary and nightmarish future which at the time feels very real and is very upsetting. He or she worries about whether they can cope with the outcome of the trial and can see themselves disappearing into a hole. Like a whirlwind the worry leaves a trail of emotional devastation in its wake. At some level the worrier *knows* that their worry is not true, but at another level it *feels* very, very real and produces many of the emotions that you would expect to have if this was happening for real.

Does this pattern seem familiar to you? Notice how the worry, like an *express elevator,* takes the person away from an event or situation that they might be able actually to *do something* about, in this case an argument with their partner. This part of the worry is potentially solvable, by, for example, waiting for a quiet moment and sitting down together and talking things through.

### TABLE 5.1 MORE EXAMPLES OF *REAL EVENT VS. HYPOTHETICAL EVENT WORRIES*

| Real Event Worry | Hypothetical Event Worry |
|---|---|
| <div align="center">May telescope to →</div> | |
| I've just had an argument with my partner and we're not talking. | Things will get so bad that I'll break the court order (see above) and the trial will go on for months and then I'll be left with nothing, my partner will have it all. |

| | |
|---|---|
| I have to meet my boyfriend at the airport and I'm worrying about how to get there. | There could be a terrorist attack. |
| My wife is late home from work and we have some tickets for a show later. | My wife could have had a car accident. |
| I have a fever and feel dreadful. | I might become seriously ill and die alone. |
| I've lost the passwords to my Internet banking account. | Somebody will 'hack' into my account and take all my savings. |
| My child has a temperature. | I'll be interviewed on local television about how I failed to spot a serious illness. |
| My youngest is not wearing his cycle helmet to school. | He'll fall off his bike and get a head injury and then go off the rails and end up in care. |
| My neighbours are noisy. | I'll never be able to sell the house, I'll be stuck here for ever. |
| My car was stolen. | It will be used in a bank raid and I'll be prosecuted for this and end up in jail. Alone. |
| The drain outside the house needs fixing, there are two inches of water everywhere whenever it rains. | The house might be flooded or there may be a landslide. |
| We've been invited to have dinner with my partner's boss, and I don't want to go | My partner will go without me, meet someone have an affair and leave me. |
| I fell out with my neighbour. | They'll make a complaint and I'll get into trouble with the police and be forced to move. |
| I have an itchy rash and the doctor doesn't know what it is. | I will die from some horrible illness. |
| My child is disobedient and getting into trouble at school. | I'll be visiting him in prison, how will I fit the visits in with work? |
| I can't concentrate on work. | I'll lose my mind if I keep worrying. |
| I have too much work to do. | I'll lose my job and end up on the streets. |
| My three year old watches too much TV. | I'll have a 20-stone teenager. |

What do you make of the table above? Does the pattern seem familiar to you? Does it give you any clues as to what you might do to overcome your worry?

*Hypothetical Event Worry* can lead to real event worry, although the route is less direct. The *Hypothetical Event Worry* may lead to real physical symptoms of anxiety, such as irritability or concentration problems, which then become the subject of *Real Event Worry*. In these cases we need to work out which type of worry comes first and work with this: if the root worry is *Real Event*, then we move to problem-solving, but if the root event is hypothetical, then we move to face the fear at the heart of our worry. Each of these will be covered in more detail in Chapters 14–17.

The inclination to 'get on' the express elevator might begin to tell us something about what separates worriers from those who worry less. With 'big occasions' most of us have had the experience of the express elevator, but with everyday events, people who worry less might be more able to catch themselves before they reach the tenth floor or, they get to the fiftieth and come straight back down – either by saying to themselves, *Come on, where are you going with this?*, or by recognizing that they are 'in' the *elevator* and saying to themselves, *Slow down a minute, I'm getting ahead of myself*, and then getting back to either solving the problem or getting on with life. Worriers may reach the fiftieth floor before they know it and may not have noticed the ride up, or the fact that they are on the fiftieth floor, locked in and panicking while the problem or situation that triggered their worry remains on the ground floor, unresolved.

When our worry telescopes  or we ride the *express elevator* of worry the level of uncertainty that we feel increases greatly. This is not surprising. When we launch ourselves into the future everything becomes hypothetical because none of it has happened. All the potential problems, the solutions to the prob-lems and the potential problems within the solutions (every silver lining has a cloud) are all possible. The imaginary or hypothetical future is indeed uncertain because none of it is real! However, it also feels scary, and we learned in Chapter 3 that we have evolved with the capacity to feel fear because if the threat is real, rather than hypothetical, fear readies us for appropriate action. This uncertainty, and the scary, doom-laden feeling that go with it, in turn triggers more worry.

To overcome your worry it is important to become much more aware of when this 'telescoping' happens so that you don't 'get ahead of yourself' in your worry. To help you with this there are some exercises and questions in the next section. But recognizing the pattern is a first step.

## Separating *Real Event* and *Hypothetical Event* Worry

'When I look back on all these worries, I remember the story of the old man who said on his deathbed that he had had a lot of trouble in his life, most of which had never happened.' Winston Churchill

For now let us consider how we can separate out the two types of worry. The questions below aim to help you to see when your worry has become much more hypothetical. The first few questions ask you to think carefully about the context of your worry, in particular where and when the things you are worrying about are taking place. With *Hypothetical Event Worry* the feelings of uncertainty and anxiety created are very real, so when this happens reflect on the content of your worry and ask when and where is this worry happening. If the answers suggest that your worry is set in the future (tomorrow, next week, or especially at some indeterminate time in the future) and the worry has transported you somewhere else (not where you are right now) then you are much more likely to be dealing with *Hypothetical Event Worry*. The 'time code' (some time in the future) will give you the strongest clue. If you get a sense that you are dealing with a *Hypothetical*, then track this back to the start (press ground floor in the express elevator). What first triggered this chain of worry? Was the trigger a *Real Event* or was it *Hypothetical*? Is it something you can do something about?

In order to take this further, the next question to ask is how real the worry is. In very concrete terms, could you 'show it' to someone else? For instance, would they see the bailiffs knocking at your door, or would they just see your credit card bill? Would they see your partner talking to a divorce lawyer or just your partner in a huff? Would they see a doctor rushing you into hospital or just telling you to come back next week if it doesn't clear up? The last question is about taking action; if the worry is about a real event, then can you actually *do* something about it rather than *worrying* about it?

**EXERCISE 5.1: SEPARATING *HYPOTHETICAL EVENT WORRY* FROM *REAL EVENT WORRY***

Bring a current worry to mind. Sit with a notebook and pen and try to answer the following questions.

- Where is your worry set? Is it in the present or the distant future?
- Compared to where my worry has taken me, where am I right now? What day is it, what year? (Bring yourself back to the present). What was I doing just before my worry took hold?

- Have I got ahead of myself? Where did this line of worry start? Did it start with a real event (then track back), or did it start with a hypothetical event (imagined concern)? *Where did I get on the express elevator?*
- Is the thing that I am worrying about something that *actually exists now*? Can I describe the issue that I am worrying about in concrete terms, with a time, date and a place? Would someone else be able to 'see' the issue – the credit card bill, the disgruntled partner, the pile of work to do, the kids being difficult, and so on?
- Could something be done about it? Could someone else solve this? (In theory, is this issue solvable?)
- If yes, then could I do something about it (even though you may worry that you may not be able to do it right)?

As we have said before, sometimes it is possible to find worries that are about real events that have hypothetical implications. For example, if I attended a meeting and my workmates rejected my proposals, this is real; but I may then go on to worry about whether I'll lose my job or if I'll ever get another job again, which is more imagined. Or my financial worries could well be real, but I also worry that I'll never be able to find my feet again financially and that I'll live a life of ruin in an imagined and desperate future. Hypothetical events can also trigger further hypothetical worry. For example, if I worry (without any evidence) that my partner will leave me, this may lead to the worry that I'll die alone and in poverty. We will learn more about solving these kinds of difficulties in Chapter 17. To make sure that you have got the idea, think about the following examples and try to think whether the worry is *Real or Hypothetical* or a bit of both.

## EXERCISE 5.2: SPOTTING *REAL* VS *HYPOTHETICAL EVENT WORRY*

Think about *Real* vs *Hypothetical* first. What makes this item hypothetical? What makes it real? Is there a bit of both? Can you separate out each element? Tick to indicate which type of worry you see.

| Worry | Real | Hypothetical | Both |
|---|---|---|---|
| 1. I've completed a piece of work that I've never done before and I'm worried about whether my boss will like it. | | | |
| 2. I'm about to go on holiday and am worried that my plane will be delayed, although the weather is fine, and there have been no security alerts or baggage handler strikes. | | | |
| 3. I've been to the bank, and there is less money in there than I expected. | | | |
| 4. There are new streetlights in my road and I'm worried that I won't be able to get to sleep at night. | | | |
| 5. I'm having a baby and am worried about whether my employer will allow me the extra maternity leave I want to take. | | | |
| 6. My daughters are two and four years old: I'm worrying how I will cope with them as teenagers with boyfriends. | | | |
| 7. The double-glazing is old, the frames are cracking and there is condensation between the windowpanes: we need to replace it. | | | |
| 8. We need to get the plumber in to fix a leaky pipe. How will I be able to pay if the leaky pipe damages all the electrics? | | | |
| 9. I need to make a minor insurance claim of £200. I'm worried about filling the forms in correctly and that the company may not process the claim properly and my premium will go up, or that they will refuse to pay and accuse us of submitting a false report. | | | |

**Possible ways of answering**

1 = Mostly Real.
2 = Hypothetical: I haven't even got to the airport.
3 = Real: I could show this to the bank manager.
4 = Hypothetical and Real: if I haven't spent a night in bed with the new lights then this is Hypothetical, if I have and I couldn't sleep then this is Real and I could do something about this.
5 = Mostly Real. The baby is not the issue; the response of the employer to my pregnancy is the issue, which is uncertain.
6 = Hypothetical: set in the distant future.
7 = Real.
8 = Both: we have a leaky pipe (real problem), with a hypothetical ending (what if the leak damages the electrics?).
9 = Both: similar to 8. We are worrying about completing a form (real) and this leads to a Hypothetical Worry where the company messes up our application, even though it has not been sent (time code and place offer clues).

By now you will have a better idea of what you are trying to spot in your worry. It's time to turn your attention to your own worry. In order to help you do this you will find a Worry Diary below (see also Appendix 2), which you may like to use. If it's too small, then why not copy it out onto a larger piece of paper? You will need to keep this diary for at least a week and record your worries three to four times a day (see the 'Practical tips' in the next section if you need to).

Before you start recording your worry consider the following questions and write down your answers.

- What do you think you are likely to find if you do this?
- What worries do you have about doing this? What predictions might you make?
- What do you worry about most?
- Can you spot themes in your worry already?
- How much time do you think you spend worrying?
- Is there any pattern to your worry?

| WORRY DIARY | | CONTENT | DISTRESS | WORRY TYPE |
|---|---|---|---|---|
| Day | Time | What was the worry about? | How intense was the worry? How uncontrollable did it seem? Scale 0 = mild 100 = very severe | Is the worry about a real, current problem: does the problem actually exist? Yes/no If no, is it hypothetical? Have I got ahead of myself? |

Once you have kept this diary for a week, ask the following questions:

- What have you learnt about your worry?
- Did anything surprise you?
- If so, what was it?
- When and where do you worry the most?
- What are the things that you worry about most often? What are the recurring themes? What do you make of this?
- Do you get a sense of how long you spend worrying?
- Does one worry lead to another?
- Do your worries represent real events?
- Do your worries ever predict the future?
- How often do your hypothetical worries come true? What does this tell you?

You may like to make a list of the bad things that you 'see' in your worry. How many of these actually come true?

## Practical tips

The following tips apply to all the exercises that appear in this book, so read this carefully and return to it if you need to.

Keeping a diary is difficult, so it's worth thinking about what might help you to remember to write it up and what might get in the way of completing it. The bottom line is that the sooner you sit down to write things down, the clearer your memory will be. The longer you leave it, the worse your memory. And it's often better to have the raw material rather than the processed version – a bit like the difference between tinned and fresh strawberries. So the sooner you sit down to record the better the quality of the information.

If you need to record information three or four times a day then you might find it useful to link up the diary to events in the day such as morning tea, lunch, the six o'clock news or a daily soap. Some people decide to record their worry at four-hour intervals. If you use a computer during the day, then you might want to copy the diary sheet onto the desktop. Mobile phones usually have an organizer function that 'bleep' when it's time to do something. It can be helpful to carry a notebook or diary to jot down a few quick notes, before returning to the diary sheet a little later.

The pattern that you decide to work with and how you remember to complete the diary has to work for you. The important thing is that you start to reflect on your worry more often. So have a think about what is realistic and achievable for you.

Despite the best-laid plans, our lives often have a habit of interfering with our goals. What might hinder, interfere or put you off completing the worry diary? Are you concerned about keeping it from the eyes of others? You may also worry about losing it, and then thinking, *What if someone reads it?*, leading to another bout of worry. Thinking these issues through before-hand will help, but beware of avoiding putting pen to paper because of worry – and, let's face it, you probably will worry about this.

The information you start to collect here will be used in many of the exercises throughout this book, so it will help if you start to get into the habit of recording your worry.

**PIT STOP**

Let's stop and think about what you have just been reading. Can you summarize the key ideas you have taken on board? What is sticking in your mind? Maybe write them down. If you have any questions, jot these down too. You can return to them once you have had a chance to digest the information.

What is sticking in my mind from my reading so far?

1.

2.

3.

**6**

# Marking out the route to feeling better – setting goals

## Goals

In Exercise 1.1 (pages 16–17) there are some questions aimed at getting you to think about what you want from this book; more specifically, what are your goals. Setting goals is an important step in overcoming worry and there are many good reasons for this. For example: if, in our work as cognitive behavioral therapists, we start working with clients before we have set ourselves clear goals, we don't really know where we are going, or what we are trying to achieve. Furthermore, although emotional or psychological change can sometimes be quick, usually it is slow and steady. Or think for a moment think about how your hair grows; you know it is happening, but it is not something you notice or can see. But if you took photos two months apart, then you would notice the difference. Psychological change has this quality: it's measured and sure, and it can go unnoticed unless reviewed and assessed. In our clinical experience, it is as if people quickly get used to the new way of being, almost as if they can't see where they've been, and this can make it much harder to 'see' progress, just as your 'new' hair length becomes just the way your hair is. So setting goals is crucial:

goals motivate us, they help us to recognize change, they give treatment a direction and purpose and, critically, they also tell us where the finishing line is. As someone once said, 'If you aim at nothing, you will hit it every time'.

In this section we review the advantages of setting personal goals and then review the things that can make goals more effective.

## Worry gets in the way of getting things done

To set goals is to challenge life's uncertainties but will in itself trigger worry. You may ask yourself, *What if I don't have any goals?* or *What if I don't know how to achieve them?* or *What if I have too many goals and don't know which to focus on?* and so on. One of the key problems you may face is how to step out of worry in order to begin work on it, without worry hijacking your efforts to get better. There is no easy answer to this. However, we need only a small ledge to get a first foothold: you need only to step outside of worry *enough* to start dealing with it. Understanding how worry works is also very useful, and will help you feel more in control of your worry.

The frameworks found in this book, the tables and diary sheets, suggest ways to help you find your feet and organize your thinking. For instance, writing things down means that you can come back to them if you are hijacked by worry. When thinking about your worry, see *it* as the problem, not yourself. Worry is only a tiny part of who you are. Treat yourself with compassion, just as you would treat anyone else struggling with worry.

To reach your goals you have to try out new things; goals are all about what you are *trying* to do, and simply *trying* is achieving, since you are moving towards your goals. As Samuel Beckett wrote, 'Ever tried. Ever failed. No matter. Try Again.

Fail again. Fail better.' It doesn't matter if you do not achieve your goal, as long as you are trying to achieve it.

In Chapter 16 we will turn our attention to problem-solving, which may help you to think about how to overcome some of these difficulties. There, we begin to think about things to do other than worrying. When thinking about setting yourself goals, you may say to yourself, *I can't cope with this, things will go wrong*, or *I can't manage to do this*. The chapter will also address such thoughts. You may wish to read on and come back to this point, but it can be very useful to have set some personal goals before embarking on overcoming your worry. Remember, a goal is a two-fingered salute to worry and uncertainty. *You can do this!*

## Advantages of setting ourselves goals

If we are looking for good reasons to break the seemingly impossible into manageable chunks, we should look no further than the story of British mountaineers Joe Simpson and Simon Yates. In 1985 they climbed Siula Grande, a 20,814 ft mountain in the Peruvian Andes. On the descent, disaster struck. They had run out of fuel, food and water, and the weather conditions deteriorated, and, to cap it all, Simpson broke his leg. Together they decided that the best and quickest way down the mountain was for Yates to lower Simpson by rope in 300 ft stages, which they continued to do into the night. During the attempt to get off the mountain, Yates, blinded and deafened by blizzard conditions, lowered Simpson over an ice-cliff and there he hung in mid-air. Yates neither had the strength to pull him up, nor enough rope to let him down. Simpson was equally stuck on the other end of the rope, unable to help himself. Neither could communicate with the other. Yates was being pulled over the edge, and finally he made the agonizing decision to cut the rope. Later, when he saw the ice-cliff and crevasse below it clearly, he was convinced that his friend must have died.

Unknown to Yates, Simpson had survived the 100 ft fall; he had come to rest on a small ledge within the crevasse. Alone, with a very badly broken knee, in excruciating pain and without food or water, Simpson took three days to crawl, scramble and drag his broken body for five miles and down 3,000 feet to their base camp, where Yates was just setting off, with another friend, Richard Hawking, to face the world to explain what had happened. Following his experience Simpson wrote the best-selling book *Touching the Void*, and a film of the same name followed. You may like to see the film or read the book.

There is much more to the story, but our focus is on Simpson. He clearly described how he motivated himself to get down the mountain. Given his situation, he knew that if he thought about or focused on the whole torturous journey ahead, he would have probably given in and died. Instead, he set himself small achievable goals such as, *I'll get to that rocky outcrop in 30 minutes* (an easy task had he been able to walk), but he defied excruciating pain to meet his goal. Or, *I'll get to the edge of that crevasse in 20 minutes*, and so on. His survival was truly remarkable, and by breaking this impossible journey into manageable, achievable stages, or goals, he was able to defy the odds and survive. Unsurprisingly, he is now a motivational speaker, helping others to find a way to overcome their problems. (Incidentally, another factor that motivated him was his reluctance to die with a song he hated ('Brown Girl in the Ring' by the 1970s pop group Boney M) playing over and over in his mind – fair enough!).

So why are goals so important? First, they contain within them the idea that things can be different, that change is possible. Second, they help us to focus on future possibilities, rather than the problems that impede us; they help us to 'think outside the box'. Third, they help us become a more active part of the process of change, and, in so doing, help us to feel more influential in, or responsible for, change. Fourth, they impose structure on the seemingly unwieldy. Fifth, they give us targets that we can achieve, offering a taste of success and building up motivation. Sixth, they give sense of meaning to our endeavours: they enable us to find out more about ourselves, which drives personal growth and development. Finally, and probably most importantly of all, they hold out hope and can carry us through the toughest times.

Can you see how Simpson's story illustrates these factors?

## Getting better at setting goals

Our goals should aim to be **SMART** goals, that is:

- **S**pecific
- **M**easurable
- **A**ttainable
- **R**ealistic
- **T**ime limited

We would like to add:

- **C**ompassionate
- **O**rdered
- **P**ositively framed
- **E**ngaged
- **R**eviewed

We will go through each of these to help you think through your goals. There are no right or wrong ways of doing this. At the end of this chapter is a worksheet to help you develop your goals. Like many of the tasks suggested in this book, you may worry about it, which may stop you from doing it; but, once the worry has passed, return to the task, and if worry interferes again, wait for it to pass, and again, return to the task, and so on, until it is done. Ask yourself, *What was I doing before I started to worry*? and then go back to it.

## SMART, COPER

### SPECIFIC

Goals should be clear and focused. Often people have a 'headline' goal, such as *I want to feel better, I want to be happy,* or *I want to be rich*. Such goals are about where we want to get to, but tell us little about how to get there. So we need to explore them a little further to unearth a more focused and detailed version. You can do this by asking a few extra questions to make the goal more specific and break it down into manageable chunks. More specific goals give us clues about how to go about achieving them.

Reflect on the following questions to help you define your goals:

What problems does worry give me?
If worry were less of a problem in my life, how would things be different?
What would I do with my time if I worried less?
What would I notice if I worried less?
Is there anything I would like to stop doing? What could I do instead?
What activities have I avoided because of my worry?
Is there any I would like to start doing if I worried less?
What would we see you doing if you worried less?
How would my relationships/friendships/work life/social life/school, etc. be improved if I worried less?

In giving you some idea of how things might be if you worried less, your answers to these questions will provide you with good ideas for setting goals.

## MEASURABLE

With the best goals we can measure our progress. Think of your goal as a goal on a football field: you know when you have scored, or when you have achieved your goal, when the ball is in the net. So, for instance, if you wanted to worry less, how would you know that you were worrying less? You may wish to use some of the questionnaires or diary sheets found in this book to help you measure your progress. Or, more simply, use a scale of 0–100 and ask where you are on the scale at any given moment. For example, you could record on this scale how much your worry interferes with your relationships (see below). There are limitless ways of measuring change in this way: the key is to find targets to measure that make sense to you. Using these scales you can decide on what and how to measure progress. For example you could measure intensity, frequency, degree of uncontrollability, level of worry and so on.

### EXAMPLE OF RATING SCALE

How much does worry interfere with my relationships?    Date..................

Not at all                                                Interferes a great deal

| 0 | 10 | 20 | 30 | 40 | 50 | 60 | 70 | 80 | 90 | 100 |

What problems does this cause?

## ACHIEVABLE AND REALISTIC

Are the goals you have set doable? Are they feasible? Can you reach them? Are they sensitive to your situation? If you have a busy life, or have little time to think and reflect, then your goals should be in tune with this. Imagine you're setting these goals for a close friend who worried in similar life circumstances; from this point of view, are your goals workable? Is there someone you trust with whom to chat through your goals? A few minutes a day together might be achievable (doable) and realistic.

Worry is a normal everyday process, so setting a goal such as *I never want to worry again* is completely impossible – we all worry. Furthermore, setting a goal to eradicate worry from your life would quickly lead you to failure and deflation. It's important to give yourself small tasks that are sensible within the practical limits. So, a headline goal might be, *I want to learn how to worry less*; a more specific, realistic goal might be, *I want to reduce my worry about my children by 30 per cent*.

There is a series of mini-tasks throughout this book, such as assessing the extent of your worry, keeping a worry diary and spotting types of thoughts. Each task is a small stepping stone to help you reach the headline goal of reducing worry.

## TIME-LIMITED

Set a time frame for the goal. For example, *I want to read the next chapter within two weeks*. Time limits help to maintain focus and momentum. Setting a time limit that is too brief may lead to more anxiety or a poor job since you rush to complete the goal. On the other hand, time limits that are too far away may not offer the sense of urgency that helps us to complete goals. For some of us, a deadline offers something to work towards, it motivates us and helps us plan what we need to do and when we need to do it.

Broadly speaking, we know that worriers can do one of two things: they either put things off for as long as possible, or they dive in without thinking. Both these styles are influenced by how worriers react to uncertain situations (we will talk more about this later). If you recognize the first of these traits in yourself, then it might be worth giving yourself tighter deadlines; if you recognize the second you may need to give yourself more time.

## COMPASSIONATE GOALS

Goals are not cold-hearted things; they represent how we would like to see ourselves in the world and, as such, they encapsulate our intimate thoughts, feelings and aspirations. As the Irish poet W. B. Yeats wrote, 'I have spread my dreams under your feet; tread softly because you tread on my dreams.' Engaging in goal-setting is a very personal experience; it can make us feel very vulnerable. Consequently, it can be very difficult, because of the anxiety and concerns that bubble to the surface the moment change is invited into our lives. This book is about change, and no one finds that easy; so be thoughtful and sensitive to your needs in the way that you are to others. Change requires courage, but goals can help.

## ORDERED – SHORT- AND LONG-TERM GOALS AND STEPPING STONES

When you have worked out some goals, ask which can be achieved in the near future and which are longer-term goals. To help you with this, answer the following questions:

- Which of these goals are easier to meet?
- What might give you a sense of success early on?
- What can be achieved right now?
- What can be left for later?

Think of goals like a series of stepping stones: to get to the third stone you have to walk across the first and the second. If one goal is dependent on another, you may need to ask which goals *have* to happen first. For example, if your goal is to reduce worry about finances by 50 per cent, this will be dependent on another goal that focuses on developing a better understanding of your worry. Or, if your goal is to fly a helicopter, this will be dependent on a goal of attending training sessions and another one of passing exams.

### POSITIVE REFRAMING — APPROACH AND AVOIDANCE GOALS

Goals framed in a way that means we are trying to get away from something bad or negative are called avoidance goals. Goals that are moving us towards something positive are called approach goals.

Let's start with an unusual example: imagine running away from a tiger. Compare the goal of avoiding being eaten with the goal of finding safety. The first is an avoidance goal, the second an approach goal. While both are reasonable, the first keeps your mind and eyes behind you, focused on the tiger and so on all that is frightening and scary, while the second forces you to focus on the solution, not the problem. Now stop for a moment and try this suggestion.

Imagine you are being chased by a tiger. Keeping the first goal in mind (to avoid being eaten), what pops into your mind, what pictures do you see? Spend a few moments with this. Then, with the tiger still there, your goal is now to find safety. Ask the same questions. What happens?

Our reasonable goal of avoiding the tiger may bring to mind all that could go wrong, all that is horrible, images of blood and gore. However, the second part of the exercise may have brought to mind images of safety, an elephant lifting you on to its back or a helicopter lifting you away from the danger. Avoidance goals tend not to lead us anywhere in particular; they may even leave us running around in circles. On the other hand, having approach goals tends to mean that you are looking out for a particular feature to head towards. This is not to say that avoidance goals are unhelpful, it's just that approach goals may be more helpful – they don't keep reminding us of the problem. And it's more likely you achieve an approach goal than an avoidance goal..

How can I identify which is which? We can 'hear' avoidance goals in the words people use to describe them, such as 'reduce', 'get rid of', 'prevent', 'avoid', 'escape', 'quit', 'forget'. For example, *I want to reduce my worry*, or *I want to avoid feeling anxious*. Again, these goals sound very reasonable, but at the heart of the goals is the idea of worry or anxiety (the tiger). To take the worry goal, worry is a negative experience (the tiger), and trying to escape this experience provides the energy or drive for the goal. In trying to reduce worry, we are in essence trying to move away from it. However, the goal tells us little about where we should move to, and, if we succeed, we don't really gain anything positive, except to escape from the clutches of our negative feelings (the tiger). Researchers suggest that goals framed in this way are less likely to be achieved. As the exercise above has shown, such goals keep in mind the idea of threat, of what could go wrong and, as a result, they may make our worry or anxiety worse. They also put the energy for change outside of ourselves: we are fleeing or escaping something awful, rather than heading towards something positive.

On the other hand, approach goals lead us towards something positive; the goal provides direction and has an implicit reward. So, rather than saying *I want to lose weight* (an avoidance goal), an approach goal would suggest *I want to eat more vegetables*.

Here are some examples:

### TABLE 6.1 EXAMPLES OF REFRAMED GOALS

| Avoidance goal | Reframed or approach goal |
| --- | --- |
| I want to give up smoking. | I want to be able to run up two flights of stairs without stopping. |
| I want to lose weight. | I want to go for a 20-minute walk five times a week for the next month. |
| I want to stop giving all my work to my boss for her to check. | I want to handle routine things more independently. |
| I want to get rid of worry. | I want to spend more time reading. |
| I want to stop telephoning my husband when he's on his way home. | I want to write some e-mails and catch up with my friends. |
| I want to reduce the amount I look into things before I make even small decisions. | I want to manage the uncertainty by making quicker decisions. |
| I want to reduce the worry about my kids by 30 per cent. | I want to spend at least 20 minutes a day playing with my children. |

There is still much to be discovered by research about the different types of goals and their impact on us. But it would seem to make common sense to begin to think of our goals as representing the hope of a new way of being, rather than an escape from the old. But reframing requires some work. A tip – think about adding new actions or behaviors, rather than reducing or stopping existing actions or behaviors: what you can do and will do, not what you are trying to stop doing.

Usually the avoidance goals spill out first – and that's OK. Goals are often framed in avoidance terms in the early stages, since our focus is then understandably on the problems themselves. However, it may help to stop and think about your goals and ask if reframing them could offer some advantage. Having a mix of avoidance and approach goals is OK, since, as with all things, balance is the key. And you may include both the approach and avoidance aspects of your goal for example. The bottom line is that any goal is better than none.

## ENGAGED

A tip: keep a postcard or credit card-sized paper in your wallet or purse, and write on it the reasons why it is important for you to keep *engaged* with your goals, so that when the going gets tough you can remind yourself of the reasons why you are trying to change. Alternatively, find something that visually symbolizes your positive approach goal. Keep this somewhere in your mind or, better still, find something to remind you of it – a picture from a magazine, a postcard, an object, a word, a phrase, anything that keeps your approach goals in mind.

## REVIEW

It will help to set a series of review dates to reflect on your progress. You may want to put a note on the fridge or use the organizer on your mobile phone to remind you when to review your progress. What would help you to remember to review your progress?

Our goals should not be set in stone. It is helpful to review and renegotiate them as things change. As this happens you will access new information and experiences, which will alter your goals, so that reviewing and renegotiating become part of the process. As Doug Larson, an English Olympian suggested, 'Establishing goals is all right if you don't let them deprive you of interesting detours'.

Below you will find a series of questions and an exercise (Exercise 6.1, page 116) to help you to set better goals. Read carefully through the example worked out for you (Table 6.2). You will definitely need much more space than is found in this book, so sit with a notebook and write down your responses. There are many questions: not all of them will be relevant to you, so read them through and decide which questions work best. Take time, but beware of investing too much time and energy in this; are you avoiding starting to put your goals into action? And remember, having any kind of goal is better than none; so don't get hung up on trying to find the perfect set of goals.

## TABLE 6.2 DEVELOPING BETTER GOALS FOR OVERCOMING YOUR WORRY

### A: Questions to help you clarify your goals

- If worry were less of a problem in my life, how would things be different?
- What would I do with my time if I worried less?
- What would I notice if I worried less?
- What activities have I avoided because of my worry?
- Is there anything I would like to start doing if I worried less?
- Is there anything I would like to stop doing?
- What would we see you doing if you worried less?

### B: Questions to help organize your answers

- Which are short-, medium- or long-term goals?
- Which goal needs to be done first?
- Which can I ignore for now?
- Which goal would give me a sense of achievement?
- Am I picking an issue that is too tough, is there anything easier I could attempt now?
- *If my goal is an avoidance goal, would re-framing it to an approach goal help?*

### C: SMART goal questions

- Is this goal specific? Can it be broken down further?
- How can I measure progress towards this goal? How will I know when I have achieved this goal?
- Is this goal practically possible or achievable?
- Is this goal realistic?
- How long will I realistically need to complete this goal? (time limited)

### D: Revised goal/s questions

- Is your goal compassionate?
- *For when things are tough:* What are your reasons for continuing to engage with your goals?
- Is there a picture or an object that could remind you of your goals?

## EXAMPLES OF WORKING OUT YOUR GOALS

| Headline Goal | Answers to A questions | Answers to B questions | Answers to C (SMART) questions | D: Revised goal/s |
|---|---|---|---|---|
| I want to overcome my worry. | If I worried less, I would be more confident, I would need to check things out with my boss less. I would go for that promotion. I would be able to handle my concerns about doing things wrong. I would be less tired and stressed by work. | New goal/s **Shorter term:** I want to stop giving all my work to my boss for her to check it. **Positive reframe:** I want to handle more things independently. **Longer term:** Go for promotion. | I could ask her to check only work that she needs to. I could note how many pieces of work I give to her. This is doable, and realistic and she will help me. I need 4 weeks to do this. | I want to handle more things independently. <u>Plan</u> For the next 4 weeks, I will give my boss, only the work that she needs to see. I could ask for her feedback and keep a count of the work I do, that she does not see. <u>Review</u> in two weeks. Review other short-term and long-term goals. |

| EXERCISE 6.1: DEVELOPING BETTER GOALS FOR OVERCOMING YOUR WORRY | | | |
|---|---|---|---|
| Headline Goal | Questions A | B: Questions (What new goals come to mind as a result of your answers to Questions A?) | C: SMART questions | D: Revised goal/s questions |
| | | New goal(s) <br><br> Shorter term: <br><br> Positive reframe: <br><br> Longer term: | Answers to questions | Revised goal(s) (Do you need to positively reframe your goal?) <br><br><br> <u>Plan</u> <br><br> <u>Review when?</u> |

**PIT STOP**

Let's stop and think about what you have just been reading. Can you summarize the key ideas you have taken on board? What is sticking in your mind? Maybe write them down. If you have any questions, jot these down too. You can return to them once you have had a chance to digest the information.

What is sticking in my mind from my reading so far?

1.

2.

3.

# 7

# Learning about rules

As we mentioned in the traffic metaphor above, there are other things that influence the flow of traffic, such as drivers' beliefs or rules (*If I keep up with the traffic flow, I'm less likely to have an accident*). For a moment consider what would happen if you rigidly held this rule. Suppose there is heavy rain and the traffic is moving much too quickly, or imagine everyone else is going well above the speed limit – what would you do? Would you break the rule or would you keep it? Our life experience helps us to know when it is best to either update or break our life rules. It is this flexibility that helps us to adapt and adjust to new experiences or situations.

It seems that our emotional wellbeing is based on beliefs or rules that are held firmly enough to give a consistent sense of who we are. Yet, at the same time, these rules and beliefs need to be fluid enough to enable us to adapt to new experiences. If you think about it, even so-called hard and rigid things, like bridges and tall buildings, move, flex and bend to wind and loads; without this ability they would soon break and fracture.

When people have psychological problems, often this flexibility is lost and their rules have become stuck and rigid. Our feelings can be considered to act like resin or concrete, setting the rules in place and making them harder to change. In this state, they are extreme and absolute, with no shades of grey. We can see these qualities reflected in the words used to make up the rules. For example, *I must <u>always</u> worry to solve my problems; I should <u>never</u> make a decision without checking it;* or, *If I can't predict what will happen, I'll <u>never</u> be able to cope.* If we think about these rules, would you consider them to be rules that everyone should hold? If not, why not? You may consider them to be unhelpful or extreme; you may also consider them to go beyond what is considered to be common sense.

We each have a unique 'rule book', which is a set of beliefs that guide our actions and help us to make sense of the world around us. If a Martian landed in your street tomorrow, using your rulebook, he or she should be able to understand more about your world. The 'rulebook' helps us to make sense of the world because the rules are essentially predictions about what will happen next: for instance, *If I smile then others will smile back; If I hit my thumb then it will hurt; If I eat then I won't be hungry;* and so on. When we look at how people act we can begin to work out what rules might be influencing their actions. Usually we are unaware of these rules, but with a little attention and thought we can work them out. The first way to spot them is to become curious about what you or others do (or don't do) in a given situation. Our aim in this chapter is to reveal your 'worry rulebook' and then help you find ways of adapting the rules or even breaking them. The first section explores the different types of rule or belief that might be in operation, the second section moves on to helping you develop your 'worry rulebook'.

## How to spot rules

Rules are often phrased as *if–then* statements, but they can also be *shoulds, oughts* or *musts*. They can be about many things – thoughts, feelings, actions, events, memories or even bodily sensations. We can use these phrases (*if–then, shoulds*, etc.) to help us work out the rules that might be active in any given situation. Take an everyday example such as why people form a line at a bus stop.

### EXERCISE 7.1. WAITING AT A BUS STOP

How would you finish these statements? Write your answers on the dotted line.

If I stand in a queue **then** . . . . . . . . . . . . . . . . . . . . . . .
If I am at the front of the line **then** . . . . . . . . . . . . . . . .
If my feet are cold **then** . . . . . . . . . . . . . . . . . . . . . .
If I am lost in my thoughts **then** . . . . . . . . . . . . . . . . .
If I urge the bus to come **then** . . . . . . . . . . . . . . . . . .

For the first of these beliefs or rules you might say, *Then, I'll get on the bus*, or, for the fourth belief, you may answer, *I'll miss the bus*! For the final one, well of course, *It'll be late!* Completing these phrases helps us work out what rules might be operating. Can you also see how these rules tell us about what might happen next, how they are essentially predictions? (Stop for a moment to think about this.) If my feet are cold, then we might predict that I'd stamp my feet. It works the other way round, too – if I notice someone stamping their feet, then I can guess that their feet are cold, although I can't be certain without asking.

Rules can also be phrased as *shoulds*, *oughts* or *musts*, and using these phrases can help us to work out other rules. For example,

> I **must** not stand too close to the person in front.
> I **must** not talk to the driver when he is driving.
> Other people **should** never barge in.
> I **ought** to have the right change.

Rules can be culturally specific. This means that bus queues in Bristol, Calcutta, Istanbul, La Paz, Toronto, Beijing, Paris and Nairobi are all influenced by slightly different rules, which means that different things happen. If you have travelled to new places, it might take a while to understand how the 'local' rules operate – this is part of the fun (or hassle) of travelling. When we learn about how others live their lives, we are essentially sussing out the rules that govern their actions.

We can also ask questions to help us detect rules, questions like, *Supposing you didn't queue what would happen?* Or, *What are the advantages and disadvantages of queuing?* These questions trigger us to reflect on the things that are important to us and bring us closer to understanding the rules that drive our actions.

How do your rules influence your actions at a bus stop? Before reading on, review your answers in the box above and try to imagine how these rules might influence your actions. You may also want to complete the following sentences:

- At a bus stop I should . . .
- At a bus stop I ought to . . .
- At a bus stop I must . . .
- At a bus stop others should . . .
- At a bus stop others ought to . . .
- At a bus stop others must . . .

What about your worry rules? Try completing the following:

---

**EXERCISE 7.2: WORRY RULES**

If I worry, then . . . . . . . . . . . . . . . . . . . . . . . . . . . . . . .

If I don't worry, then . . . . . . . . . . . . . . . . . . . . . . . . . . .

I should worry because . . . . . . . . . . . . . . . . . . . . . . . . .

---

## Rules or beliefs? (Rules = Beliefs)

So far we have used these terms together or interchangeably. They are different ways of referring to the same thing. In CBT, rules are a type of thought and so we can call them beliefs.

### What happens when the rules are broken?

When our rules are broken, or more usually when they look as if they might be broken, we often feel strong emotions. For example, if someone looked as if they were about to 'barge in' in a queue, then we may feel irritated or even angry. If someone was standing too close to us, we may feel uncomfortable. The fact that they have threatened to break or have actually broken the rules might lead us to do something about it, like moving to plug the gap, complaining, moving away or having angry thoughts of revenge. Look at the table below and answer the following questions: do these rules make sense of the actions they support? When the rules are broken, do you understand why the person ends up feeling the way they do? Can you see how their feelings might motivate these actions?

| TABLE 7.1 STANDING AT THE BUS STOP | | | |
|---|---|---|---|
| Rule | Actions the rule encourage | Feelings produced if rule is broken | Actions taken if rule is broken |
| Others should never push in | Standing in line | *(e.g. if people push in)* Anger Irritation | Complaining Muttering to yourself Glancing at others |
| I ought to have the right change | Planning to get change Counting out change Repeatedly checking change or holding change in hand | *(e.g if I don't have any change)* Nervousness Guilt Resignation | Planning what to say Making excuses Walking home Worrying |

## Rules and worry

Worry is an everyday experience, and naturally there is a range of rules that underpin or support worry. Everyone holds some of these worry-supporting rules, but worriers probably tend to hold them much more rigidly than non-worriers. Research also tells us that if we target these rules in treatment then the symptoms of excessive worry may reduce. So it's worthwhile spending some time understanding them and then finding ways of adapting them. Rules appear in every chapter of this book; in some chapters they play a much more central role than in others, and some will be much more relevant to you than others. In the upcoming chapters note the sections that most closely describe the way you think, so that you can return to them. Many of the rules can be worked with by using *behavioral experiments*; we will tell you more about these later in this chapter.

Rules that support worry instruct us to worry in lots of different situations – when we face uncertainty or everyday problems, for example. Rules might also instruct us to do other things in addition to worry, such as avoid situations that trigger worry, seek much more information than we need, put things off so we worry later or seek reassurance. There are many others. If we are looking for signs that these worry rules are in action, then we need look no further than worry itself. The action of worry suggests that our worry rules have been activated. But these other signs – avoidance, putting things off and so forth – also give us clues as to the type of worry rule that is in action. In the forthcoming chapters you will learn how to spot the tell-tail signs that these rules are in operation.

## Understanding what keeps problems going

A helpful analogy is to think about the time when the world was thought to be flat. This idea comes with images of the 'edge of the world', where great waterfalls cascade over from the rim of the earth into oblivion. If we truly believed this, then it would make good sense to avoid the edge of the world. But because we never go to the edge of the world, we never find out that this simply isn't true, so the belief that the world is flat lives on.

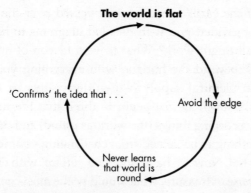

**The world is flat**

'Confirms' the idea that . . .

Avoid the edge

Never learns
that world is
round

**Figure 7.1. Flat world analogy.**

Now imagine you hold this belief very strongly and that we turn up and tell you the world is round. Would you believe us? Probably not, given that you imagine that those foolish enough to sail to the edge of the world will fall into oblivion. Next we might suggest you come with us on a journey around the world and 'over the edge'. How would you feel? What would you do? You might decide to give us a wide berth, writing us off as con artists and troublemakers (and you may be right). But supposing we brought evidence that the world was round; what if we showed you pictures, diagrams and charts, brought gifts and treasures from beyond the known world, what would you think then?

What evidence would you need to take the risk? (Think about this before moving on.)

What if we asked you to think about the balance between the advantages and disadvantages of a flat earth, and then a round earth? What if we took you to talk with other sailors to find out what they knew? What if we watched a ship disappearing over the horizon hull first, masts last? What if we told you that you would see new constellations of stars if you travelled with us? What if we observed a lunar eclipse and watched the curve of the earth's shadow as it passed over the moon? What if we provided you with detailed diagrams to help you see how it all might work? What if we told you of an island paradise just beyond the horizon with everything you could ever want in plentiful supply (we will leave this bit to your imagination)? You may just begin to think that there *may* be another way of seeing things (the world is round) and that there *may* be something to be gained from challenging your idea that the world is flat. Now we have 'softened you up' with evidence and the promise of treasure, what would be the most convincing piece of evidence to prove once and for all that the world was not flat? The bottom line is that you need to go over 'the edge' and find out for yourself.

In CBT this is what is called a *behavioral experiment* – doing things differently to find out something new. In our example, you may be beginning to think there may be something in this idea that the world is round, but you still might be doubtful. You may agree to come for a sail, and after an hour or so, we turn to you and say, *Look the world is round*. But you are not convinced and you reply, *Yes, but if we sailed further then we'd really go over the edge, the edge is just beyond this horizon*. So we sail on for another hour and the same thing happens again. So we ask, *How long would we have to sail to convince you*? And you say, *A year and day, and in and out of weeks*. And off we'd go. As we sail we might look up into the night sky to see how the constellations change, collecting evidence as we go. And finally, after a year and a day, we'd ask, *So how does this experience of sailing for all this time fit with the idea that the earth is flat?* If your flat world idea still remained then there would be nothing for it – we'd have to call NASA and get you a seat on the next space shuttle!

Why are we telling you this story? It helps to demonstrate the ideas that we will use for helping you to change. It shows how rules motivate actions, which then in turn act to confirm the original idea. For instance, if I believe that worry helps to solve problems, then it makes sense to worry. Also, in order to challenge the idea of a flat earth we needed to find evidence to gently rock the foundations of this idea. In the above example we used the same ideas and techniques used in the treatment of worry and other emotional problems.

## TABLE 7.2 FLAT WORLD – WORRY RULES COMPARISONS

| Strategies | Flat earth example: If I sail over the edge of the world I will die | Worrying example: Worrying helps me solve problems |
|---|---|---|
| Information gathering | We found objects from beyond the edge of the world and information in the form of maps and charts. | We might ask, how do people in general solve life's problems? What ideas/techniques are there to help/teach you to do this? Do good problem-solvers recommend worry as a technique to solve problems? |
| Developing an understanding of how the rules lead to actions and keep the problem going | We helped you understand how your thoughts might be influencing your behavior and keeping the idea of a flat earth alive. | We would show you that worry can get in the way of solving problems, particularly if the worry makes it hard to concentrate – the rule may end up causing more worry and prevent you from solving the problem. |

| Advantages and disadvantages | We reviewed the advantages and disadvantages of taking risks to learn new things. | We might review the advantages and disadvantages of worrying to solve problems. For instance, you may get some good ideas, but do you really want the emotional baggage that comes with solving problems in this way? |
|---|---|---|
| Evidence for an alternative view | We looked for good evidence that suggested that the earth was indeed round. | We would look for good evidence that worrying to solve problems was not as helpful as other methods. We might ask what other ways, aside from worrying, have you solved problems? Which is the best way? |
| Surveys | We talked to the sailors and learned from them. | We might ask you to survey several friends about how they go about solving problems; how many of them do you think might suggest worrying? |
| Goals | We spoke of the treasure that lay in waiting for the brave explorer. | What do you stand to gain by solving problems in another way? Is this something worthwhile to you? |

| Behavioral experiments | We took you over the edge of the world. | We might ask you to solve a minor problem by using problem-solving steps, rather than worrying; what's your prediction about what would happen? How can you push this idea? |
| --- | --- | --- |
| Reviewing learning | Given all this information and experiences, what do you believe now? | What have you learned about worrying as a method of solving problems? |
| What can you do now to push home the idea? | Sail alone around the world. | Solve bigger problems using problem-solving skills. |

In the flat world example above we used information gathering (charts, objects), we developed an understanding of the problem, we looked at the advantages and disadvantages of change, we provided evidence for the alternative idea of a round earth (stars, masts and eclipse), we surveyed other people (sailors) to find out their experience, and we reminded ourselves of the value of change (treasure). We then reviewed the idea in the light of these new experiences and the final step was trying something new. The last part is important, because doing something new normally leads to new information and ideas. It's as if you have a new piece of the jigsaw (new information), and you have to accommodate this into your existing world view, which can be quite an earth-shattering experience. This new information can be like wearing someone else's shoes for a while; it might feel odd and take a while to wear them in. This is why it's important to follow up your experiments with others until it begins to feel like second nature. The acid test is whether you start to feel differently. While sometimes this happens quickly, mostly it's a question of chipping away and doggedly moving forward.

While the story above is about actions and thoughts, it is principally about feelings. In the flat earth example, fear is the main motivating emotion. If you believe that the world is flat, it makes absolute sense to feel frightened about going over the edge of the world! The test enabled new learning by trying something new, and as a consequence the fear of the edge was dissolved. Doing things differently requires courage, and these kinds of experiences are not easy, but the benefits are huge. Anxiety and fear can lock us into unhelpful patterns of thinking and action; behavioral experiments are the key, and enable us to unlock our minds and free it from anxiety.

Behavioral experiments are among the most powerful ways of enabling change and helping people to overcome their problems. We will outline in more detail how they work later, but first let's take the flat earth experiment a little further by looking at how some of the actions people use to keep themselves safe during experiments get in the way of learning something new.

## Safety behaviors

As we have suggested above, rules and beliefs encourage or discourage actions. For instance, one way to prevent yourself falling off the edge of the world is simply to avoid sailing and never get in a boat, or at least never leave the port. However, if you do go sailing, there are some things that you might do to keep yourself safe. Let's imagine that we are in the boat and we are heading towards the edge of the world. If you are like us, then you may want to 'hedge your bets' and *do* something to make the experience less frightening. Because your safety behavior makes you feel safe, it might be something you do every time you sail out into open water and consequently you may not notice it. The idea that the world is flat may encourage you to trail a rope back to shore, so you can pull yourself back if you *feel* you are too close to the edge. You may ignore the edge and pretend that none of this is happening and stare into the bottom of the boat (missing the evidence from the stars). You may feel safe only if you can see your homeland behind you (meaning that you sail in circles for days and not towards the horizon). These actions are logical, given the idea that the earth is flat, and they function to make us 'feel' safer. However, they are based on the idea that there is something 'real' to fear. If we managed to sail closer to the edge of the world while trailing a rope, we may think that the only reason we were safe was because of the rope, that is, *If I didn't have this rope then we really would have gone over the edge.* This turns the experience into a near-miss, *Phew, I saved myself from certain death this time*, rather than allowing you to really find out that there was nothing to be frightened of. Can you see how entirely logical and understandable this is? Breaking, or the potential of breaking, our rules or other beliefs produces strong feelings and motivates us to take action to find safety where we can. This cycle in turn serves to 'rubber stamp' our original unhelpful rule, as above. To drive this idea home, here is our version of a story told by Paul Salkovskis, Professor of Clinical Psychology at the Institute of Psychiatry in London.

A man was sprinkling white powder in the fast lane of a very busy motorway. The police were alerted and arrived with blue lights flashing, stopped the traffic and arrested the man. They asked him, 'Why were you sprinkling white powder on the motorway?' The man replied, 'It's anti-elephant powder to keep the elephants off the road and stop awful accidents from happening.' The police officer exclaimed,

'But there are no elephants in Newcastle!' And the man answered, 'You see, it works!'

The things we do to keep ourselves safe (safety behaviors) have a number of unhelpful side-effects. They keep the idea alive in our minds that there is something to be frightened of (*that was a near miss, next time I won't be so lucky, be prepared*); they often make the situation or problem much worse (by being in the fast lane the man was actually putting his own and others life at risk rather than stopping accidents); and they keep our danger radar on which means that we pick up on the tiniest signs of danger or see danger where there is none. There are many safety behaviors in worry. For example, asking someone for reassurance once a decision has been made is a safety behavior aimed at reducing uncertainty and worry. Unfortunately, it keeps worry alive because the worrier never learns to trust their judgment. Each time a new decision or situation arises, the worrier doubts their ability to make a good decision and so seeks reassurance. If this is done enough times, then those close to them may start to get annoyed, which in turn triggers more worry, the very thing the worrier was trying to reduce in the first place. Also, because the worrier's 'threat radar' is on full, even decisions they are certain about trigger them to seek reassurance.

## Safety behaviors and worry

Below is a list of typical safety behaviors, with a series of questions to help you explore your own. Spotting safety behaviors is helpful because they are important in keeping worry alive, and they also give clues as to what rules might be lurking beneath them. Review the list and then try to answer the questions that follow.

## TABLE 7.3 TYPICAL SAFETY BEHAVIORS SEEN IN WORRIERS

Seeking reassurance for decisions.

Trying to push upsetting ideas out of our minds.

Seeking out excessive amounts of information before making a decision.

Avoiding certain types of information that triggers worry.

Putting off making decisions.

Overanalysing problems.

Solving problems impulsively.

Making lists as a substitute for actions.

Checking on the whereabouts of loved ones (e.g. finding excuses to telephone them).

Checking and rechecking on decisions or tasks.

Overprotecting others.

Avoiding fully committing to things to leave an 'escape route'.

Distraction.

Being overly busy; throwing ourselves into activity rather than solving problems (e.g. cleaning).

Using lots of superstitious behaviors to avoid bad luck or create good luck.

*Take a notebook and try to answer the following questions:*

- Which of these behaviors are typical of you?
- What other things do you do to reduce worry or uncertainty? Make a list of these.
- What rules might be driving your safety behaviors?
- Supposing you didn't have or dropped your safety behavior, what do you fear would happen?
- Supposing you 'amplified' your safety behavior, then what do you think would happen? (For example, what might happen if on purpose, you checked more often than you usually would? What effect might this have?)
- How might these safety behaviors make your worry worse?

## Summary

So far we have explored the rules (or assumptions) that underpin worry; we have seen how they have an influence on how we feel and what we do, and how, unfortunately, these actions tend to backfire as they keep our worry alive and also make it worse. It is important then to find a way of challenging these unhelpful patterns.

# Modifying our worry rulebook – behavioral experiments

If worry is a problem for you, then we have to help you to challenge the rules that underpin your worry. We do this by taking the stance of a scientist wanting to explore and work out how things relate to one another or how things happen. Like a scientist, we want to set up experiments to see if we can learn something new when we change what happens. We want to look for evidence or facts to test the validity of particular rules. You, and more specifically your worry, will be the subject of these experiments and so it's very important that you understand why we are suggesting them, how these experiments might make things better and what to expect when you are doing them. Behavioral experiments are all about predictions, that is, *what we expect to happen vs what actually happens.* If what *actually* happens is very different from what we *expect*, then we would do well to update the way we think in the light of this new information. Behavioral experiments are powerful because they help us change by giving us *an experience of doing something new, rather than just thinking or talking about it.* Remember Kolb's learning cycle in Chapter 2.

## Planning behavioral experiments

What follows is a series of steps that offers a blueprint to show you how you can start challenging some of the rules. You will find a table summarizing the key points at the end of this chapter.

In each chapter there will be further signposts towards what behavioral experiments you might want to engage in. We have put the blueprint here because it offers some basic principles that apply, no matter what kind of experiments we do. Nearly all the techniques within CBT can be thought of as attempts to examine the helpfulness of particular rules or beliefs, or, put another way, to find out what is really going on. Behavioral experiments and other techniques try to help answer this question by bringing all the information into play, rather than just information selected by the filter of our emotions, habits, avoidance, safety behaviors, unhelpful thinking styles or other processes. In order to bring a more helpful perspective into play, we have to approach the experiment with an open mind, ready for new learning. We have to become curious about previously unexplored information and, like an explorer, we need to seek out, discover and then understand new or previously ignored or avoided experiences, and then be prepared to engage in them.

## Planning behavioral experiments: steps to discovery

First, we need to put the rule 'on the table' in everyday language, that is, to name it in a way that we know what we are dealing with. For argument's sake, let's work with a common rule in worry: *Worrying helps me to solve problems*. We should try to nest the rule within our everyday experience. As it stands, the rule is phrased in a very general way. What might this rule sound like when brought to the 'coalface' of our lives? For example:

*If I worry about problems at home then I can find better ways of solving them.*

Second, although we have our rule in everyday language, it is still a little too vague and we need to tie it down to an everyday example. We also need to get a little more specific and find out what problems the worrier is trying to solve by worrying and what exactly might happen if they *did not* worry.

*If I didn't worry about what to do with the kids over their summer break, then I'd have a nightmare on my hands; they'd be bored and get annoyed with me.*

The more specific we get the easier it is to find ways of challenging rules. More global or general rules are much harder because they don't give us clues about what we might be able to do to challenge them. The following questions can help to get down to the level of detail needed.

Supposing you didn't worry about this; what would be so bad about that? Supposing you didn't worry about this; what would that say about you, or what would that mean to you?

Like all rules, this rule is a prediction – it tells what would happen if the worrier did not worry – and it also helps us to understand why the worrier is so keen to act upon the rule by worrying. Pause for a moment and see if the rule above makes sense to you.

Third, there is a need to get a sense of how big an influence the rule has in our lives. To do this we rate how strongly the worrier believed the rule on a scale of 0–100 per cent, with 100 per cent corresponding to *I absolutely believe this to be true*. We can check this rating later to see if things have changed.

Fourth, we need to think of other ways of seeing things. Essentially, we are trying to find other information or evidence that suggests that this rule may not be wholly helpful. Remember the flat earth example. It's as if these two (or more) ways of thinking are placed on a set of weighing scales: which of these two ideas makes the most sense, when we consider all of the information available? There are several questions that the worrier can be asked to help bring this information to the surface. For example, is your worry actually solving the problem, or are you just going over and over the same concerns? When you worry about this, how does it leave you feeling and how do your feelings influence your ability to think of solutions? Is there a more helpful way of preparing for the summer break, rather than worrying? Even if, you could think of nothing to keep your children occupied, what would be the worst thing that could happen, or what would it say about you as a person?

This fourth step is often a tricky one, since the worrier has been stuck in a particular way of seeing the world and stepping outside of this viewpoint can be difficult. Questions like *Is there another way of seeing this?* or *What ideas would you give to a friend who was struggling with the same problem?* might help. By posing these questions we are trying to soften the rule and enable a new rule to emerge. When it does, then rate this new idea on the same scale.

NEW PREDICTION

*Worrying doesn't seem to be the best way of solving problems. If I worry, I get anxious and can't think straight, so I need to do something instead of worrying.*

Fifth, we need to think of a way of challenging this unhelpful rule. We have to progress towards testing the prediction out by doing something new. In this example, to start with we may decide to focus on finding ideas for a weekend rather than the whole summer break. By doing this we are testing things out in a small way first, where there is more chance of success, and so we will develop better ideas about how things work. The worrier could worry as usual for one weekend and then do something new the following weekend. So for the first weekend they would worry as usual and see what activities they come up with for the children. For the second weekend, we would ask them to write a list and ask the children what they might want to do and then decide together. Which of these two strategies work best?

**Test 1**

*I'll worry about what I can do with the kids over the weekend.*
– How many ideas can you come up with by worrying?

**Test 2**

*This time, I'll write a list and ask the kids to do the same and then decide together what we can do.*

Sixth, we need to consider the things that could get in the way of finding out something new. A useful question is, *If you did this, would it help you to think and feel that worrying was not the best way of finding solutions to problems?* If the answer is no, then we need to think again about how to test this rule out. By asking this we are trying to get the 'yes buts' out in the open before we embark on an experiment. It's like a dry run in your mind to see if the experiment will help. So be prepared to redesign the experiment if needed. Treat each step forward or back as an opportunity to learn something new.

The most important thing is to do something in a different way and break the pattern of your worry, so don't get too hung up on the details. Try it out and review, try again.

## Looking for safety behaviors

With most rules, there are often subtle safety behaviors that coexist. These may become more obvious as you try to challenge and change you worry rules. These mostly small, inconspicuous actions are very powerful, and while they reduce our fear in the short term, they have the unfortunate side-effect of keeping the problem alive. When we use safety behaviors we learn – *Phew, I solved that one, but that was a close call* – rather than learning that worrying isn't the best way to solve problems. So we simply need to drop the safety behaviors when doing our behavioral experiments. But not all at once: do so one at a time, dropping the easy ones first and then moving on to the ones held most strongly, moving finally to do something new without any safety behaviors at all.

If you believed the rules above, what might you end up doing to make you feel safe if your rules were threatened? What might your safety behaviors be? If the worrier was not worrying to solve problems then they may increase other actions to compensate, like seeking reassurance, or looking for subtle signs of disapproval, or being extra nice to the children, just in case.

**Improving test 2**
*This time, I'll write a list and ask the kids to do the same and then decide together what we can do. I won't ask my partner for advice or help, or keep checking with the kids that they are happy with the plan.*

Seventh, we need to do the experiment. Eighth, we need to review what happened, what things you noticed and what you have learned. With this rule, the worrier might notice a sense of relief as they hand over some responsibility to their children, or their relationship with their children might improve as they spend more time talking and discussing things rather than telling them. Often, people find that there are many more advantages to the new way of doing things than were first apparent when working through the test. At this stage we return to the rule or belief that we held and ask how this new experience has challenged this. We then re-rate the beliefs. Finally, we need to think about how we can push the idea much further. So, where else might this rule have an influence? What other situations, relationships or events might be influenced by this rule? What other experiments could help to challenge the rule?

There is a simple experiment planning sheet (see Exercise 7.3 overleaf) to help you plan your behavioral experiment on worry. In each of the following chapters we shall refer back to this sheet and the steps outlined above.

When trying new things out, expect the unexpected. This unexpected information helps develop our understanding of how things work. Whether things go to plan or otherwise, the new learning will add to your understanding. Finally, while we have focused a lot on ideas, beliefs and rules, behavioral experiments are really about changing the way we feel. And this is the acid test: as a rule of thumb, if your feelings don't change, then think about what you are doing and ask if there are any safety behaviors that you have not spotted and dropped. Is the experiment real enough? Is it triggering some anxiety or is it too safe?

## EXERCISE 7.3: CHALLENGING YOUR WORRY RULES – BEHAVIORAL EXPERIMENTS

### 1. Spot the rule or idea to be tested
Use the safety behavior list, the sentence completion tasks, the questionnaire information, your worry diary, etc., to spot an idea or rule.

### 2. Putting the rule 'on the table'
Name it, so that we know what we are dealing with. Frame it in *if–then* terms. Make it real by linking it to a real situation. What is your prediction about what will happen if you broke, bent or disregarded the rule? Write it here . . .

### 3. Rate your prediction
Put a cross on the line below.

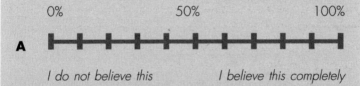

0%                    50%                    100%

A

*I do not believe this*          *I believe this completely*

### 4. Alternative prediction
Is there another way of seeing this? What ideas would you give to a friend who believed this? When you are less worried, do you see things any differently? What else might happen if you broke your rule? Write it here . . .

Rate your alternative prediction: put a cross on the line below.

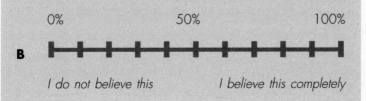

0%                    50%                    100%

B

*I do not believe this*          *I believe this completely*

## 6. Figuring out what to do

How could you test your prediction out? Start simple, start small, and build towards more emotionally loaded experiments. What exactly will you do? What safety behaviors might you need to consider? Can you drop them one by one and see what happens? What else might stop you from learning?

**My experiment is**

## 7. Do it! (Guard against perfectionism and putting thing off.)

## 8. Review what happened

What things have you noticed? What have you learned? How do you feel now? How does this new experience sit with your prediction? Re-rate both your predictions. What does it tell you about your rule?

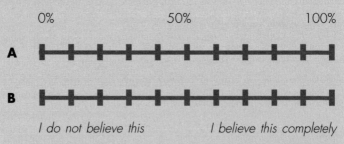

|  | 0% | 50% | 100% |
|---|---|---|---|

**A**

**B**

*I do not believe this*          *I believe this completely*

**What now? What other experiments can you do?**

**PIT STOP**

Let's stop and think about what you have just been reading. Can you summarize the key ideas you have taken on board? What is sticking in your mind? Maybe write them down. If you have any questions, jot these down too. You can return to them once you have had a chance to digest the information.

What is sticking in my mind from my reading so far?

1.

2.

3.

**8**

# Learning to tolerate uncertainty

In the traffic metaphor in Chapter 1 we suggested that there is a level of uncertainty in travel, with unforeseen delays, breakdowns and so on. We noted that when the flow of traffic was very heavy or if conditions were bad, as in heavy rain, then these other factors acted together to increase the level of uncertainty and made journey times especially unpredictable. Living with this kind of uncertainty is something we have to tolerate, if we are to get to our destinations without feeling exhausted and stressed. Uncertainty is the fuel for worry and it drives much of our worry; and so, like learning to tolerate the uncertainties in driving, we need to learn to tolerate life's uncertainties. The following chapters will help you do this.

## Introducing uncertainty

Uncertainty is a state almost *all* of us find unbearable. When we are uncertain we have less knowledge than we would like to have, nothing appears to be clear-cut, and it is often impossible to predict what exactly will happen next, although some things are more likely than others. It arrives with feelings of unease, apprehension and sometimes a mental paralysis, as we rapidly oscillate between solutions, unsure of which path to follow. Some situations leave us in a state of limbo, and, when relative certainty materializes, there seems to be a sense of relief as a degree of predictability and order returns. Take the example of a family waiting in an A&E department for news of a loved one involved in an accident; sometimes the uncertainty, or not knowing, is the hardest thing to bear. Once they know what the situation is, whether it is good news, bad news or somewhere in between, they can start to deal with it.

Uncertainty, like gravity, is a constant feature of our world, and it influences many aspects of it. A quick look at the world news tells us that uncertainty has influence at both government and individual levels. Stock markets and oil prices are influenced by uncertainty caused by conflict, climate change, politics and industry. At an individual level, a person's mood and wellbeing might be influenced by the uncertainty found in their relationships, their health or their work. Life is full of novel experiences and these come with a degree of uncertainty – indeed, uncertainty, like gravity, seems to be a part in the jigsaw of life.

As uncertainty is universal, it appears to be something we *all* have to learn to manage and tolerate. Worry and uncertainty are intimately linked: uncertainty is seen as the fuel for worry and because worrying generates more uncertainty, this in turn fuels more worry (see Figure 8.1 overleaf). While all of us want to decrease life's uncertainties and so worry less, we can never eradicate them entirely, and efforts to do so often result in more uncertainty (we will explore this in more detail later). So we cannot decrease the levels of uncertainty in the world, but we might be able to help you to adjust your reaction to it. Remember that CBT is about your view, or your appraisals, of what is happening (see Chapter 4). This is also true with uncertainty. Your view or appraisal of uncertainty is critical in helping to understand your reaction to it. If we can offer you other ways of thinking about uncertain situations, then we will help you to tolerate the not knowing, to worry less and react in more helpful ways. We know from research that worriers have difficulty accepting uncertainty, they become upset by it, and then have difficulty acting in helpful ways when facing it. One of the things they do instead of acting is worrying. As uncertainty fuels worry, our task in this chapter is to help you to manage and tolerate uncertainty, and, in doing so, manage and reduce your worry.

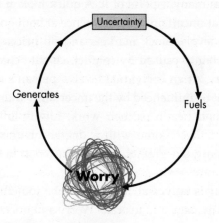

**Figure 8.1. Worry and uncertainty.**

Worry is a natural reaction to uncertainty, and it can be seen as a way of trying to predict the future and manage the experience of uncertainty. When we face uncertain situations, worry tends to spiral following well-worn paths about relationships, finances, family and so on, while at the same time rapidly following an infinite number of smaller tracks within these themes, as the worrier 'seeks' solutions. This frenetic mental activity unfortunately tends to reveal new problems, which in turn stimulate more worry. We all experience this when faced with uncertain, life-changing events. One of the problems for worriers is that this activity is used to try to solve all life's uncertainties and not just the big, life-changing events, where this activity can actually be useful.

As we saw in the case stories at the beginning of the book, worriers often avoid facing uncertainty at all costs. Sometimes they would even prefer bad things to happen immediately rather than live with the sense of not knowing what will happen next. It's not that they want the bad thing to happen, but not knowing if, or when, something may happen feels terrible and intolerable. They find it hard to put plans into action because they can't be sure their plans will work out; or, at the slightest hint of things not going to plan, uncertainty may stop them in their tracks. Of course, uncertainty is ever present, so it is not the situations themselves that are the problem, nor is it the presence of uncertainty. Rather, it appears that worriers seem on the whole to be much more sensitive to even tiny amounts of uncertainty in everyday situations. Uncertainty can be obvious to us all – for example, being called in for an unexpected appointment with the bank manager, or a family member falling ill. It can also be subtle, and might be found in conversations – for example, someone saying *I'll be in some time after nine*. Worriers may prefer certainty, which is, unfortunately, frequently impossible to have. Consider the following example.

Ellie worried about whether her husband could find his way home following sales trips. He had done so nearly every working day for the past ten years from all parts of the country and he had *never* got lost. Despite knowing this, she also knew that there was a slim chance he *could* get lost, that his car *could* break down, that he *could* be delayed by an accident, stuck in traffic or that he *could* even have had an accident. It was these *splinters of doubt* that gave rise to uncertainty, which, in turn, fuelled her worry. She wanted to be 100 per cent sure, but even after ten years she could not be certain – even though he had never been more than two hours late and always phoned if he was stuck in traffic. Despite being highly unlikely, it was possible and this was enough to start her worrying. Her worry had become such a habit that she was barely aware of it, though she did notice feeling exhausted and tense most of the time.

In their excellent book on cognitive behavioral treatment for GAD, Professor Michel Dugas and Dr Melisa Robichaud helpfully suggest that the intolerance of uncertainty can be thought of as an allergy. With something like hay fever, you only need a tiny amount of pollen to cause an allergic reaction. This is also true of worry; you only need a tiny amount of uncertainty to trigger excessive worry and anxiety. For many worriers, if there is a million to one chance that something bad could happen, then because there is this *splinter of doubt* that it could happen, they worry. The *splinter of doubt* then fuels the whirlwind of worry. It might be a good time to reread the case stories at the beginning of the book; compared to when you first started to read, what do you notice now?

As with Ellie above, it was the tiny amount of uncertainty, or the *splinter of doubt*, that triggered her worry. Because of its very nature, once worry has started it generates its own uncertainty, which means that it will continue under its own steam until something interrupts the flow.

## Horror film analogy

Uncertainty is a feeling we all experience while watching horror films. Usually there is a sense of suspense, since we know that something frightening is about to happen. In the best films, we're not quite sure what will happen, where, when or how it will happen, or even whom it might happen to. In fact, we can't even be sure if it will happen at all, as numerous close shaves tend to build up the sense of suspense. There is, however, a sense of inevitability that something bad will happen, and the best directors push this to its limits. When people are in this state of suspense, it's not unusual for them to try to do something to take control of the situation. They may, for example, cover their eyes to stop seeing the film, or cover their ears to block out the music. Their actions are motivated by the real and uncomfortable feelings that go with this sense of impending terror.

In this state of uncertainty, because we do not know what, when, where, how or even if bad things will happen, it makes it much harder for us to do anything about them in any *real way*. From this uncertainty emerges a spiral of thoughts about what might happen. The *what ifs* and the subsequent whirlwind of worry are an attempt to predict what will happen next. It's almost as if worry is used as a bridge to span the abyss of uncertainty. At these moments of uncertainty, because our worries feel real, we have a genuine desire to stop the bad things we worry about from happening and we then try to think of ways of avoiding the imagined horrors. But our solutions start us thinking about other things that could happen, and we may begin to worry about those instead. Our worry quickly becomes a way of trying to wrestle certainty from the jaws of uncertainty, but, unfortunately, it has completely the opposite effect, making things feel more uncertain. Furthermore, *the solution of*

*using worry to try to resolve uncertainty becomes a one-size-fits-all*
*approach for trying to take control over the uncertainties in life.*
Unfortunately, it is impossible to be absolutely certain, as we
shall soon see.

## Insurance metaphor

If uncertainty feels like the suspense we experience in a horror
film, then we can think of worry as like an insurance policy for
the uncertainties of life. Insurance can't stop things from
happening, it just reduces the financial losses if they do. Some
insurance makes sense in many cases, but if the cost (premium)
is too high, is it really worthwhile? Likewise, worry can't really
stop bad things from happening; it just seems to offer the chance
of reducing the losses. However, the cost (premium) in hours
of wasted worrying, the knot in the stomach, the loss of sleep
and enjoyment, the furrowed brow and the tension between the
shoulder blades, is just too high. Worry appears to offer the
promise of a solution to uncertainty, but never quite delivers.
If we spent a little less money on insurance against things that
could go wrong (but may never happen), we could spend more
on the things that really matter to us. Likewise, if we spent a
little less energy on worrying about things that could go wrong
(but may never happen), we could spend it on pursuing things
that really matter right now, such as family, friends, fun and
the things we really want from our future.

## Learning to spot uncertainty

Although worriers are sensitive to uncertainty, they do not often
notice the experience, for many reasons. First, it is often embedded
in life events (see Ellie's example above and Oscar's below).
Second, worry is a habitual response to uncertainty, almost like

a reflex, so we may not pay attention to what triggers the worry. Third, worry is the overwhelming experience at the time, making it hard to think of other things. Fourth, worriers tend to need only tiny amounts of uncertainty to trigger worry. Fifth, worry is everywhere, like gravity, and, like gravity, we are blind to it unless we look for it. In order to clarify the relationship between uncertainty and worry, we would like you to start to paying closer attention to everyday events and see if you can spot the uncertainty within them. Then turn your attention to your worry to see if you can do the same there. Each of the exercises below is followed by questions. These revolve around uncertainty and are repetitive, but they aim to stimulate your thinking – a question phrased in a slightly different way can often do this.

## EXERCISE 8.1: BEGINNING TO NOTICE UNCERTAINTY

Read a recent news article or a story in a magazine and see if you can spot the uncertainty within it. Or watch your favourite soap and pick one character and see if you can spot the uncertainty they experience. Alternatively, you can use books or films, or you can put uncertainty into an Internet search engine and see what news or current affairs come up. Or think about someone you know well: what uncertainty do they have to deal with? Use the following questions to help you to think this through:

- What makes this/their situation uncertain?
- What are the unknowns? What are they unsure about?
- What might be the gaps in their knowledge?
- How does their uncertainty influence their actions?
- How do they try to manage their uncertainty?

- Would anyone feel uncertain in this situation? If not, then what other things make the situation uncertain for them?

## EXERCISE 8.2: NOTICING MY EXPERIENCE OF UNCERTAINTY

Spotting uncertainty in situations that trigger worry. By now you will have been keeping a diary of your worry and have become better at spotting the *what if* statements, the types of worry and the themes of worry. You can use you Worry Diary to help you to reflect on uncertainty in each bout of worry. The following questions may help you to do this:

- If you consider worry as a way of bridging uncertainty, then what are the unknowns in that situation?
- In this situation what were you unsure of?
- Was there something unknown to you, what was it?
- How did uncertainty influence your actions?
- How did you try to manage the uncertainty?
- Thinking of all the worry episodes; what did you notice in your body, thoughts or behaviors that might act as an early warning sign for uncertainty?

## EXERCISE 8.3: RECOGNIZING MY STRENGTHS

Finally, as a consequence of thinking these issues through, have you noticed situations in your life where uncertainty does not lead to worry?

- Are there situations in your life in which you can manage the uncertainty? How do you do this, and what makes these situations different?
- What does this tell you about how you react to uncertain situations? How do others cope with uncertainty?
- What can you learn or take from them? Ask a friend or observe a colleague.

What have you learned from the exercises above? Have they helped you to understand how uncertainty and worry are linked? What have you learned about uncertainty, or how you and others cope with it? Write down your responses.

## PIT STOP

Let's pause again and think about what you have just been reading. Can you summarize the key ideas you have taken on board? Make a note of any new ideas that are sticking in your mind? What have you taken from this chapter so far? If you were to put your learning on a t-shirt, what would the slogan be? If you have any questions, jot these down too. You can return to them once you have had a chance to digest the information.

1.

2.

3.

## Why do worriers react to uncertainty?

Research tells us that worriers have a particular way of seeing the world. When faced with uncertain or unclear situations, worriers tend to assume the worst. They also have a remarkable sensitivity to uncertainty. Just as a dog's or cat's sense of hearing is much more sensitive than a human's, the worrier is much more sensitive to uncertainty and is tuned in to the 'sound of uncertainty'. Consider the following:

> Following a routine check-up a doctor gave Oscar, a worried man, some feedback. The doctor told him, 'there is only a very small chance that your chest pain is anything to worry about, but I think it's best we meet in three to four weeks to see how things are'. The doctor gave the man some reasonable advice, but, because of the way he approached the world, Oscar fell into the trap of assuming the worst and started to worry even more. He began thinking, *If it was nothing, then my doctor wouldn't be concerned; what if he's not telling me something? What if he's saving the bad news for next time? This isn't fair. I can't handle this, I need to know now.* Before he drove home, he tried to telephone his doctor from the car park outside the surgery.

In this story there are three things to notice. First is Oscar's tendency to assume the worst. Second is his hypersensitivity to the uncertainty found in the situation. There are several sources of uncertainty: the language the doctor uses – he says there is a *very small chance* and what Oscar wants to hear is that there is *no chance*; the apparent contradiction between 'nothing to worry about' and coming back in for another appointment; and, finally, the self-generated uncertainty found within Oscar's worry. Third is that he also found uncertainty nerve-racking and upsetting and could not tolerate it; put another way, he is *intolerant of uncertainty*. Research has shown that this is one of the most important influences on our tendency to worry: intolerance of uncertainty forms the cornerstone of the psychological ideas that explains GAD and the self-help treatments found in this book.

## What is intolerance of uncertainty?

This is an important idea, so it is vital that we spend some time thinking this through. A very straightforward way of describing this is to say that *worriers hate not knowing*. It is the no man's land between the knowing and not knowing that they find so unbearable. Why do they find this so difficult? Individuals with an intolerance of uncertainty have a way of seeing the world, or an outlook, that is underpinned by a set of rules and beliefs about uncertainty. These rules carry with them negative predictions about what might happen if they are exposed to uncertain situations or events. For example, a rule might sound like this: *If I'm not totally sure about something, then I'm asking for trouble*, or, *If I do something new, I cannot be sure I'll cope*. As you know, these rules influence our actions. In both these examples, a person holding these rules would understandably avoid situations that threatened to break them.

Let's look more closely at the first of these rules in the example below.

Peter's Rule: *if I'm not totally sure about something, then I'm asking for trouble*.

Peter is trying to buy a washing machine and he quickly realizes that there is an overwhelming number of brands and choices. His rule tells him to be careful and make the right decision. It also instructs him to be totally sure of his choice. Every time he comes close to making a decision, another type of machine pops up and he starts to worry that the washing machine he is about to choose may not live up to its five-year guarantee or that the model out next week may be better and he'll end up regretting the choice he's made. He walks in and out of the shop. He stares long and hard at the details of the machines on display without really taking much in. He leaves and heads into another store where the process starts all over. Eventually he makes a snap decision, not based on the information he now has, but as a way of escaping the awful feelings of uncertainty.

This type of experience might be common. For some worriers, their rules may paralyse them and they may never feel confident enough to make a decision. For others, any decision, even the wrong one, is better than being stuck with the horrible feeling of not being sure.

### Emotional impact

For people who are intolerant of uncertainty, the whirling stream of ideas and doubts created by their worry begins to erode their confidence in their ability to make good decisions. If we are less confident about our decisions, then we will worry about whether we have made good choices. So, the product of worry, namely anxiety, then kicks us while we are down, both by eroding our confidence and by triggering more worry.

## Assessing your tolerance to uncertainty – tuning in

To assess your tolerance to uncertainty can help you to tune into the feeling of suspense described in the horror film analogy above and you can begin to become more aware of when the intolerance appears, noting what triggers it and what you did to handle this feeling. It's almost as if we have to tune into what tells us we are in an uncertain situation. Of course, worry is the most likely thing that you will notice, but there may be other things, such as physical sensation, a mood, a feeling, a sharp intake of breath, a statement or phrase you say, a thought which jumps into your mind or one you think habitually, a habit you fall into, an action you can't help doing, a mannerism, and so on. The list is endless, but for a moment stop to think: is there anything you do that might alert you to the fact that uncertainty is around – like a smoke detector? Use the cognitive model to help you: think through your thoughts, feelings, actions and bodily sensations.

On the following page is a questionnaire developed by a team of Canadian researchers. It is called the Intolerance of Uncertainty Scale, or the IUS for short, and just as it says on the tin, it tries to measure an individual's intolerance of uncertainty. This can be a useful questionnaire to repeat every week as you progress towards overcoming your worry. As we have suggested, the intolerance of uncertainty fuels worry. If we can reduce the fuel by enabling you to become more tolerant of uncertainty, then we can reduce worry.

To score the questionnaire, simply add up the numbers that you have circled. People who suffer with GAD or excessive worry tend to have higher scores, and on average will score about 87. Scores above 50 suggest some problems with uncertainty. So, as a rule of thumb, if your score is above 50 then it might be worth spending some time thinking about and then challenging how you react to uncertainty.

The questionnaire will also give you a feel for what intolerance of uncertainty is. When you complete it, focus on each item. Which items stand out for you? What are you surprised by? Does completing it give you any further insights into your worry? Does it raise any questions for you? Are you surprised at your score, and if so why?

## EXERCISE 8.4: INTOLERANCE OF UNCERTAINTY SCALE

*You will find in the scale below a series of statements that describe how people may react to the uncertainties of life. Please use the scale to describe to what extent each item is characteristic of you. Write the appropriate number in the column on the right.*

| Not at all characteristic of me | | Somewhat characteristic of me | | Entirely characteristic of me |
|---|---|---|---|---|
| 1 | 2 | 3 | 4 | 5 |

1. Uncertainty stops me from having a firm opinion.
2. Being uncertain means that a person is disorganized.
3. Uncertainty makes life intolerable.
4. It's unfair not having any guarantees in life.
5. My mind can't be relaxed if I don't know what will happen tomorrow.
6. Uncertainty makes me uneasy, anxious, or stressed.
7. Unforeseen events upset me greatly.
8. It frustrates me not having all the information I need.
9. Uncertainty keeps me from living a full life.
10. One should always look ahead so as to avoid surprises.

11. A small unforeseen event can spoil everything, even with the best of planning.
12. When it's time to act, uncertainty paralyses me.
13. Being uncertain means that I'm not first rate.
14. When I'm uncertain, I can't go forward.
15. When I'm uncertain, I can't function very well.
16. Unlike me, others always seem to know where they are going with their lives.
17. Uncertainty makes me vulnerable, unhappy, or sad.
18. I always want to know what the future has in store for me.
19. I can't stand being taken by surprise.
20. The smallest doubt can stop me from acting.
21. I should be able to organize everything in advance.
22. Being uncertain means that I lack confidence.
23. I think it's unfair that other people seem sure about their future.
24. Uncertainty keeps me from sleeping soundly.
25. I must get away from all uncertain situations.
26. The ambiguities in life stress me.
27. I can't stand being undecided about my future.

Source: K. Buhr and M. J. Dugas, 'The intolerance of uncertainty scale: psychometric properties of the English version', *Behavior Research and Therapy*, 40 (2002). With permission from Elsevier.

## Underlying rules

There appear to be three main sets of rules that underpin the intolerance of uncertainty. One group tries to work together to reduce the risk of bad things happening in uncertain situations, another tells us to value certainty and to act only when certain, and the third reminds us of the awfulness of uncertainty and why we should avoid it. The rules around certainty and uncertainty seem to be locked in an antagonistic embrace that spirals relentlessly. From this conflict emerge jittery tension and feelings of being ill at ease. We will explore these rules in more detail below.

Let's look first at the rules that aim to reduce the risk. This makes good sense when the stakes are high, in life-changing events such as getting married or divorced, having children, buying a house, changing a job, and so on, but makes much less sense in everyday events such as taking your car to get its MOT, visiting the doctor for a routine check up, or going to meet your children's teachers. The focus is entirely on what could go wrong and how this could be stopped from happening. Despite their efforts at prevention, worriers believe that they may not be able to cope if this happened. It becomes much safer to assume the worst than to take the risk of assuming that everything will be fine – its almost like bracing for bad news. In this way worriers reduce the uncertainty by convincing themselves of the nightmare version and acting, or being ready to act, as if this really were the case. Sometimes, even though the nightmare version is awful, it feels much more certain and safer than the alternative of uncertainty. For example, if there is some uncertainty about a relationship, then for the worrier it seems much safer to assume that the relationship will break down. Then, they might be able to do something to try to prevent this from happening. If the worst thing did happen, then they should not assume that they could cope; in fact they should assume that they will *not* cope. By doing this, they can prepare themselves for the worst-case scenario. Worry takes us on a tortuous journey around the hellish things that could go wrong, and because these experiences feel very real, we want to make sure that they don't happen. In short the worrier believes that it is *always better to be safe than sorry*.

Another set of ideas that underpins the intolerance of uncertainty concerns certainty and uncertainty themselves. With regards to certainty, worriers believe that they can, and should, achieve absolute certainty, and, because of this, they should delay or put off acting until they are sure. But to be sure means to cover all the bases; and as we check out one detail we become more aware of even more possibilities and so become less certain. As we will discover, certainty is a belief and is rarely achievable and so the worrier's pursuit of certainty is often in vain. Beliefs about uncertainty suggest that it is very unpleasant and should be avoided at all costs. But to avoid uncertainty we have to hang on to what seems most certain – and then anything that might happen that does not fit the plan becomes very unsettling. This means that trying to avoid uncertainty gives rise to rigid plans that are then easily undermined as circumstances change. Flipping between trying to find certainty and avoiding uncertainty leads to a sense of disorientation and, paradoxically, to an increase in the levels of uncertainty. While experiencing this flip-flopping, the worrier is at the same time trying to be safe and certain, which is nearly impossible given how they are feeling. It's like trying to take a photograph while holding a pneumatic road drill; trying to focus and hold still while being jolted all over the place. They begin to experience a state of *not knowing*, which is unbearable for them. From this unbearable state rises worry, which is an attempt to find certainty within uncertain situations. In summary, *it's better to be safe than sorry, but how can I be safe when I can't be sure?* – which makes uncertainty intolerable.

These three sets of beliefs appear in the diagram below. They are related to one another, as you will see. The beliefs about it being better to be safe than sorry follow on from one another. The beliefs about certainty and uncertainty create a tension between them, which pushes us even harder towards being safe rather than sorry. The questions in Exercises 8.5 and 8.6 (page 171) aim to bring this idea alive for you.

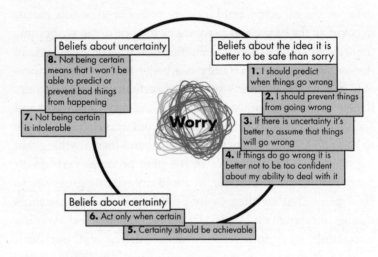

Figure 8.2. Beliefs that are thought to underpin the intolerance of uncertainty.

### EXERCISE 8.5: OUTLINING YOUR THINKING IN A WORRISOME SITUATION

This exercise helps you to outline your thinking in a worrisome situation. Think about the last few times you worried and then answer the following (note that only some may apply to you). Each question corresponds to a box on the diagram above.

1. Were you trying to predict that bad things might happen?
2. Once these were in mind, did you try to prevent them from happening in some way, either in thought or deed?
3. Did you feel unsure or uncertain in this situation? If you did, did it feel safer to assume that something bad would happen?
4. If this bad thing did happen, did you doubt your ability to cope with it?
5. Do you believe that you should be absolutely sure or certain?
6. Did you need to feel certain before making a decision or taking action?
7. Was the sense of not knowing intolerable?
8. As you felt more uncertain, did this make it harder to prevent bad things from happening?

Each set of rules will have dozens of variants, some of which seem to be held by some people and some held by others. Likewise, some apply to many situations, and some to only a few.

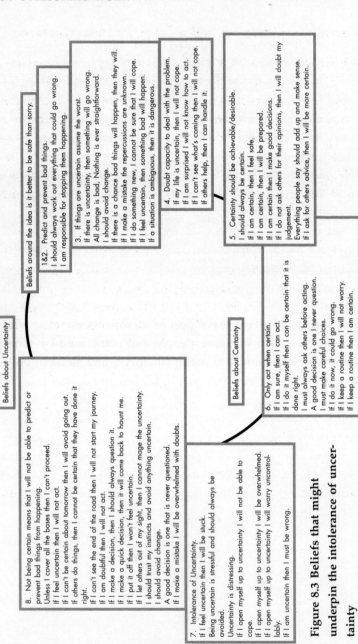

**Beliefs about Uncertainty**

Beliefs around the idea is it better to be safe than sorry.

1&2. Predict and prevent bad things.
I should always work out everything that could go wrong.
I am responsible for stopping them happening.

3. If things are uncertain assume the worst.
If there is uncertainty, then something will go wrong.
All change is bad. Nothing is ever straightforward.
If there is a chance bad things will happen, then they will.
If I do something new, I cannot be sure that I will cope.
I cannot make a mistake the repercussions are unknown.
I feel uncertain, then something bad will happen.
If a situation is ambiguous, then it is dangerous.

4. Doubt capacity to deal with the problem.
If my life is uncertain, then I will not cope.
If I am surprised I will not know how to act.
If I can't see what's coming then I will not cope.
If others help, then I can handle it.

5. Certainty should be achievable/desirable.
I should always be certain.
If I am certain, then I feel safe.
If I am certain, then I will be prepared.
If I am certain then I make good decisions.
If I do not ask others for their opinions, then I will doubt my judgement.
Everything people say should add up and make sense.
If I ask for others advice, then I will be more certain.

8. Not being certain means that I will not be able to predict or prevent bad things from happening.
Unless I cover all the bases then I can't proceed.
If I feel uncertain then I will not act.
If I can't be certain about tomorrow then I will avoid going out.
If others do things, then I cannot be certain that they have done it right.
If I can't see the end of the road then I will not start my journey.
If I am doubtful then I will not act.
If I make a decision, then I should always question it.
If I make a quick decision, then it will come back to haunt me.
If I put it off then I won't feel uncertain.
If I let others out of my sight, then I cannot mange the uncertainty.
I should trust my instincts and avoid anything uncertain.
I should avoid change.
A good decision is one that is never questioned.
If I make a mistake I will be overwhelmed with doubts.

**Beliefs about Certainty**

6. Only act when certain.
If I am sure, then I can act.
If I do it myself then I can be certain that it is done right.
I must always ask others before acting.
A good decision is one I never question.
I must make careful choices.
If I do it now, it could go wrong.
If I keep a routine then I will not worry.
If I keep a routine then I am certain.

7. Intolerance of Uncertainty.
If I feel uncertain then I will be stuck.
Being uncertain is stressful and should always be avoided.
Uncertainty is distressing.
If I open myself up to uncertainty I will not be able to cope.
If I open myself up to uncertainty I will be overwhelmed.
If I open myself up to uncertainty I will worry uncontrollably.
If I am uncertain then I must be wrong.

**Figure 8.3 Beliefs that might underpin the intolerance of uncertainty**

## Certainty and uncertainty – the broader picture

We will now broaden the focus to consider uncertainty in a broader context. We suggest this, in part, to help you understand how the pursuit of certainty and the eradication of uncertainty are equally problematic. This section is important because it begins to question some of the assumptions we make about uncertainty and certainty, assumptions that underpin the intolerance of uncertainty. Following this section, we will ask you to reflect on what you think are the relative merits of each assumption.

Life is full of uncertainties and rarely are things clear-cut; but if we do know where we stand, we are less likely to worry. On the other hand, some life situations are highly distressing and uncertain and the lack of clarity can be disabling for us all. Almost all of us will worry in response to these highly stressful and ambiguous situations (e.g. learning that a close relative has a serious and life-threatening illness). Most of life, however, lies somewhere between these two extremes, and it is usually neither clear-cut nor highly distressing and uncertain. It is not the highly uncertain nor the clear-cut situations that make people who are intolerant of uncertainty stand out. Rather, it is the normal, everyday and moderately uncertain situations that mark them out from others. Those who worry less in these situations are aware of the uncertainty, accept and/or expect it, and although they would like things to be more clear-cut, they just seem to deal with it.

Figure 8.4. Uncertainty as the fuel for worry.

## The impossibility of certainty

In our uncertain world we play the odds every day of our lives. For example, when a woman rides a bicycle to work she weighs up the probability of being in an accident against the benefits to her health, the environment and her purse. She makes her best guess and plays the odds. Or, think about the road where you live. You may have crossed it several times in the last few days. While having an accident might be awful, the probability of having an accident is low, but it is not, nor ever can be, zero. Or, over your lifetime you may have eaten hundreds of sandwiches bought from supermarkets. While it would be terrible to get food poisoning, the probability of getting ill from eating a sandwich from a reputable supermarket is very low, but, again, it is not zero. We can never cover every eventuality because we live in a world characterized by novelty and uncertainty. As the ancient author and natural philosopher Pliny the Elder suggested in AD 79, 'the only certainty is that there is nothing certain'.

Indeed, being certain about something locks you into a

particular way of seeing the world, and prevents you from seeing other views. Consider Clayton:

> Clayton thought, *I'm certain that I won't like London*. He was so sure that he never went and never entertained the idea that London could offer him anything. His view locked him into a particular way of thinking, which influenced his actions and thoughts, and denied him the possibility of discovering something new and exciting. One day, his work took him to King's Cross Station in London. Having a few moments before his train arrived, he wandered up the Euston Road. Looking up he saw St Pancras Station and was captivated by the structure of the building. He wondered to himself how he could have been so foolish as not to have come sooner.

In Chapter 2 we talk about keeping an open mind: unfortunately, certainty has a way of closing our minds. Think about the last time you were convinced that you would not like a film, a book, a restaurant, a pub or an evening out, and were then pleasantly surprised. So being certain can be unhelpful. Certainty is also an illusion. We cannot be certain about anything, because certainty is a belief, not a fact. If we are certain about something we tend to have to blur the edges of the world, since ambiguity and uncertainty are inherent within all things. Trying to iron out the uncertainty in life is like trying to squeeze a large octopus into a glass box. This is a very difficult thing to do, particularly if the octopus doesn't want to oblige. But if we succeed in containing it, we lose its rich shape and form; the octopus becomes little more than a colourful cube. What we mean here is that reality has to be distorted, cleansed, and sanitized if uncertainty is to be excluded. If this were possible, then what kind of world would we be left with?

The idea that life can be certain also brings with it the suggestion that the future can be predicted in some precise way, which, at some level, is partly true – as day follows night – but usually life brings with it uncertainty. Of course, let's not get carried away: we need relative certainty as much as we need relative uncertainty and, as with most things, balance is important. The bottom line is that protecting ourselves against uncertainty is an unattainable goal, like trying to walk on your shadow. Uncertainty is in everything, it's everywhere and is part of life. In this respect it's like gravity, death and taxes: we can't avoid it or will it away.

'To be absolutely certain about something, one must know everything or nothing about it.' Olin Miller, author, 1918–2002

## A certain world

While you may argue that your life would be wonderful if all uncertainty was excluded, think this through for a moment. What would life be like without surprises, without unknowns, without mystery? As an exercise, why not try to imagine a world where uncertainty was excluded. The film *Groundhog Day* plays with this idea. Bill Murray's character experiences the same day over and over and over again, but even here the main character is able to learn new skills, like jazz piano and ice sculpture. And, while the events happen predictably, his reactions to them add a degree of uncertainty. So, even the world of *Groundhog Day* is not completely certain.

What would your uncertainty-free world be like? In your imagined world, don't just exclude worry and make certain all those situations that trigger worry: you need to exclude uncertainty completely. Here's one scenario: so the Number 37 bus might always run to time and you might always get a seat, and Newcastle United might win the Premiership and the Champion's League every year. But your children would never surprise you with new ideas, each new film that was released would not have a twist or a surprise ending, none of the books you read would tell you anything new – in fact, there would be no new films, books, bands, CDs or DVDs. You would be passed by the same cars and people everyday, you would have the same conversations, you would know it was the third Tuesday in the month because you would be eating meatloaf, you would never have the opportunity of tasting a new fruit or a new chocolate cake.

A newborn baby is a wonder, but they bring uncertainty, as life itself is uncertain. So would there be any children if we excluded uncertainty? Would we ever take the risk of having them in our uncertainty-free world? We could go on. It would be a mechanistic, mechanical world, where nothing new ever happened. It would appear that uncertainty is a critical stimulant to life, and that without it our lives would be poorer, impoverished and empty. Erich Fromm, a German psychotherapist, suggested that *creativity requires the courage to let go of certainties*. If Fromm was right, certainty might stifle freethinking, and, taking his idea a little further, reaching absolute certainty might destroy a fundamental characteristic of what it is to be human, namely freewill or the ability to choose.

Would you want to live in this kind of world?

## Routines and shrinking worlds

On reading the above, some of you might see your lives reflected in the description: this would not be surprising for at least two reasons. First, life has patterns and routines and sometimes we feel stuck in a rut, as if all we do is sleep, eat and work. Routine and patterns are helpful as they give a sense of rhythm, they ground us, they give an idea of where we are in the world and a sense of purpose. But sometimes we run too tightly around these routines and patterns. At these moments we often crave novelty or uncertainty to help us get out of the rut. The second reason relates to one of the consequences of worry: worriers reduce the circumference of their world in order to manage their worry. They try to run on safe and familiar tracks largely to avoid uncertainty, but this can also place *real* limits, taking away new opportunities, new beginnings, new relationships or keeping people stuck within unhelpful roles or relationships. Another possible consequence of this limited lifestyle is low mood and depression, especially when people are stuck in familiar but unrewarding situations, roles or relationships. This makes the whole thing much worse because with low mood, it is often much harder to motivate ourselves to do new things or in fact to do anything at all.

The reasons why worriers might have started to run on such tight rails is less clear. But for some worriers, if their early lives were typified by uncertainty and insecurity, these patterns and routines might have offered one way of establishing certainty or, put another way, of managing their exposure to uncertainty. They become familiar and comforting, but later, as we grow, we may begin to realize how they might also limit us.

If there are parts of the uncertainty-free world that you recognize, do you like what you see? Is that a world you want to remain in? If the answer to this is yes, then fine. We suspect however, that the answer will be no – because you are reading this book, which tells us that you want to change something. An implication from all this is that injecting a small amount of uncertainty into your life could be a way of making your life much more enjoyable, and this is what we aim to help you do in this chapter.

## EXERCISE 8.6: FINDING THE EDGES OF MY WORLD

Take a moment to reflect on the following questions. Jot down the answers in your notebook. Are there any things you would like to do as a consequence of thinking these through? Any new goals?

How has worry or uncertainty impacted on the circumference of your world?

Is there anything you avoid doing now?

What does worry stop you from doing?

What have you stopped doing since worry became a problem? When can you get back to it?

Are there things that you would like to start doing? What are they? When can you start?

What are the advantages of letting go of certainty and letting new experiences in?

Are there any disadvantages?

### An uncertain world

Now back to our extremes. At the other end of the spectrum from complete certainty is complete uncertainty. So, as we approach complete uncertainty, we would expect to encounter a pretty awful experience. Professor David Wilkinson, who works at Cranfield University in the south of England, has investigated how leaders cope with high levels of uncertainty and ambiguity in business settings and in the aftermath of events like terrorist attacks. He views ambiguity on a sliding scale from total certainty to total ambiguity or chaos. At the certain end of the scale, cause and effect are linked and there is clarity and order; the world makes sense and day still follows night. But, with increasing uncertainty and ambiguity, the relationship between cause and effect becomes weakened and eventually breaks down; day no longer follows night, things fall apart, the centre cannot hold, order is lost and nothing makes sense. Despite the nightmarish vision at the highly ambiguous end of the scale, he sees chaos as a positive state and as a moment of creativity and new learning. He suggests that 'at the moments of the most intense fear, the moments when there appear to be huge threats all around, when ambiguity is at its highest, when we know little and understand less, these are the moments of most potential for moving into a new world and taking the advantage'. These uncertain moments offer 'the most degrees of freedom to act'; he means that highly uncertain situations offer us the most choices and opportunities for acting in different ways.

This reminds us that, even at the extreme end of the spectrum, uncertainty can still be seen by some as positive and useful. As we said earlier, the key is how each one of us views uncertainty.

Whether we 'buy' this perspective or not, it also shows that there are always other ways of thinking about high levels of uncertainty. While we may all be in awe and a little envious of those individuals who are able to cope and act in these extreme situations, we need to bear in mind two things: first, in our everyday lives we rarely, if ever, meet chaos, as there is usually some degree of order; and, second, at this extreme end of the scale the difference between worriers and non-worriers disappears. The 'big events' that Professor Wilkinson refers to are extreme, rare and highly unusual, and so both worriers and non-worriers would cope similarly. As we know, worriers tend to worry about everyday events, and it is this that marks them apart. We all worry about the big occasions, and there is nothing to indicate that someone who worries about everyday events would, in more pressing circumstances, be less able to cope. Indeed, in our clinical work we have heard many stories of worriers who have successfully coped with and overcome 'big occasion' or life-changing problems only to seek help for managing the everyday ones. Also, we believe that absolute chaos would be as awful as absolute certainty, and that, as we have said before in this book, balance is the key.

## The cost of uncertainty

Finally, there is *always a cost* associated with the strategies we use to manage uncertainty. The following exercises will help you to think this through.

### EXERCISE 8.7: ACTIONS AND COSTS RELATED TO THE INTOLERANCE OF UNCERTAINTY

Spend a moment reviewing each item and then score the questionnaire, spotting those aspects that are closer to your experience of worry. As a rule of thumb, if you are scoring 5 or more on an item, you may want to consider setting a goal to change this or consider a behavioral experiment. Because not all the items will apply to you, if an item reminds you of another aspect of your life then write this down. As you read, be thinking about what benefits might come your way if you learn to sit with uncertainty and tolerate it. Secondly, you can use this as another way of helping you to spot how the intolerance of uncertainty might influence the way that you live your life. As uncertainty is everywhere, a huge amount of energy and effort is put into trying to eradicate it: imagine having this energy and effort for other things.

Using the scale below, read each statement and decide how closely each statement matches your actions and then circle the appropriate number.

| Very unlike me | | | | | Very like me | |
|---|---|---|---|---|---|---|
| 1 | 2 | 3 | 4 | 5 | 6 | 7 |

Asking for reassurance on a decision you have made, and then feeling stupid for having asked in the first place because you knew you were right.    1 2 3 4 5 6 7

Checking emails, letters or cheques several times before sending them, and then getting behind on other jobs.    1 2 3 4 5 6 7

Reading all the cinema reviews and then asking your friend to make the decision about what to see because you just can't be sure they will like the film and then feeling disappointed from missing the film you really wanted to see.    1 2 3 4 5 6 7

Telephoning home while shopping in the supermarket because you just can't decide on what to eat and then feeling indecisive and down on yourself.    1 2 3 4 5 6 7

Always going to the same shop and buying the same food in case you bought something you or others wouldn't like, and then complaining about the lack of variety in your diet.    1 2 3 4 5 6 7

Finding excuses why you should not delegate jobs at work; consequently you end up doing everything yourself.    1 2 3 4 5 6 7

Not allowing your kids to do things for themselves in case they don't quite get it quite right. And then feeling annoyed that you have to do everything yourself.    1 2 3 4 5 6 7

Pacing the house if your partner is five minutes late home from work and being stressed out when they arrive.    1 2 3 4 5 6 7

You've bought something you have always wanted, but now can't enjoy it because you keeping questioning your decision.    1 2 3 4 5 6 7

Asking someone to check your work, even though at some level you know it's perfectly fine and then criticizing yourself for lacking confidence. 1 2 3 4 5 6 7

Wanting to know where everything is, and feeling unsettled if things are out of place, even when you don't need to use them right now. 1 2 3 4 5 6 7

Wanting to know where important people are and feeling unsettled if they are not where you expect them to be. 1 2 3 4 5 6 7

Needing to have the plans for an evening clearly laid out beforehand and getting upset when they don't go as planned, even though everyone is having fun. 1 2 3 4 5 6 7

Doing things in the same routine and complicated way for fear of going off track and then complaining how boring life is. 1 2 3 4 5 6 7

Taking over driving from your partner because you worry about them driving and then not enjoying the trip. 1 2 3 4 5 6 7

Avoiding committing yourself to something just in case it might go wrong. 1 2 3 4 5 6 7

Finding good but imaginary reasons for not doing things and then realizing that you have missed out on something you would have enjoyed if you had taken the chance. 1 2 3 4 5 6 7

Procrastinating or putting things off until they become bigger, and more problematic. 1 2 3 4 5 6 7

Finding other tasks to do rather than do the one that needs your attention, and then letting things mount up. 1 2 3 4 5 6 7

Avoiding (or keeping contact to a bare minimum) people who may act unpredictably and then missing out on other aspects of their company. 1 2 3 4 5 6 7

Making snap decisions that you may regret later because it feels better than being stuck with not knowing what to do. 1 2 3 4 5 6 7

Following the crowd and doing things you don't really like to do because it feels less difficult than making decisions.　1 2 3 4 5 6 7

Getting lots and lots of information to help you make a decision, and then not being able to make sense of it all.　1 2 3 4 5 6 7

## PIT STOP

Let's pause again and think about what you have just been reading. Can you summarize the key ideas you have taken on board? Make a note of any new ideas that are sticking in your mind? What have you taken from this chapter so far? If you were to put your learning on a t-shirt, what would the slogan be? If you have any questions, jot these down too. You can return to them once you have had a chance to digest the information.

1.

2.

3.

To overcome your worry, it is essential that you become more tolerant of uncertainty by challenging your uncertainty rulebook and the actions that they influence (such as avoidance). The next section will tell you more about why the intolerance of uncertainty is central in understanding worry; it will explain why we need to help you to tolerate it more, it will help you to spot it, it will outline what worriers tend to do to manage uncertainty, and then it will suggest some ways to help you to tolerate it better.

## EXERCISE 8.8: ADVANTAGES AND DISADVANTAGES

This exercise will help you think about all you have read so far.

What are the advantages of accepting a little more uncertainty into your life?

What are the advantages of letting go of a need for absolute certainty?

Are there any disadvantages?

Are there any disadvantages?

## EXERCISE 8.9: EXPLORING UNCERTAINTY

When you feel uncertain do you assume that bad things will happen? If so, how often are your worry predictions right? Why not write them down and see how many come true?

Is it always better to be safe than sorry? What are the disadvantages of this stance? When might it not be helpful?

What tells you that you cannot cope? Feelings, actions, thoughts?

If certainty is not achievable, then how do you ever feel safe?

## How does the intolerance of uncertainty link to worry?

If a situation can be read in many different ways or when things are unclear or uncertain, worriers, who are generally more intolerant of uncertainty, tend to assume the worst and predict that bad things are going to happen. Because they genuinely believe that these bad things will happen, this leads to further worry and anxiety, making these uncertain situations more threatening and disturbing than the situation objectively deserves. Furthermore, if these bad things do happen, worriers assume that they won't be able to cope with them, leading to further worry. It makes sense that what worriers really want is absolute certainty, certainty that either something bad will never happen, or, if it does, that it is guaranteed that they will be able to cope with it.

As we have said, overcoming worry demands that we learn how to deal more effectively with our reactions to uncertainty. We know that worriers find uncertainty intolerable and they will do many things in addition to worrying to try to minimize it. Unfortunately, nearly everything they try has the tendency to make uncertainty and worry much worse. It's important that you know this in order to enable you to tolerate uncertainty: you need to start exposing yourself to it. There is simply no other way around this. We have explored the rules that underpin uncertainty, but just thinking these through will not enable you to change. You have to *do* things differently.

### What drives the intolerance of uncertainty?

Worriers tend to experience uncertainty as stressful and upsetting; they feel that an uncertain future is unfair and intolerable, that surprises are threatening and unsettling and that uncertainty interferes with their ability to live. People who are intolerant of uncertainty are driven towards seeking certainty while at the same time they are driven away from uncertainty. What drives them is a number of rules and ideas about how awful uncertainty is, as well as a number of rules valuing certainty; these rules have developed throughout their lives (see page 55). These rules set the scene for how the worrier responds to situations where the outcome is uncertain, such as making a decision.

## A pattern for the interface between worry and uncertainty

On the following pages we outline one way of thinking about how worry and uncertainty fit together. Within this picture you will find elements of the diagram of worry that we have been following throughout this book:

**Trigger ⇨ What if . . . ⇨ Worry ⇨ Anxiety ⇨ Demoralization and Exhaustion**

Here we are adding to this the intolerance of uncertainty and its relationship to worry. It is important to understand how the intolerance of uncertainty influences your worry for a number of reasons: first, to map out your problems; second, to help you understand your worry; third, because this understanding also tells us what we need to do to help you change. There are two diagrams (Figures 8.5 and 8.6): one is the bare bones, the second has some thoughts and statements added that worriers typically suggest. You may have to read it through a few times, but we will pull out the key points later on. As always, read with a pen and paper to hand.

When faced with an everyday decision where the outcome is uncertain, worriers tend to *assume the worst, fall into worrying* and then believe that they *cannot cope* with the worst-case scenario they imagine through worrying. They may think, *What if I make the wrong decision?* Or *What if I can't cope with this?* These *what if* statements simultaneously trigger worry and a demand for certainty. As the worrier searches for certainty (*I must get this right, I must be certain*), another set of conflicting thoughts or questions appear that hint at how impossible certainty is (*I could get it wrong; How can I be certain?*), triggering yet more worry. The worrier is now caught in a trap between the futile pursuit of certainty and the avoidance of uncertainty. This generates a number of strong feelings including anxiety coupled with an intense feeling of indecisiveness, which further erodes the worrier's confidence in their ability to make decisions. The feelings are often accompanied by strong bodily sensations.

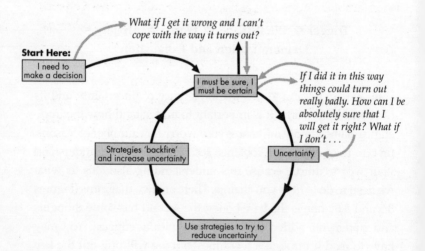

Figure 8.5. The uncertainty cycle.

Understandably, the worrier then falls into habitual ways of acting to try to reduce the level of uncertainty. Unfortunately, many of the actions they take have the opposite impact – rather than reducing uncertainty they tend to increase it, triggering further worry. They may avoid making a decision, for example, which increases the pressure on them to make a decision. With each cycle, the worrier feels less certain and more overwhelmed.

In the next diagram overleaf we have added more detail, in particular how worry interacts with each stage of the uncertainty cycle. We have added more detail in terms of what someone might think at each stage to help you understand the cycle. This appears as handwritten text. We have also added worry, which sits at the centre of the diagram.

Worry is both *fuelled* by uncertainty and in turn *generates* uncertainty. Each stage of the uncertainty cycle produces more uncertainty and so more worry (see the double arrows between worry and each stage). Let's take the first block, *I must be sure, I must be certain*. Here these statements lead to worry – *What if I am wrong? What if I mess up?* – which then generates more *uncertainty*, both fuelling more worry (see double headed arrows) and also leading on to the worrier using *strategies to try to reduce the uncertainty*. Unfortunately, these strategies tend to generate more uncertainty (double headed arrows), leading to more worry but also propelling the worrier back around the cycle to pursue certainty.

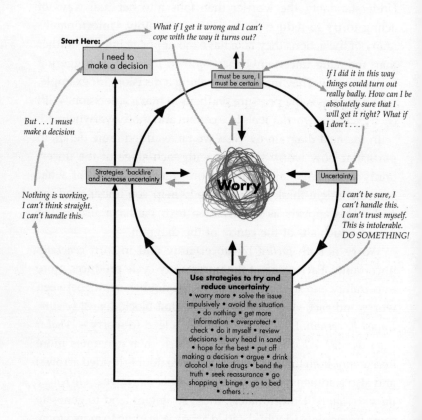

Figure 8.6 The relationship between the intolerance of uncertainty and worry.

**9**

# Unhelpful strategies in reducing uncertainty

By now you will have looked at spotting uncertainty within worrisome situations (see Exercise 8.2 above) and looked at the rules that underpin the intolerance of uncertainty. Spending time working out how you react to uncertainty is important because it's another way of stepping out of our habitual patterns; it also means that we are *stepping under worry* to focus on what drives it. This and the following chapters tie together the rules about uncertainty, actions and worry. As you know, working out how the intolerance of uncertainty impacts on our lives requires some thought. One way of spotting this is to pay closer attention to what we do in worrisome situations. To help you do this, review the twelve strategies listed below and complete the mini-questionnaire that follows each strategy. As you find those that fit with your experience, then a key question to ask yourself is, *If I was less bothered by uncertainty, then what might I do differently?* Or, to put it another way, *If I was more tolerant of uncertainty what might I do differently?* In each section we have added some typical rules that people hold to help you understand what might drive the strategies that people use. When you read the rules ask yourself if they make sense of the strategy; do they help you understand why someone might do this, based on these underlying rules? As you read, keep the idea of change in mind. Are there things, situations or events that come to mind that would be good opportunities for facing uncertainty? If 'yes', write them down.

## Strategy 1. Looking for lots of information

Consider the case of Alison in the stories at the beginning of the book. Here is part of the story again:

> Recently she wanted to buy a new digital camera to take pictures at her son's 21st birthday, but she couldn't decide which one to get. She visited nearly every shop and got conflicting advice. She worried, *What if I make a bad decision? If I do I may not understand the instructions and if I took the photos I could annoy everyone by being intrusive.* Her worries went on and on. She felt paralysed by her worry and in the end gave up on buying the camera. She regretted this and felt ashamed that her worry had got the better of her.

Unfortunately, looking for more information to help her come to a decision just stoked up the uncertainty and triggered more worry. This can happen in a number of ways. Often, the additional information does not necessarily make things clearer, but just gives us more to consider and worry about. Alison also held the belief, *If I get enough information then I can be sure*, but this led to a number of unhelpful outcomes. She got too much information, which made the task unwieldy and impossible, leading her deeper into worry. In addition, with the mass of information there was the increased risk of finding contradictory facts, which again led to more uncertainty and worry, triggering the search for even more information to resolve the issue. Another thing that made this worse was her feelings. She felt anxious, and the sense of vulnerability that came with her anxiety eroded her confidence still further and led her to doubt her ability to make good decisions. So, even if she had reached a decision, she may then have worried about whether she had made the right choice, again opening up uncertainty, fuelling worry. Even if she gathered all the information together, in the end she may still have worried about whether her decision was a wise one.

## EXERCISE 9.1: LOOKING FOR LOTS OF INFORMATION

How typical or characteristic is this strategy for you?

| Not like me at all | A little like me | Somewhat like me | Moderately like me | Mostly like me | Nearly like me | Completely like me |
|---|---|---|---|---|---|---|
| 0 | 1 | 2 | 3 | 4 | 5 | 6 |

Can you think of a personal example where you might have looked for more information than the situation demanded?

In this example, what impact did collecting more information have on how certain or sure you felt about the decision you had to make?

| Felt very uncertain | Felt moderately uncertain | Felt mildly uncertain | Neither certain or uncertain | Felt mildly certain | Felt moderately certain | Felt very certain |
|---|---|---|---|---|---|---|
| 0 | 1 | 2 | 3 | 4 | 5 | 6 |

What impact did collecting too much information have on the sense of uncertainty? What impact did it have on your worry? How much energy and effort do you put into managing uncertainty by using this strategy? Could your energy be used elsewhere?

What rules or beliefs do you have that might underpin this strategy? Examples: Unless I am certain that I have all the information, then I will not act. If I am absolutely certain, then I will make a good decision.

If I were less bothered by uncertainty, then what might I do differently? Could I collect less information and sit with my uncertainty?

*Hint: What are the advantages and disadvantages of collecting lots of information before making a decision? How does this help or hinder decision-making? Does getting more information actually make you feel more certain? What would happen if you decided to limit the time or the amount of information you could look at? Could you perform a behavioral experiment to find out what might happen? How might doing this improve your confidence? To get started, what could be a small decision to try new things out on?*

## Strategy 2. Scanning for uncertainty – the uncertainty radar

Because worriers find uncertainty unbearable, understandably they are on the look out for it nearly all the time. Think about someone who has a phobia of spiders: they tend to be on the alert, scanning for spiders because being surprised by them would be awful. As a consequence of living on high alert, even things that are not spiders, but look like them, can trigger their phobia – a knotted up piece of wool blowing across a floor, for example. Psychologists call this hypervigilance. It functions to help us to detect threats quickly (in this case uncertainty) in our environment; but it also turns things that are not threatening into threats. As a consequence of scanning, worriers are able to spot uncertainty quicker and pick up on it more often than others. It's almost as if their minds zoom in on uncertainty and then magnify it, until it 'fills the screen'. When this happens everything about a situation then feels uncertain. Let's return to our case stories:

> Alex was the 23 year old who was full of nervous energy. He listened to music on his MP3 player, but pulled the headphone off to make sure he had not missed anything. He checked his ticket for the number of the bus, even though he knew he was on the right one.

Alex worried on his journey into work, and this was partly responsible for his pulling off his headphones. But, at the same time, he was searching for uncertainty, scanning his environment looking for things that were uncertain. He looked at his bus ticket (*Am I on the right bus?*), he listened (*Have I missed something?*), he may have also looked out of the window to check the bus was taking the right route into town (*Does the bus driver know where he's going?*). By doing this he was actually making the problem worse. Like the spider phobic above, any vague sign of uncertainty will trigger anxiety. For example, if the engine of the bus made an unusual sound, or if the driver opened and closed the door a few times, this would be perceived as a sign of uncertainty, followed quickly by *What if the bus breaks down?* Any *splinter of doubt* will fuel worry, and as we live in an uncertain world, Alex would always have found it, and therefore something else to worry about. Scanning also kept the threat of uncertainty at the front of his mind, leading him to feel apprehensive and edgy (remember the approach vs avoidance goals in Chapter 6). Even if he 'failed' to spot anything uncertain, he may still have worried that the uncertainty was yet to 'arrive'. This process also stopped him from enjoying his journey and his mind was on 'red alert', which is exhausting. Scanning for uncertainty would be like scanning for gravity, always on the look out for it and always finding evidence for it. Scanning does not mean that uncertainty is reduced – quite the opposite, it 'cranks it up'.

## EXERCISE 9.2: SCANNING; THE UNCERTAINTY RADAR

How typical or characteristic is this strategy for you?

| Not like me at all | A little like me | Somewhat like me | Moderately like me | Mostly like me | Nearly like me | Completely like me |
|---|---|---|---|---|---|---|
| 0 | 1 | 2 | 3 | 4 | 5 | 6 |

Can you think of an example where you noticed that you were looking out for something that didn't quite fit the pattern and so could be a sign of danger?

In this example, what impact did scanning have on how certain or sure you felt about the situation you were in?

| Felt very uncertain | Felt moderately uncertain | Felt mildly uncertain | Neither certain or uncertain | Felt mildly certain | Felt moderately certain | Felt very certain |
|---|---|---|---|---|---|---|
| 0 | 1 | 2 | 3 | 4 | 5 | 6 |

What impact did scanning for uncertainty have on your worry? How much energy and effort do you put into managing uncertainty by using this strategy? Could your energy be used elsewhere?

What rules or beliefs do you have that might underpin this strategy?
Examples: Uncertainty is awful and I should avoid it. If I am surprised I will not know how to act. Unless I keep a look out, something terrible may happen.

If I were less bothered by uncertainty, then what might I do differently? Could I stop scanning and sit with the feeling of not knowing or being certain?

*Hint: Do you know when you are doing this? What are the tell-tail signs? What are the advantages and disadvantages of this? How does looking for uncertainty make you feel better? What could you do instead? What could you tell yourself when you find yourself scanning for uncertainty? Where would be a place or situation to let your guard down a bit and just go with the flow?*

## Strategy 3. Avoiding committing yourself

The title of this strategy says it all. Rather than choosing to commit themselves or not commit themselves, worriers avoid doing either, which leaves them hanging in uncertainty. This increases the sense of uncertainty rather than decreasing it. Worriers often avoid commitments because they can't be sure how things will turn out. This might include intimate relationships, where love or fidelity can't be absolutely guaranteed, and may result in the worrier avoiding relationships completely or partially engaging, with one foot in and one foot out the door just in case things go wrong. The worrier may find relationships unfulfilling, as they cannot give themselves to the relationship just in case it fails. Also their focus is on what could go wrong, which generates more uncertainty and more worry. The worry gets in the way of simply enjoying the time they have with their partner, which may put the relationship at more risk. Avoiding commitment also applies to social engagements or work commitments – for example, worriers might avoid a night out where the plan has not been laid out clearly enough and they don't know when and where they will be going. Or worriers might avoid committing to a training event at work because they can't be sure that they will understand what they are taught and will then worry about not being able to give good enough feedback to their colleagues.

## EXERCISE 9.3: AVOIDING COMMITTING

How typical or characteristic is this strategy for you?

| Not like me at all | A little like me | Somewhat like me | Moderately like me | Mostly like me | Nearly like me | Completely like me |
|---|---|---|---|---|---|---|
| 0 | 1 | 2 | 3 | 4 | 5 | 6 |

Can you think of a personal example where you avoided making a commitment?

In this example, what impact did doing this have on how certain or sure you felt about the situation you were in?

| Felt very uncertain | Felt moderately uncertain | Felt mildly uncertain | Neither certain or uncertain | Felt mildly certain | Felt moderately certain | Felt very certain |
|---|---|---|---|---|---|---|
| 0 | 1 | 2 | 3 | 4 | 5 | 6 |

What impact did it have on your sense of uncertainty? What impact did it have on your worry? How much energy and effort do you put into managing uncertainty by using this strategy? Could your energy be used elsewhere?

What rules or beliefs do you have that might underpin this strategy? Examples: If there is a chance that bad things will happen, then they will; if I feel uncertain, then something bad will happen; if I can't see the end of the road, then I won't start my journey; if bad things happen, I won't be able to cope.

If I were less bothered by uncertainty, then what might I do differently? Could I quickly commit to something and sit with the uncertainty?

*Hint: What is helpful about doing this, what is less helpful? What's the worse thing that would happen if you just 'dived in'? To get started, what would be a 'time-limited' commitment where you could try this out (e.g. an evening out, attending a meeting, or agreeing to go to a one-off talk, or gym class)?*

### Strategy 4. Avoiding people or social occasions

As we have mentioned above, some worriers reduced the circumference of their world in order to reduce the uncertainties. They have tight routines, which they rely on to manage the uncertainty in the world. To do this, they may have decided to avoid certain people and social events – indiscrete people, for example, or 'colourful', spontaneous or impulsive people. Worriers may avoid these characters because they bring uncertainty with them: do you know anyone who fits this bill? Sometimes this avoidance comes with a sense of responsibility within the worrier for the actions and behavior of others, which motives further avoidance. Often these people are unavoidable because they are work colleagues or family members or they are part of the worrier's social circle. This makes the worriers feel much worse, since they may be 'on guard' or hypervigilant when there is a chance that they will meet them. They might think, *What if she's there tonight? Oh no, I can't go tonight, but if I don't go, then what if they think I am rude? They may never ask me to come out with them again,* or, *What if I end up sitting next to him . . .?* This uncertainty can lead to more worry.

On the other hand, avoiding people or social events can be another way of avoiding commitment, which leaves the worrier hanging, for example, by avoiding people who show a genuine interest in you because they ask meaningful or thoughtful questions. This may lead the worrier to think, *What if they get to know me and don't like me?* Or, *What if I say the wrong thing and they get the wrong end of the stick?*, which leads to strong feelings of anxiety and this motivates avoidance.

Another side-effect of worry is irritability, so sometimes we end up avoiding people because we can't be sure that we won't say something we might later regret. Poor concentration can also pose difficulties; difficulty concentrating may lead worriers to struggle to follow conversations and they may worry that they will not remember what has been said. As you can see, both these side-effects load more uncertainty into the conversation and with it more worry, which makes the problem worse. Unsurprisingly, worriers tend to avoid situations where their difficulty in concentration or irritability may be exposed. Worriers may then avoid social situations, because they may worry about making the wrong impression or worry about what others might think of them.

The feeling of being unable to relax (restlessness) also impacts on social situations. Worriers may be skilful social butterflies, moving from one conversation to the next, keeping out of the lime-light, never really talking about themselves and finally moving on before, or just as, the focus turns on them. This activity is tiring and stressful and while worriers keep their distance and try to reduce the uncertainty associated with becoming involved, the constant flitting around just loads it all back in again. It's like being the host of every social gathering you've ever been to – exhausting.

## EXERCISE 9.4: AVOIDING PEOPLE OR SOCIAL SITUATIONS

How typical or characteristic is this strategy for you?

| Not like me at all | A little like me | Somewhat like me | Moderately like me | Mostly like me | Nearly like me | Completely like me |
|---|---|---|---|---|---|---|
| 0 | 1 | 2 | 3 | 4 | 5 | 6 |

Can you think of a personal example where you avoided someone or a social occasion?

In this example, what impact did doing this have on how certain or sure you felt about the situation you were in?

| Felt very uncertain | Felt moderately uncertain | Felt mildly uncertain | Neither certain or uncertain | Felt mildly certain | Felt moderately certain | Felt very certain |
|---|---|---|---|---|---|---|
| 0 | 1 | 2 | 3 | 4 | 5 | 6 |

What impact did it have on the sense of uncertainty? What impact did it have on your worry? How much energy and effort do you put into managing uncertainty by using this strategy? Could your energy be used elsewhere?

What rules or beliefs do you have that might underpin this strategy? Examples: Everything people say should add up and make sense; I should understand and remember everything that is said; if I let people know me then I will feel unsure of myself; if I am uncertain or unsure, then I must be wrong; if I do something new I cannot be sure that I will cope.

If I were less bothered by uncertainty, then what might I do differently? Could I accept, rather than avoid these people and sit with the uncertainty?

*Hint:* People: *Is there anything about the people you avoid that you like or miss? What would your social/work/family circles be without them? Is this the only part of their character, what else do you know about them? Would you bump into them any more or less if you stopped avoiding? How does being on the look out for them affect how you feel? Are you responsible for the actions of others?* Side-effects of worry: *Would your friends be that bothered if you lost the thread of a conversion or forgot something? If this happens to someone talking to you then what would you think? If a close friend told you that they worried about concentrating or worried that they were more irritable than usual, what would you tell them? What are the advantages and disadvantages of avoiding people or social events? How does this leave you feeling?*

## Strategy 5. Avoiding situations

Some situations inevitably have a level of uncertainty built into them. For some you go there to find out what, if anything, might be wrong – for example, a check up at the doctors or dentist, an MOT on your car. For some there are factors clearly beyond your control – a wedding where you don't know who you will sit next to, or a train trip (delays, noisy passengers, disasters), or the exact contents of an exam paper, and so on.

Worriers would like to avoid these situations, which usually makes the problems worse and increases the opportunity for worry. For example, avoiding a trip to the dentist because they can't be sure that they won't need a filling only means that they are putting themselves more at risk of needing one further down the line, which then triggers more worry. If the worrier can't avoid a situation, then sometimes they revert to safety behaviors to manage the situations. A very common one is to have a few quick drinks at a wedding to 'oil' the wheels of conversation, and to take the edge off their worry.

### EXERCISE 9.5: AVOIDING SITUATIONS

How typical or characteristic is this strategy for you?

| Not like me at all | A little like me | Somewhat like me | Moderately like me | Mostly like me | Nearly like me | Completely like me |
|---|---|---|---|---|---|---|
| 0 | 1 | 2 | 3 | 4 | 5 | 6 |

What kinds of situations have you avoided recently?

Thinking of one typical example, did avoiding the situation make you feel more or less certain?

| Felt very uncertain | Felt moderately uncertain | Felt mildly uncertain | Neither certain or uncertain | Felt mildly certain | Felt moderately certain | Felt very certain |
|---|---|---|---|---|---|---|
| 0 | 1 | 2 | 3 | 4 | 5 | 6 |

If it made you feel less certain, then how did it do this? What impact did avoiding have on your worry? How much energy and effort do you put into managing uncertainty by using this strategy? Could your energy be used elsewhere?

What rules or beliefs do you have that might underpin this strategy?
Examples: Uncertainty is awful and I should avoid it; if I am surprised I will not know how to act; unless I keep a look out, something terrible may happen.

If I were less bothered by uncertainty, then what might I do differently? Could I approach these situations and live with the uncertainty that arises?

*Hint: What are the advantages and disadvantages of doing this? Getting started: what upcoming situations have some likely benefits, even though the uncertainty may be a little uncomfortable?*

## Strategy 6. Procrastination – avoiding painful feelings

Another form of avoidance is procrastination. This is where worriers find every excuse under the sun to avoid dealing with an uncertain problem or issue. Examples of this include putting off a conversation with a friend or colleague because they can't be sure how it will turn out, or spending time cleaning the house because they know the bills need sorting out, or putting off phoning their bank for an overdraft because they don't know if the bank will agree to it or not. As with the example of the dentist above, not dealing with something straight away means that the problem or issue remains. And if left, it may get worse, bringing more uncertainty than the problem contained in the first place. In addition, by trying to ignore something, our minds have a wonderful way of reminding us of unfinished business by sporadically dropping the issue or problem into our thoughts. This can happen when we are least able to do anything about it (say at 3.00 a.m.), and so triggers more worry. Or, the person is caught up worrying about the implications of their failure to address the problem, which means they again fail to do anything about it.

## EXERCISE 9.6: PROCRASTINATION

How typical or characteristic is this strategy for you?

| Not like me at all | A little like me | Somewhat like me | Moderately like me | Mostly like me | Nearly like me | Completely like me |
|---|---|---|---|---|---|---|
| 0 | 1 | 2 | 3 | 4 | 5 | 6 |

What kinds of situations or events have led you to procrastinate?

Thinking of one typical example, did putting things off make you feel more or less certain?

| Felt very uncertain | Felt moderately uncertain | Felt mildly uncertain | Neither certain or uncertain | Felt mildly certain | Felt moderately certain | Felt very certain |
|---|---|---|---|---|---|---|
| 0 | 1 | 2 | 3 | 4 | 5 | 6 |

What impact did avoiding have on your worry? How much energy and effort do you put into managing uncertainty by using this strategy? Could your energy be used elsewhere?

What rules or beliefs do you have that might underpin this strategy?
Examples: All change is bad; if I do something uncertain, I cannot be sure that I will cope; if I feel uncertain then I cannot act.

If I were less bothered by uncertainty, then what might I do differently? Could I do it now, rather than later, and then sit with the feelings of uncertainty.

*Hint: What are the advantages and disadvantages of doing this? Do not wait for certainty to act, experiment with being certain enough. What happens to your worry when you put things off? Can you actually solve problems by putting them off? Getting started: where could I make a start on something where even doing only a bit can have some benefit?*

## Strategy 7. Looking for reassurance – avoiding taking responsibility

This is a very common way of dealing with uncertainty. Reassurance-seeking is helpful in the short term because we usually feel much better once someone has told us that everything will be OK, but its effect is generally short lived. Uncertainty drives the worrier's thirst for reassurance and before too long they need more. How does this happen? They may seek reassurance when feelings of uncertainty are triggered by a decision or when they have solved a problem and want to know that they did OK. Any certainty that may have emerged as a result of seeking reassurance is both short lived and then undermined by *what if* questions as they take the reassurance to pieces. As they do this, the levels of uncertainty increase and the worrier is then driven to demand more reassurance to stave off the uncertainty, and the cycle starts again. Reassurance has another side-effect that triggers more uncertainty and worry: worriers will often ask the people closest to them for reassurance. Worriers can do this repetitively, which after a while may irritate the people they ask and lead them to respond in a dismissive and unconvincing way or perhaps even to say unintentional but hurtful things – this can trigger more worry.

Worriers can be either very direct or very subtle about how they seek reassurance. For example, when wanting to find out if their friends enjoyed an evening out at the cinema the worrier might ask a series of questions. The straightforward questions would be, *Did you enjoy yourself?* and *How did you find the film?* The more clandestine questions would be, *Do you like that type of film?* Or, *Did you notice that X didn't seem to enjoy it?* Seeking reassurance means that we never learn to tolerate uncertainty or take responsibility for our actions. It undermines our confidence in dealing with uncertainty and erodes our confidence in our decision-making. Worriers can also use a 'hanging statement'. This is a half-question, a question without an ending, and the worrier implies the ending – for example, *I wasn't so sure about that . . .* (the question is, *What do you really think?*), or *It wasn't as good as the others he made . . .* (the question is, *Did you really like this one?*). Of course the big problem with these hanging statements is that the other person doesn't really know where the worrier is coming from. It's a sort of bear-trap, where the ambiguous or unexpected response may unknowingly trigger more worry.

---

### EXERCISE 9.7: LOOKING FOR REASSURANCE

How typical or characteristic is this strategy for you?

| Not like me at all | A little like me | Somewhat like me | Moderately like me | Mostly like me | Nearly like me | Completely like me |
|---|---|---|---|---|---|---|
| 0 | 1 | 2 | 3 | 4 | 5 | 6 |

What kinds of situations or events have led you to seek reassurance?

Thinking of one typical example, did seeking reassurance make you feel more or less certain? (Please rate this twice, for the feeling just after seeking reassurance and then over the next few hours.)

| Felt very uncertain | Felt moderately uncertain | Felt mildly uncertain | Neither certain or uncertain | Felt mildly certain | Felt moderately certain | Felt very certain |
|---|---|---|---|---|---|---|
| 0 | 1 | 2 | 3 | 4 | 5 | 6 |

What impact did the reassurance have on your worry in the short and long term? How much energy and effort do you put into managing uncertainty by using this strategy? Could your energy be used elsewhere?

What rules or beliefs do you have that might underpin this strategy?
Examples: If I ask others, then I feel more certain; I must always ask others before acting; if I make a mistake I will be overwhelmed with doubts; I can only handle uncertainty with the help of others.

If I were less bothered by uncertainty, then what might I do differently? Could I stop seeking reassurance and tolerate the uncertainty instead?

Hint: What are the advantages and disadvantages of doing this? How will you develop your confidence if you continue to ask others for reassurance? Getting started: what is something I could do without asking for reassurance when I have to, but would normally ask someone if they were around?

## Strategy 8. Overprotecting others – avoiding giving others responsibility

Worriers tend to look out for others and at the same time worry about them. As a way of reducing uncertainty and worry they may prevent their children or other family members from doing everyday activities. They may take on tasks themselves, rather than putting other people at risk. We saw this in Abby's example on page 53: while pregnant she took on running errands for her husband so that *he* would not be put at risk when driving. She did this because she genuinely cared about him, but she also wanted to manage her uncertainty. Worriers genuinely care about their families and friends, but because of the nightmare scenarios they have when they worry, they are often motivated to protect others from these awful hypothetical experiences. This strategy is a 'just in case' strategy. If the awful thing really happened, then they also worry that they would not be able to cope, leading them to protect, irrespective of the costs to themselves or others. Being the subject of overprotection can be annoying: children and other family members may 'rebel' and their behavior become much more uncertain and unpredictable, which leads to more worry. Furthermore, for parents, there is a delicate balance between allowing children to grow up and become autonomous through taking age-appropriate risks, possibly making mistakes, versus trying to keep them completely safe from all possible harm.

## EXERCISE 9.8: OVERPROTECTING OTHERS

How typical or characteristic is this strategy for you?

| Not like me at all | A little like me | Somewhat like me | Moderately like me | Mostly like me | Nearly like me | Completely like me |
|---|---|---|---|---|---|---|
| 0 | 1 | 2 | 3 | 4 | 5 | 6 |

Who do you overprotect? Why do you do this? When was the last time you did this?

In this example, did doing this make you feel more or less certain?

| Felt very uncertain | Felt moderately uncertain | Felt mildly uncertain | Neither certain or uncertain | Felt mildly certain | Felt moderately certain | Felt very certain |
|---|---|---|---|---|---|---|
| 0 | 1 | 2 | 3 | 4 | 5 | 6 |

What impact did overprotecting have on your worry? How much energy and effort do you put into managing uncertainty by using this strategy? Could your energy be used elsewhere?

What rules or beliefs do you have that might underpin this strategy? Examples: If I let people out of my sight, then I cannot manage the uncertainty; I could not handle it if something happened to my loved ones; I should work out what could go wrong; I am responsible for it, if it happens.

If I were less bothered by uncertainty, then what might I do differently? Could I drop your guard a little and sit with the uncertainty? Then drop it a little more?

*Hint: What are the advantages and disadvantages of doing this? How do the people feel who are the subject of your protection? If you continued to overprotect them, what might be the outcome? Are there better ways of protecting your loved ones, apart from stopping them from doing things or doing things for them? Getting started: is there something that I know others can do, but I still do it for them or instead of them? Can I let them do it this time and sit with the uncertainty?*

## Strategy 9. Failing to delegate – avoiding giving others responsibility

As we mentioned above, some people bring uncertainty and sometimes worriers avoid them because of this. Another way of reducing the uncertainty is for worriers to do things them-selves rather than relying on others. It's not that they don't trust others, but it means they can manage the uncertainty by doing the task themselves. But this has knock-on effects. First, it may leave the worrier exhausted, as they try to do too much. Second, those around them may begin to take the worrier for granted, or feel undervalued themselves. Third, we never learn to manage the uncertainty attached to delegation and our worry is maintained.

## EXERCISE 9.9: FAILING TO DELEGATE

How typical or characteristic is this strategy for you?

| Not like me at all | A little like me | Somewhat like me | Moderately like me | Mostly like me | Nearly like me | Completely like me |
|---|---|---|---|---|---|---|
| 0 | 1 | 2 | 3 | 4 | 5 | 6 |

What do you fail to delegate. To whom? (Remember it could be tasks for your partner, or children, or housemates or work colleagues.) When was the last time you did this?

In this example, did failing to delegate make you feel more or less certain?

| Felt very uncertain | Felt moderately uncertain | Felt mildly uncertain | Neither certain or uncertain | Felt mildly certain | Felt moderately certain | Felt very certain |
|---|---|---|---|---|---|---|
| 0 | 1 | 2 | 3 | 4 | 5 | 6 |

What impact did failing to delegate have on your worry? How much energy and effort do you put into managing uncertainty by using this strategy? Could your energy be used elsewhere?

What rules or beliefs do you have that might underpin this strategy? Example: If others do things, I cannot be sure that they have done it right; if I do it, then I can be certain that it is done right; others' reactions are uncertain – to avoid this I should do it myself; if I do it myself, then I am sure of the emotional fallout.

If I were less bothered by uncertainty, then what might I do differently? Could I delegate and learn to tolerate the uncertainty that comes?

*Hint: What are the advantages and disadvantages of doing this (for you and for others)? How might doing this be unhelpful to you? If you continued to fail to delegate, what might be the outcome? Getting started: is there something small enough, that wouldn't be a disaster if it didn't work out perfectly?*

## Strategy 10. Smoke screen

Sometimes we avoid uncertainty by putting up a smoke screen to 'distance' ourselves from the uncertainty. Often the smoke screen is made up of 'every idea under the sun' why we shouldn't deal with an uncertain situation or event apart from the real reason, namely finding the feelings of uncertainty intolerable. For example:

An office worker was offered a promotion in which he would get much more money, work on the same floor of the same building, have a bigger office, a nicer desk and view, work with a lovely team and so forth. The promotion was offered because he was more than able for the new role. But he declined because he said he preferred his desk in the office, he felt settled in his job, he knew his way around, he had a nice routine and wanted to stay close to his friends. Each idea was reasonable, but may have masked the real reason for declining the promotion, namely that the uncertainty it would bring would have been intolerable. The smoke screen meant the worker never really got to grips with the underlying ideas that motivated him to avoid the risks and new experiences that came with the promotion.

While we have used a work-related example, the pattern can be seen in relationships, in our financial dealings, in the way we think about our health or in our avoidance of social events. So how does the smoke screen keep us worrying? As we have mentioned, by not addressing the underlying issue, the idea that we would be unable to cope with uncertainty is kept alive. We never find out that, if we blew away the smoke screen, we would probably be able to cope and thrive. The uncertainty turns an opportunity into a threat. The smoke screen also has a secondary impact: the worrier avoids opportunities for growth and development, which may in the longer term have a profound impact on how they feel about themselves.

## EXERCISE 9.10: SMOKE SCREEN

How typical or characteristic is this strategy for you?

| Not like me at all | A little like me | Somewhat like me | Moderately like me | Mostly like me | Nearly like me | Completely like me |
|---|---|---|---|---|---|---|
| 0 | 1 | 2 | 3 | 4 | 5 | 6 |

What kinds of new situations or events have led you to put out a smoke screen or reasons and excuses?

In this example, did doing this make you feel more or less certain?

| Felt very uncertain | Felt moderately uncertain | Felt mildly uncertain | Neither certain or uncertain | Felt mildly certain | Felt moderately certain | Felt very certain |
|---|---|---|---|---|---|---|
| 0 | 1 | 2 | 3 | 4 | 5 | 6 |

What impact did avoiding have on your worry? How much energy and effort do you put into managing uncertainty by using this strategy? Could your energy be used elsewhere?

What rules or beliefs do you have that might underpin this strategy?
Examples: All change is bad; if I open myself up to uncertainty, then I will not be able to cope; I should avoid change.

If I were less bothered by uncertainty, then what might I do differently? Could I recognize I am making a blockade of excuses, accept the uncertainty that exists and engage with the problem?

*Hint: What are the advantages and disadvantages of doing this? Getting started: is there a time-limited situation, or a small enough action (e.g. a purchase) where I could drop the smoke screen and become a man/woman of action?*

## Strategy 11. Checking and rechecking – avoiding making mistakes

This is very common. Worriers often feel uncertain about decisions or choices that they have made and consequently revisit decisions or choices to see if they did the right thing. As with many of the strategies mentioned so far, the *what if* question sows doubt and the worrier is drawn into checking to answer the doubts raised by their worry, thus increasing rather than decreasing uncertainty.

## EXERCISE 9.11: CHECKING

How typical or characteristic is this strategy for you?

| Not like me at all | A little like me | Somewhat like me | Moderately like me | Mostly like me | Nearly like me | Completely like me |
|---|---|---|---|---|---|---|
| 0 | 1 | 2 | 3 | 4 | 5 | 6 |

What kinds of situations or events have led you to check and recheck? Consider a recent example.

In this example, did doing this make you feel more or less certain?

| Felt very uncertain | Felt moderately uncertain | Felt mildly uncertain | Neither certain or uncertain | Felt mildly certain | Felt moderately certain | Felt very certain |
|---|---|---|---|---|---|---|
| 0 | 1 | 2 | 3 | 4 | 5 | 6 |

What impact did checking have on your worry? How much energy and effort do you put into managing uncertainty by using this strategy? Could your energy be used elsewhere?

What rules or beliefs do you have that might underpin this strategy? Examples: If I make a decision, then I should always question it; if there is a chance that something will go wrong then it will; if I make a mistake I will be overwhelmed with doubts.

If I were less bothered by uncertainty, then what might I do differently? Could I reduce your checking and sit with the uncertainty, and then reduce and stop checking?

*Hint: What are the advantages and disadvantages of doing this? Getting started: is there something I routinely check and where it wouldn't be a complete disaster if not checking meant that it was not perfect? To learn how checking influences you, pick something you don't usually check, and now check this as frequently as you check when worried. What do you notice?*

## Strategy 12. Post-mortem worry

Once worriers have made up their minds with regard to a decision or problem, they may then begin to doubt whether they have made the right choice. On their way to making a decision, they would have wrestled with uncertainty until they 'bit the bullet' and decided. Once the decision is made, then uncertainty opens up again. The worrier will ask, *What if I have made a bad decision?* and then worry about the implications of their decision. Their questioning stimulates uncertainty and breaks simple decisions into a thousand pieces, and the worrier becomes lost within the labyrinth of ideas and begins to doubt their decision and themselves. Imagine a parrot sitting on your shoulder asking you these questions: why did you do that, what if it goes wrong, why didn't you get more advice, how could you be sure? (And so on). How would you feel towards the parrot? The questions are undermining and critical, based on the idea that the worrier does not have the capacity to make good decisions or choices. Remember that we are referring to everyday decisions – a choice about where to go for lunch with a colleague, or what car seat to put your child on, or which account to put your money in. These everyday choices are taken apart and scrutinized and, not surprisingly, we feel much more uncertainty when we do this, leading to more worry. The story above about Peter also hints at a secondary problem that comes with post-mortem worry, namely that the worrier is denied the chance to feel enjoyment or contentment in their decision-making. For example, a student worried about which laptop to buy. She eventually chose one and took it home. Once connected to the Internet her post-mortem worry started and she searched the Internet for cheaper and better laptops and soon felt stupid for choosing the one she had. This kind of post-decision worrying is particularly problematic when coupled with impulsive decision-making linked to escaping uncertainty.

## EXERCISE 9.12: POST-MORTEM WORRY

How typical or characteristic is this strategy for you?

| Not like me at all | A little like me | Somewhat like me | Moderately like me | Mostly like me | Nearly like me | Completely like me |
|---|---|---|---|---|---|---|
| 0 | 1 | 2 | 3 | 4 | 5 | 6 |

What kinds of decisions, situations or events have led you to worry after you have made a decision? Choose a recent example.

In this example, did doing this make you feel more or less certain?

| Felt very uncertain | Felt moderately uncertain | Felt mildly uncertain | Neither certain or uncertain | Felt mildly certain | Felt moderately certain | Felt very certain |
|---|---|---|---|---|---|---|
| 0 | 1 | 2 | 3 | 4 | 5 | 6 |

What impact did this have on your worry? How much energy and effort do you put managing uncertainty by using into this strategy? Could your energy be used elsewhere?

What rules or beliefs do you have that might underpin this strategy? Examples: If I make a decision, then I should always question it; if there is a chance that something will go wrong then it will; if I make a mistake I will be overwhelmed with doubts.

If I were less bothered by uncertainty, then what might I do differently? Could I recognize that nothing is to be done when the horse has bolted? Could I sit with the uncertainty and wait and see what really happens?

*Hint: What are the advantages and disadvantages of doing this? How does pulling your decisions to pieces help? Have you ever found that the decisions you made were good despite pulling them to pieces? If so, how often? When you recognize yourself doing this what could you say? Would you do this if it were someone else making the decision; if not, why not? Getting started: is there a small decision you need to make which you know you will pull to pieces afterwards? Make your decision and then sit with the uncertainty. When you start to pull it to pieces ask, Why am I doing this? and tell yourself that your decision is good enough.*

## Other strategies

Some people use drugs or alcohol to take the edge off their worry. These strategies tend to make their problems worse, as they do not address the underlying issue or problem that triggered the worry in the first place. They also have the effect of increasing uncertainty, as we tend to be much less predictable and ordered when we are under the influence of drink or drugs. There are also long- and short-term costs. For example, in the short term there may be immediate emotional costs as we 'beat ourselves up' for using alcohol or drugs to cope and because we have avoided our problems by drinking. In the longer term we may begin to become reliant on drink or drugs to help us cope, or the problems that we continue to avoid become bigger and more problematic, leading us to drink more to manage them. If you are worried about how much you are drinking or worried about the drug you are taking, then please go and see your family doctor and discuss this with them.

Some worriers tend to comfort eat or binge to manage feelings of uncertainty. Of course these strategies do not address the real uncertainty, only the unpleasant feelings that come with it. A similar pattern of short- and long-term costs is associated with this strategy, too. The long and short of all the strategies that we have mentioned is that their aim is to reduce uncertainty, but they have the opposite effect because we fail to engage with our problems enough to solve them.

We mentioned that worriers tend to reduce the circumference of their world because of uncertainty. Uncertainty will also keep worriers stuck in unhelpful relationships because the worrier believes that leaving or ending them will generate much more uncertainty than keeping things as they are. We have often heard the phrase 'better the devil you know than the devil you don't know' when working with people who are in these situations. If you are struggling within a relationship, or are being abused in any way, if you can find the courage to tell your family doctor, they will know where to find help. No one has the right to hurt or abuse you. In the first instance, you may need to talk it through to get your mind around what is going on and help you to make a decision about what will happen next. In the UK, the website NHS Direct has information about violence or abuse within the home (see Further Information at the end of the book).

## EXERCISE 9.13: PULLING THINGS TOGETHER

This exercise summarizes the key points in this chapter.
What are the key strategies that you use to manage uncertainty?

Overall, how much energy and effort are you putting into managing the unmanageable, that is managing uncertainty?

Are there any key rules that kept popping up? What are they?

What general ideas did you come up with to help challenge your intolerance of uncertainty? What behavioral experiments can you think of to help you learn to tolerate uncertainty?

In all these strategies the common process is that of increasing uncertainty rather than diminishing it, and the simple message is that we should learn to tolerate uncertainty by challenging the rules that underpin it and doing things differently.

**PIT STOP**

It may be helpful to stop here and think about what you have just been reading. Can you summarize the key ideas you have taken on board? What things are sticking in your mind about uncertainty? Maybe write them down. If you have any questions, jot these down too. You can return to them once you have had a chance to digest the information.

What things are sticking in my mind from my reading so far?

1.

2.

3.

In the next chapter we will give you some examples of behavioral experiments to help you to become more tolerant of uncertainty.

**10**

# Behavioral experiments – dealing with uncertainty

Before reading this chapter, it may be helpful to review Chapter 7 to remind you of how to go about developing behavioral experiments.

Behavioral experiments are about finding out something new, by doing something differently. This means changing the way you react to uncertainty and, rather than avoiding it, beginning to seek it out on purpose to see what happens. We do not expect you to dive into the deep end of uncertainty; it's much better to begin thinking about small, manageable and realistic steps. Expect to feel anxious and to worry more when trying new things out – we all do. Remember do not to wait until you feel motivated: go out and seek motivation by doing. *Motivation does not come before action, it follows it.* Act first, and the motivation will arrive.

## What would these steps look like?

Take a strategy that you now recognize and begin to think about all the situations where this strategy appears in your life (we have asked you to think about this in the exercises above). Don't get too hung-up on trying to separate the strategies out since they overlap a great deal. The important thing is that you have thought about what you do in the face of uncertainty, and spotted some of the unhelpful patterns you fall into.

Let's take seeking reassurance as an example. Here is a list of situations that Abby wrote down about where she looked for reassurance:

- About the clothes she's wearing
- Which clothes to buy while shopping
- What food to cook
- About her appearance
- About whether she's a good enough partner (parent, friend, etc.)
- About her financial dealings
- About whether she has upset others
- About other people's whereabouts
- About whether her partner still loves her.

Next we put this list in order, starting with the 'shallow end' stuff first. Imagine you are putting each of these on a ladder, with the toughest one on the top rung and the easiest on the first. Abby did this with her list: she found that the easiest step for her would be to stop asking her partner what she should cook for supper. For her, the hardest steps were about her relationships, and she left these until she had got some experience of tolerating uncertainty under her belt.

In our example, we would ask Abby, 'Supposing you did not ask for reassurance, what is the worst thing that could happen?'

This question is very helpful for getting to the hidden conse-quences that often underpin our rules. In Abby's case, she feared upsetting her partner by not asking him. She developed the following prediction:

*If I don't ask my partner about what food to cook for supper, then I'll feel awful and he will be upset with me for making something he doesn't want.*

At this point is might be helpful to think about the other side-effects of seeking reassurance, such as the costs to you or how it maintains poor self-confidence or the impact on those around you. The cost in this case might simply be that Abby knows what she wants for supper, but she may not actually want to eat what her partner suggests. The idea is to begin to rock the foundation of the rules, and to help you understand why challenging them would be useful and to develop alter-native ideas about what might happen. Abby came up with the following alternative:

*If I don't ask my partner about what food to cook for supper, then I may feel awful for a while, but if I do this, I'll feel more confident and I can surprise my partner with something new and I can prepare something I want to eat.*

Now that Abby has set up the experiment she now needs to do it and see what happens. She may need to remind herself of her goals and why it is important that she remains engaged with them. She needs to guard against perfectionism and be mindful of stalling because of the fear of uncertainty, which is only natural. She also needs to be aware of her safety behav-iors and ask herself: *Am I finding reassurance in another way?*

*What am I doing to keep myself safe?* For example, she may realize that she is seeking reassurance by asking her friends about their ideas about what she could cook for her partner's tea, or she may add in something else that she is sure he will like just in case he gets annoyed with her. In these instances, once she realised this, she had to stop doing this. Lastly, she had to watch that she was not compensating by doing more of the other strategies mentioned above. For example, she noticed that she started scanning her partner's conversations for any sign that he did not like his supper.

Once Abby has done this, she needs to think about keeping this going, while tackling another of the situations in which she seeks reassurance. This is a little like plate spinning – keeping one thing on the go while introducing something new – but after a while it can become second nature. When thinking about your experiments you may want to use the worksheet found on page 141 to help you plan them out.

While this may feel like a trivial example, worry and GAD are about the everyday. They're not about big occasion worry, because in this situation we all worry and some aspects of worry can be helpful. In order to help you to worry less, we need to help you to tolerate uncertainty in the everyday, not the spectacular and unusual. So keep this in mind.

### How do I know it is working?

As you actively seek out uncertainty it is perfectly normal to notice uncomfortable feelings and worry. In the normal course of things (and according to your previous rules) this would be a signal to stop what you are doing and to try to decrease the uncertainty. If you are using your level of worry, your anxiety or your discomfort with uncertainty as an indicator of whether the new way of doing things is working, the logical conclusion would be: *This isn't working!* So, how worried, anxious, or uncomfortable you are feeling at the time are not the right indicators. The *right indicators* are the outcomes (namely, what happened) and how you feel about them afterwards. As far as the outcomes are concerned, did disaster strike? Was the outcome at least OK? Was it any better than OK? Did anyone else notice anything? Did anyone else notice something good? Did you discover anything new? Did you experience something new? How did you feel about what actually happened? OK? A bit better than OK? Any positive feelings like pleasure, satisfaction, surprise? Are you proud of your attempt to do something differently? Are you motivated to try something else? Did you manage (even if it was uncomfortable) to tolerate uncertainty?

If your answers to at least some of these questions are in the right direction, then you are making progress. This is why the post-experiment review where you compare the outcome with your predictions is absolutely critical. Although a few people can experience 'A-ha' moments from experiments, when a blinding flash of realization leads to a new way of looking at the world, for most people change comes from chipping away at everyday experiences. It is only when we look back after a few weeks that we can see how far we have come. Remember, also, that the intention is not to become carefree, spendthrift, lackadaisical, irresponsible, uncaring or any other extreme change. The intention is to become flexible, responsive and capable of spontaneity, all according to the situation. Although certainty may remain attractive but elusive, pursuit of it is no longer the main guiding principle.

## TABLE 10.1 IDEAS FOR BEHAVIORAL EXPERIMENTS THAT STIMULATE TOLERANCE OF UNCERTAINTY

Don't ask for reassurance on a decision you have made.

Take a gamble, go and see a film you know nothing about.

Arrive 10 minutes later than you normally would at an informal social occasion.

Go to a different shop for your groceries.

Having something you have never tried in a restaurant.

Allow your kids to do age-appropriate things for themselves.

Stop asking others to check your work.

Put a cap on the amount of time or information you need to make a decision.

Take opportunities to meet new people.

Within your acquaintances, let people get to know you.

Book a visit to your GP, accountant, dentist or bank manager, or anyone else you are avoiding.

Stop checking emails, letters or small cheques before sending them.

Buy food you have never bought before.

Take responsibility for something small and time-limited. Go ahead, don't ask for reassurance.

Delegate small jobs at work or at home.

Go to a restaurant you have never been to (and don't read the reviews).

Once you have bought something new, use it and keep using it.

Make a smallish, impulsive buy.

Stay in the here and now; go with the flow when in familiar settings.

Try new activities out; take a taster session for a club or a hobby.

Sit still in social occasions; lose the butterfly wings.

Move things around in the home; break your patterns and order.

Ask your loved ones to *not* tell you exactly where they are, or exactly when they will be home.

Break your routines and go 'off track'.

Make a minor commitment.

Act while the problem is still small.

Be generous and less critical of yourself.

Find your own path; don't follow the crowd for the sake of it. Do your own thing.

Don't stick rigidly to a plan; act spontaneously if an opportunity presents itself.

Let others drive if you always drive yourself. Drive yourself if you always let others drive.

Find good reasons for doing things instead of not doing things – then do them.

Do the task that needs your attention and not the thousands of others that get in the way.

If you make too many snap decisions, use the time it takes to have a coffee to think things through.

Say yes more often to small invitations.

Now, time for action and challenge your intolerance of uncertainty. As the inspirational poet and writer Sark suggests, it's time to 'make friends with freedom and uncertainty'.

**PIT STOP**

Let's stop and think about what you have just been reading. Can you summarize the key ideas you have taken on board? What is sticking in your mind? Maybe write them down. If you have any questions, jot these down too. You can return to them once you have had a chance to digest the information.

What is sticking in my mind from my reading so far?

1.

2.

3.

# 11

# The cradle of worry

For a moment, let us return to the traffic metaphor. Remember that in order to try to manage traffic, we needed to understand and then challenge driver rules or beliefs, which influenced the flow of traffic (for instance, *I must always keep up with the flow of traffic; If I drive at the speed limit, then I could annoy the drivers behind me*). Both these rules motivate faster driving. There are a number of rules and beliefs that have a very strong influence on our propensity to worry. We shall explore these rules in this chapter.

## The link with uncertainty

There are three broad groups of beliefs or rules that influence worry and they all tend to make us worry more. What is important is where they are thought to appear in the timeline of worry. They provide the platform or framework for worry, which we have called the *worry cradle* (see figure 11.1 on page 227). Some of the rules that make up the worry cradle tell us that worrying is, by and large, a helpful or useful thing to do. For instance, *Worrying shows that I care*. Other rules tell us that worrying is an unhelpful thing to do. For instance, *If I worry, bad things are more likely to happen*. The final group of rules are more general rules related to our thoughts, for instance, *All my thoughts are important* or *I should always think things through properly*. All three types of rule 'set us up to worry' and we will explain how they do this in more detail below.

So the cradle of worry is made of three groups of rules:

- Positive worry-promoting rules
- Negative worry-promoting rules
- General worry-promoting rules.

The next sections of this chapter will take in turn each of the rules and beliefs discussed and provide more detail on what they are and how they might influence worry.

## Positive worry-promoting rules

We will now focus on the first set of worry-promoting rules. We can think about these positive rules as if they were a *cradle*, providing the 'space' where worry can form, develop and grow. Just as in the bus stop example, the rules provide a framework or cradle for the actions that follow them; remember, the whirlwind of worry is considered as an action or mental behavior. The diagram below shows how a situation activates the *cradle of worry*, which both starts us worrying and keeps us worrying. The worry itself then opens up doubt and uncertainty and triggers more worry. We now return to the example of Tom waiting at the train station.

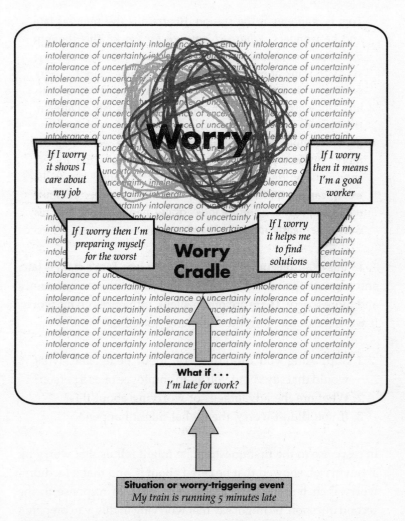

**Figure 11.1. Building the picture: the cradle of worry.**

Tom is standing at the station. His train is five minutes late and he wonders, *What if I am late for work?* This thought opens up doubt and uncertainty and he starts to worry. He starts to think about the implications of being late for work and how this will impact on his job, his relationship and his life. His worry quickly turns into a nightmarish daydream. His worries feel very real, they arrive thick and fast and generate more doubt and uncertainty, so he worries all the more. His worry feels out of control and he starts to feel very panicky. He is barely aware of his surroundings as his worry carries him further away. He starts to *feel* anxious, tense and restless and he looks about nervously. Lost in his worry, he nearly misses his train.

In this example, uncertainty appears when Tom's train is late, and triggers the *what if* questions that create more uncertainty and more worry. There are other 'silent' influences on his worry. If we were to ask Tom the following questions:

1. Supposing you didn't worry about being late, what would that say about you as an employee or as a person?
2. What are the advantages of worrying about this?
3. If you didn't worry, then what might happen?

In response to the first question, he might tell us that worrying about his job showed that he cared about it, and that if he didn't worry then he would be a bad employee. In response to the second question, he might say that worrying in this way prepared him for the awful day ahead. If we asked him how worry helped him do this, he might tell us that it is almost as if he were steeling himself for the events to come by worrying about them first, even though they were highly unlikely to happen. To the last question, he might add that worry helped him to find solutions to the problems and if he didn't worry things through, then he may miss important problems. There are several silent rules in operation here:

- If I worry then it means I'm good worker.
- If I worry it shows I care about my work.
- If I worry then I'm preparing myself for the worst.
- If I worry it helps me to find solutions to problems.

These rules are the silent partners in the development of worry; they support worry and enable it to develop and grow. Stop for a moment and ask if you can see how Tom's rules supported his propensity to worry. These rules 'instruct us to worry', they 'tell us' that if we worry we can be better prepared, or that we can show we care, or that we are better people for worrying. As you no doubt realize, there are much better ways of preparing, or bettering ourselves, or showing we care. For instance, if you were to write a list of all the things that made a good employee, father, partner, daughter, guest, host, colleague, friend and so on, would you include worry on your list?

## Discovering worry rules

By concentrating, we can guess what rules might be operating. In the bus stop example in Chapter 7 we could work out what rules were operating by looking more closely at what actions people took or noticed when strong feelings were triggered. This leaves us with a problem: with worry, worrying *is* the action and we can't see it! If we can't see it, then how can we work out what the worry rules are? We know that there are lots of actions motivated by worry and we can use these actions to help us spot worry rules, for example, by avoiding situations that trigger worry. And we use questions to help us discover worry rules. The series of questions below will help you work out your worry rulebook. It might be helpful to take a notebook and work through them to see if you can understand more about what rules might support your worry. Later in this book there are other ideas to help you develop a better understanding of the rules that might influence your worry. Research has found a number of different themes that worry rules might circle around, such as *worry motivates me; worry can protect me from awful feelings; worry helps me to find solutions; worry prevents bad things happening* and *worry shows that we are good people*. There are others, and they will be explored in more detail later in this chapter, and we will also spend more time helping you to sketch out your worry rules in Chapter 13.

### EXERCISE 11.1: SPOTTING YOUR WORRY RULES

This exercise will help you work out and spot your worry rules. You will need your notebook to make a record of your answers. In the blank space insert the name of a loved one, child, family member, colleague, or friend, or an event like an exam, a meeting at work, work or money. Think of what you worry about most and answer the questions focused on that. In Block 1, there are two versions of each question, a general (a) and a more focused version (b). Think about two or three different things to fill in the blanks with. It will feel a little repetitive, but that's OK; we are looking for themes and links to emerge and this will help.

*Block 1*

1a. Supposing you didn't worry, what would that say about you?

1b. Supposing you didn't worry about _____ then what would that say about you?

2a. Supposing you worried less, then what would that say about you?

2b. Supposing you worried less about _____, then what would that say about you?

3a. Supposing you stopped worrying tomorrow, would you be bothered by this? If so, why?

3b. Supposing you stopped worrying tomorrow about _____, would you be bothered by this? If so, why?

4a. Supposing you worried less, would anything happen?

4b. Supposing you worried less about _____, would anything happen?

5a. What are the advantages of worrying?

5b. What are the advantages of worrying about _____?

6a. What are the disadvantages of worrying?

6b. What are the disadvantages of worrying about _____?

7a. Does worrying help you in any way? If so, how?

7b. Does worrying about _____ help you in any way? If so, how?

*Block 2*

1. If I didn't worry (about _____) so much, then ...........

2. If I didn't worry (about _____), then ......................

3. I should worry (about_____) because ....................

4. Worrying (about_____) helps ................................

5. Worrying (about_____) stops .............................

6. I ought to worry (about_____) because ...................

7. I should worry (about_____) or .................... may happen.

8. I worry (about_____) to ....................................

9. I worry to stop (_____) .......................................

Review what you have discovered in this exercise. Does it help you to understand why you worry in certain situations? Or does it help you to understand what motivates you to worry? What comes to mind? Write it down and return to it once you have read more. What rules have you discovered? Write them down.

Our worry rules are grounded in, and have developed from, our past, and so it is often helpful to think about our experiences as children, teenagers or young adults. Again, review the following questions with a notepad and try to work out what rules might have been developing.

Think about what influenced you as you grew up; what were things that people did or did not value in you? What kinds of experiences do you think influenced the type of person you have become?

### EXERCISE 11.2: EXPLORING EARLY INFLUENCES

This exercise helps you to explore these early rules. Again, write down your answers in your notebook.

1. If your early life had uncertainties, how did you deal with them? What did you say or do to manage these uncertainties?
2. What were you protected from? Were you overprotected or underprotected?
3. Who else worried in your home? Who did you learn to worry from?
4. What were the family sayings about worry?

5. What were you told were good or bad things to worry about?
6. What responsibilities did you have? Did you ever feel overwhelmed with responsibility, but still managed to cope?
7. What messages did you get about your ability to cope with life? Who gave them to you?
8. What were you praised for, and what were you criticized for?
9. When you worried, how did others react? When you worried, how did you react?
10. What memories come to mind when you worry?
11. If you focus on the feeling that you get when you worry, when do you remember feeling this for the first time?
12. When did you notice that you were a worrier? What was going on for you at the time?

It might be useful to have your responses to this exercise to hand as you read the next chapter. We have added some further questions in the pages that follow and hope that by the close of this chapter you will have a better understanding of the rules that make up your cradle of worry. Meanwhile, after the pit stop, we will go on in this chapter to explore in more detail the rules and beliefs that influence our tendency to worry, the rules that make up the worry cradle.

**PIT STOP**

Let's pause again and think about what you have just been reading. Can you summarize the key ideas you have taken on board? What things are sticking in your mind? Maybe write them down. If you have any questions, jot these down too. You can return to them once you have had a chance to digest the information.

What things are sticking in my mind from my reading so far?

1.

2.

3.

## Positive worry-promoting rules – the detail

Here we will look in more detail at the positive rules or beliefs that support worry. These rules suggest that worry is useful and that it leads to positive outcomes. The positive beliefs have been found to break down into five categories, namely that worry helps to

- find solutions
- motivate
- protect
- prevent bad things from happening
- show that we care.

We will explore each of these below. Remember that these worry beliefs are common across the spectrum of worry, so people with GAD will have them, as will people who worry less.

Now we will consider the different types of positive belief considered to be important in supporting worry. You might like to view these as components of the *cradle of worry*. As you go through this section, you will find it helpful to keep notes, as we will be asking you later to think in more detail about which of the following ideas apply to you. To help you with this we have added some rating scales to fill in immediately after you have read each section. In addition, you may want to under-line passages or statements, or if you have questions then write them down and you can come back to them once you have read further. We also want you to begin to think about how useful, all things considered, these rules are. And, as with uncertainty, we would like you to think about what you could do differ-ently, using behavioral experiments for example.

The following rules overlap to some extent. It's the central ideas we want you to take from them, since these will help you to think about your own rules and to develop personal versions of them.

### Belief group 1: Worry finds solutions to problems

These rules are based on the idea that worry is a useful strategy that helps to find solutions to problems. They suggest that worry enables us to look ahead and prepare for what might go wrong or, that worrying can help us to decide what we should to do if this happens. Linked to this belief is a sense that if we worry we are more likely to produce well thought-out and effective solutions.

*How this belief makes worry worse.* This all sounds very reason-able, and to a certain extent this belief can be useful in life-changing or 'big occasion' events. But in these circumstances, the loss of sleep, muscle tension, restlessness and so on are 'accepted' as part of the deal. Unfortunately, worriers tend to use these rules to help them work with everyday events or issues, and the worry here brings the same intensity of side-effects, which can make everyday problem-solving much more difficult. If our worry is at a manageable level, then it can contribute towards developing better solutions. However, worriers can't regulate the flow of their worry and usually it comes at two levels of intensity, either high or none at all. If we worry a lot, our worry begins to interfere with our capacity to act and to solve problems. Also, by being overly alert for potential problems, each solution we come up with is 'shot full of holes' and, worse still, as we see how each solution will fail this then triggers the spiral of worry.

TYPICAL BELIEFS

If I worry then I will know what to do.
If I worry this problem through, I will find the best way to deal with this.

**EXERCISE 11.3: WORRY FINDS SOLUTIONS TO PROBLEMS**

How typical or characteristic is this group of rules for you?

| None | A little | Some extent | Moderately | Somewhat | Mostly | Completely |
|------|----------|-------------|------------|----------|--------|------------|
| 0 | 1 | 2 | 3 | 4 | 5 | 6 |

How strongly do you agree with the idea that worry helps find solutions to problems?

| None | A little | Some extent | Moderately | Somewhat | Mostly | Completely |
|------|----------|-------------|------------|----------|--------|------------|
| 0 | 1 | 2 | 3 | 4 | 5 | 6 |

Can you think of a personal example from this set of worry rules? Write it down here.

How strongly do you believe this to be true?

| None | A little | Some extent | Moderately | Somewhat | Mostly | Completely |
|------|----------|-------------|------------|----------|--------|------------|
| 0 | 1 | 2 | 3 | 4 | 5 | 6 |

What impact does this rule have on your worry? What impact does it have on your capacity to solve problems?

What could you do to challenge this rule?

*Hint: Is this the best way to find the best solutions to your problems? What else could you do? Is there a less costly approach? What are the advantages and disadvantages of this approach? Does worrying actually solve your problems, or are you just going over and over the same stuff without moving forward? Does anxiety, produced by worry help or hinder your ability to solve problems?*

## Belief group 2: Worry motivates

This is one of the commonest beliefs in people with excessive worry. In a recent tutorial a student said, *My worry motivates me to work; if I didn't worry then I wouldn't work.* This belief is only helpful if it does just enough to get us working; it then needs to 'leave us alone' to get on with the job in hand. With this set of rules it's almost as if worrying somehow guarantees that things get done and that worrying somehow increases the quality of whatever needs to be done.

*How this belief makes worry worse.* People who worry a lot tend to find that in general their worry tends to distract and reduce concentration and so this stops them from working efficiently, leads to avoidance and procrastination and may even stop them completely rather than motivating them. In the example above the student 'needed' to worry to start working, but if his worry increased to a significant level it would begin to interfere with his ability to concentrate and no doubt have a negative impact on the quality of his work, thus further increasing worry. It would be much better to be preparing an assignment without worrying as there are other more important things to think about – inspiration, creativity, concentration and maybe even enjoyment! We know that the emotional consequences of worry such as anxiety and exhaustion will reduce motivation and can lead to a vicious cycle where worry produces anxiety and demoralization, which then make it harder to work, leading to more worry, and so on. The other important issue to mention with regards to this type of belief concerns yet another belief that silently sits within; namely, that worrying about your work is the same as actually caring about it. If you worried less about your work or other life events, would it mean that you cared less about them? It seems clear that for most of us worry is thought to be useful at some level. As a result, it will be much harder to free ourselves from it unless we challenge the idea that it is useful. So we need to be clear about the advantages and disadvantages of worrying and then ask where the balance lies: is it an overall advantage or disadvantage to worry?

TYPICAL BELIEFS

If I worry about it, then it'll get done.
I should worry or else I'll never do things.
If I worry, then I'll do a better job.
If I worry, then it shows how much my job means to me.

## EXERCISE 11.4: WORRY MOTIVATES

How typical or characteristic is this group of rules for you?

| None | A little | Some extent | Moderately | Somewhat | Mostly | Completely |
|------|----------|-------------|------------|----------|--------|------------|
| 0 | 1 | 2 | 3 | 4 | 5 | 6 |

How strongly do you agree with the idea that worry motivates you?

| None | A little | Some extent | Moderately | Somewhat | Mostly | Completely |
|------|----------|-------------|------------|----------|--------|------------|
| 0 | 1 | 2 | 3 | 4 | 5 | 6 |

Can you think of a personal example from this set of worry rules? Write it down here.

How strongly do you believe this to be true?

| None | A little | Some extent | Moderately | Somewhat | Mostly | Completely |
|------|----------|-------------|------------|----------|--------|------------|
| 0 | 1 | 2 | 3 | 4 | 5 | 6 |

What impact does this rule have on your worry? How does worry motivate you to work?

What could you do to challenge this rule?

*Hints: Is this the best way to motivate yourself? What else might your worry do as well as motivating you, what are the costs or side-effects? What could you do instead? Is there a less costly approach? What are the advantages and disadvantages of this approach? Does this way of approaching work make the quality of your work better? Does it mean that you care more about your work because you worry about it? Is there anyone at work who does not worry, but still cares about their work? What would be so bad about not worrying about work?*

### Belief group 3: Worry protects

In this group the worrier believes that to worry before a difficult event will somehow protect them against the onslaught of feelings when the event materializes. Of course, the assumption is that the event will actually happen and trigger overwhelming feelings. Some worriers think that if they worry beforehand this might somehow reduce the degree of awful emotions experienced *if* indeed the awful thing happens, which it very rarely does. It's almost like inoculating yourself against bad things by worrying first, or training yourself to cope with the overwhelming feelings by practising dealing with them first in your worries (a sort of mental gym), or, put another way, dosing yourself with medicine before you show any signs or symptoms.

*How these beliefs make worry worse.* It's as if the worrier is holding a heavy shield and a full suit of armour to protect themselves, even when there are no dragons to slay. Carrying the shield keeps the worrier on their toes, but it's exhausting to be on guard all the time. One of the key problems is that the worrier is nearly always expecting to experience really nasty feelings (which rarely happen), and this awful sense of apprehension can trigger more worry as we scan for danger. The other critical problem with this approach is that it really doesn't help us to cope with bad things when they do actually happen. None of us can prepare for unexpected bad news such as a death. Our shield may be entirely useless against a foe that is not a dragon, such as a flood. Even though we would dearly like to, it's impossible to know exactly what is around every corner.

## TYPICAL BELIEFS

I should always worry because you never know what is around the corner.

If I worry now then it will not affect me so much later.

If I don't worry about it and it happens, then I will feel guilty for not worrying about it (so I should worry).

---

### EXERCISE 11.5: WORRY PROTECTS

How typical or characteristic is this group of rules for you?

| None | A little | Some extent | Moderately | Somewhat | Mostly | Completely |
|------|----------|-------------|------------|----------|--------|------------|
| 0 | 1 | 2 | 3 | 4 | 5 | 6 |

How strongly do you agree with the idea that worry can protect you?

| None | A little | Some extent | Moderately | Somewhat | Mostly | Completely |
|------|----------|-------------|------------|----------|--------|------------|
| 0 | 1 | 2 | 3 | 4 | 5 | 6 |

Can you think of a personal example from this set of worry rules? Write it down here.

How strongly do you believe this to be true?

| None | A little | Some extent | Moderately | Somewhat | Mostly | Completely |
|------|----------|-------------|------------|----------|--------|------------|
| 0 | 1 | 2 | 3 | 4 | 5 | 6 |

What impact does this rule have on your worry? What impact does this rule have on your ability to protect yourself or others?

What could you do to challenge this rule?

*Hint: Is there a better way to protect the ones you love? Is there a better way of dealing with strong emotions? How many times has this strategy worked for you? Has anything that you worried about ever happened? What else could you do? Is there a less costly approach? What are the advantages and disadvantages of this approach? What does it feel like to be waiting for this awful thing to happen? What will it feel like in a year when it still hasn't happened?*

## Belief group 4: Worry prevents

These beliefs hinge around the idea that the act of worrying alone can influence what actually happens, like a 'telepathic' hand reaching out from our minds and grappling with the world. In these kinds of beliefs, thoughts and actions appear to be fused together, and so worrying about something bad will make it less likely that the bad thing will happen. For example, Angelina, a 17 year old, constantly worried about her health, but she never got ill. She started to believe that the reason for this was her worry, and so it made sense for her to keep worrying. But this way of thinking avoided considering all the other potential influences on her health, like her age, her diet, how unlikely serious illness is or the other things that she does to keep herself healthy. Her kind of worry also involves tunnel vision, where all other explanations, in this case of her good health, are ignored. It's like focusing on one thing to the exclusion of all others. On the other hand, some worriers believe that worrying about something good will make it more likely to happen. For example, Stan worried about whether his friends would enjoy a film they had gone to see. When they left the cinema Stan quietly asked them what they thought. To his relief, they all enjoyed the film. This reinforced Stan's idea that if he worried about the film beforehand it would be more likely his friends would enjoy the film. As you can imagine, this has the potential to go either way: Stan's friends could have hated the film. But a general and powerful psychological principle is at play called 'intermittent reinforcement'. This means that to reward what you do occasionally has a more powerful reinforcing effect than being rewarded every time. So if Stan only gets it right some of the time, this is still enough to make him believe that it works. Also, as we have said in the last chapter, on uncertainty, worriers tend to hold a set of beliefs that promote the idea that it is always better to be safe than sorry, and Stan certainly seems to uphold this.

*How these beliefs make worry worse.* This rule means we learn that worrying is the best way of preventing bad things from happening, which makes it more likely that we will worry. In another example, Kate worried that her relationship was doomed to fail, but it always seemed to just survive. She learned that worrying stopped her relationship from folding, so in order to keep the status quo she needed to keep worrying. Worrying in this way fuses thoughts with actions, which tells us that worrying can have a real influence on the world. Worrying, rather than doing anything else, becomes the strategy of choice. The tunnel vision that comes with this type of worry ignores all other information, which means that it's very hard to stop to see what else other than worry might be influencing the outcomes.

## TYPICAL BELIEFS

If I worry about it, then it is more likely to happen.
If I worry about my work, then it usually goes well.
If I worry about my children, then they will be safe.

---

### EXERCISE 11.6: WORRY PREVENTS

How typical or characteristic is this group of rules for you?

| None | A little | Some extent | Moderately | Somewhat | Mostly | Completely |
|------|----------|-------------|------------|----------|--------|------------|
| 0    | 1        | 2           | 3          | 4        | 5      | 6          |

How strongly do you agree with the idea that worry prevents bad things from happening?

| None | A little | Some extent | Moderately | Somewhat | Mostly | Completely |
|------|----------|-------------|------------|----------|--------|------------|
| 0    | 1        | 2           | 3          | 4        | 5      | 6          |

Can you think of a personal example from this set of worry rules? Write it down here.

How strongly do you believe this to be true?

| None | A little | Some extent | Moderately | Somewhat | Mostly | Completely |
|------|----------|-------------|------------|----------|--------|------------|
| 0    | 1        | 2           | 3          | 4        | 5      | 6          |

What impact does this rule have on your worry? What impact does this rule have on you?

What could you do to challenge this rule?

*Hints: Is worrying the best way to prevent bad things from happening? What else could you do? Is there a less costly approach? What are the advantages and disadvantages of this approach? Can you prove that worrying actually prevents bad things from happening? What else might be influencing the outcome? Are there aspects of the things you are worrying about which you are ignoring or failing to take into account? What about making good things happen: try thinking about winning the lottery, would this work? If not why not?*

### Belief group 5. Worry shows I care

This set of beliefs is very common. Here the beliefs circle around the idea that worrying means the worrier is a thoughtful, caring, or loving person and, worse still, that if they didn't worry they were inconsiderate, careless or unfeeling. Examples of this belief are, *if I worry about my kids, then I'm a good father* or, *if I worry about my friends, I'm a good person and they will like me all the more*.

*How these beliefs make worry worse.* The trouble with this set of worry beliefs is that the worrier believes that their self-worth is dependent on how much they worry. So these types of belief suggest that you really should worry because this is valued by others. But do you really need to worry to be approved of by your friends, family or work colleagues? If you told them that you were worrying about them in this way, what would they say? Might they tell you that you can show you care in lots of other ways? Might they value other things as more important than your worry (like your time, friendship, honesty, etc.)? Supposing you didn't worry, what would be so bad about that? You may fear that this means you don't care, but why not ask and find out if this is true?

## TYPICAL BELIEFS

If I worry, then it shows I am thinking about my family.
If I don't worry about my children, then I would not care.
If I worry, then it shows that I care.

---

### EXERCISE 11.7: WORRY SHOWS I CARE

How typical or characteristic is this group of rules for you?

| None | A little | Some extent | Moderately | Somewhat | Mostly | Completely |
|------|----------|-------------|------------|----------|--------|------------|
| 0 | 1 | 2 | 3 | 4 | 5 | 6 |

How strongly do you agree with the idea that worry shows you care?

| None | A little | Some extent | Moderately | Somewhat | Mostly | Completely |
|------|----------|-------------|------------|----------|--------|------------|
| 0 | 1 | 2 | 3 | 4 | 5 | 6 |

Can you think of a personal example from this set of worry rules? Write it down here.

How strongly do you believe this to be true?

| None | A little | Some extent | Moderately | Somewhat | Mostly | Completely |
|------|----------|-------------|------------|----------|--------|------------|
| 0 | 1 | 2 | 3 | 4 | 5 | 6 |

What impact does this rule have on your worry? What impact does it have on your ability to show care and attention to your loved ones, friends or colleagues?

What could you do to challenge this rule?

*Hint: Is worrying the best way to show that you care? What else could you do instead? Is there a less costly approach? What are the advantages and disadvantages of this approach? If the person you were worrying about knew that you were worrying like this, what would they say? Has anyone ever reacted badly to your worry or complained about it? Do you consider that 'good people' are those who worry? What other traits might your value? Do you know anyone who is a good person who does not worry? What does this tell you? If worry really was a method of demonstrating that you were a good human being, then why would anyone want to stop worrying?*

## Conflicting rules

These rules or beliefs about worry can conflict with one another, making for more uncertainty and therefore more worry. For example, if I believe that *worrying prepares me for things that could go wrong*, this belief tells me, or instructs me, to worry. However, I could also believe at the same time that *if I worry about something, then it is more likely to happen*. So, because on the one hand some beliefs instruct us to worry and on the other hand others are telling us to not worry, we flip between worrying and trying not to worry, which has the overall effect of increasing our worry.

## The cradle of worry and the intolerance of uncertainty

As you now know, the *what if* questions can be thought of as signs that uncertainty has been 'spotted' by the worrier. The *what if* statements then activate the cradle of worry, which, in a sense, instructs the worrier to worry. Once the worry has started, it will, of course, generate its own uncertainty. But the rules that make up the cradle of worry also interact with uncertainty – for instance, *What if I do not worry enough to prevent bad things from happening?* or, *What if I am not worrying enough to show that I care?* and so on. The worrier may doubt whether the worry will do the job they hope it will, leading to more worry and more uncertainty. When is enough enough?

## Negative worry-promoting beliefs

So far we have focused on the positive rules that promote worry. These suggest that worrying is useful and leads to positive outcomes. Closely related to these are other beliefs, namely, the negative and general rules. There are two main negative rules – *foreboding* and *raining on my parade* – and three main general rules – *all thoughts are important, tying up loose ends* and *instant and perfect answers*. We will outline each of these below. These worry rules tends to lead to unhelpful or negative outcomes.

According to these rules, if I worry about bad things happening then they will happen (*foreboding*), and if I worry about good things happening, then they won't (*raining on my parade*). So I am damned both ways. Take Lela, who is going on holiday. She started to worry about losing her luggage. She worried that, because she was thinking about it, it was more likely to happen (*foreboding*), which left her more stressed and worried. In another example, Jim was thinking about the money in his bank account when he started to worry about Internet fraud. Because he thought that worrying about something would make it more likely to happen, he started to believe that his money wasn't safe (*foreboding*). He worried all the more. Finally, Wendy was looking forward to going to a music festival, but she started to worry about it. She believed that thinking about nice things meant that they wouldn't happen (*raining on my parade*). Every time a nice thought popped into her mind she thought, *it's not going to happen now*. She started to worry about what other things she might think about and 'stop' from happening.

TYPICAL BELIEFS

If I think about it too much, then it might happen.
If I think about good things, then they won't happen.
If I think about bad things, then they will happen.

### EXERCISE 11.8: FOREBODING

How typical or characteristic is this group of rules for you?

| None | A little | Some extent | Moderately | Somewhat | Mostly | Completely |
|---|---|---|---|---|---|---|
| 0 | 1 | 2 | 3 | 4 | 5 | 6 |

How strongly do you agree with the idea that if you worrying about bad things happening that they will?

| None | A little | Some extent | Moderately | Somewhat | Mostly | Completely |
|---|---|---|---|---|---|---|
| 0 | 1 | 2 | 3 | 4 | 5 | 6 |

Can you think of a personal example from this set of worry rules? Write it down here.

How strongly do you believe this to be true?

| None | A little | Some extent | Moderately | Somewhat | Mostly | Completely |
|------|----------|-------------|------------|----------|--------|------------|
| 0    | 1        | 2           | 3          | 4        | 5      | 6          |

What impact does this rule have on your worry? What impact does it have on your ability to enjoy future events?

What could you do to challenge this rule?

*Hint: What are the advantages and disadvantages of this approach? How often are your forecasts right? If you worried about your toaster blowing up, do you think you could make this happen, just by worrying?*

## EXERCISE 11.9: RAINING ON PARADE

How typical or characteristic is this group of rules for you?

| None | A little | Some extent | Moderately | Somewhat | Mostly | Completely |
|------|----------|-------------|------------|----------|--------|------------|
| 0    | 1        | 2           | 3          | 4        | 5      | 6          |

How strongly do you agree with the idea that if you worry about good things happening then they won't?

| None | A little | Some extent | Moderately | Somewhat | Mostly | Completely |
|------|----------|-------------|------------|----------|--------|------------|
| 0    | 1        | 2           | 3          | 4        | 5      | 6          |

Can you think of a personal example from this set of worry rules? Write it down here.

How strongly do you believe this to be true?

| None | A little | Some extent | Moderately | Somewhat | Mostly | Completely |
|------|----------|-------------|------------|----------|--------|------------|
| 0 | 1 | 2 | 3 | 4 | 5 | 6 |

What impact does this rule have on your worry? What impact does it have on your ability to look forward to anything nice?

What could you do to challenge this rule?

*Hint: What are the advantages and disadvantages of this approach? How often have you worried in this way and got it wrong? What happens when you try to push any thought out of your mind?*

## General worry-promoting beliefs

So far we have discussed two types of thought that influence worry, the positive and negative rules or beliefs (*the cradle of worry*). In addition to these beliefs, there are other general rules that can have an influence. For instance, when something pops into our mind, we may believe that we should think it through to resolve it, or that it has popped into our mind because it's important. Here's an example:

Dawn was having a 'special' night out at the theatre with friends when an issue she had faced at work that day popped into her mind. Because she believed that *all her thoughts are important*, she could not dismiss it and began to wonder why the thought had appeared. She then began to think it through, trying to find a *quick* answer that was also *perfect*. However, the more she thought it through the more it unravelled and the more she worried. It did not help being in a theatre watching a play and so being unable to talk with her work colleagues about what she could do. To manage her uncertainty, she tried to *tie up the loose ends* in her mind, but couldn't as there were just too many unanswered questions. She didn't remember much of the play nor the conversations with her friends at the interval. Unsurprisingly, she didn't enjoy her evening out.

In Dawn's example there are several beliefs or rules influencing worry. The first is that *all thoughts are important*; the second that *if a thought comes to mind, I should think it through* (tying up loose ends); the third is that *I should resolve, or solve the issue straight away and perfectly (instant and perfect answer)*, rather than 'parking it' for later and enjoying the play.

Use the templates that we have used for the other worry-promoting rules above to assess the degree to which you agree with each of these rules. Here are some tips you may wish to use:

*All thoughts are important*: Is it true that all thoughts are important, or are you choosing some to pay attention to? What thoughts are not influenced by this rule? Would this thought be important to you if it was the end of the world in an hour's time? Does it need all that attention? What's the worst thing that could happen if you didn't think things through? What are the advantages and disadvantages of this rule?

*Tying up loose ends*: What's the worst thing that could happen if you didn't do this? How successful has thinking every thought that comes to mind been for you? Are there better ways of doing this, such as writing stuff down, or talking it through with a colleague or friend? What are the advantages and disadvantages of this rule?

*Instant and perfect answers*: What are the advantages and disadvantages of this rule? What's the worst thing that could happen if you didn't come up with an instant and perfect answer? What else could you do instead and what advantage might this have? What additional, unhelpful side-effects might come with this rule?

If you challenged your specific rules, what do you think would happen to your worry? Or, put another way, what would happen if you weakened and undermined the cradle of worry? Without these rules to help worry grow and develop, you would worry less. Before we move on to how to do this, there is one last belief we should consider.

Return to the exercise we mentioned on pages 230–1. What rules are now standing out for you? Write them in the box below.

My positive beliefs about worry are:

My general worry-promoting beliefs are:

## The turbo-charger – more negative beliefs about worry

We have been discussing the second group of beliefs, or negative beliefs about worry. Professor Adrian Wells, a clinical psychologist and researcher working in Manchester, has written and studied worry for many years, and he termed this type of worry as *meta-worry*, or *worry about worry*. Typically, once worrying has started these negative beliefs kick in and 'turbo-charge' the worry.

These beliefs tend to add an intense element of anxiety to the whirlwind of worry and in doing so they stimulate more worry.

A typical thought might be *I'm losing my mind.* When thoughts like these appear they feel very real and so believable that they bring with them severe levels of anxiety or panic, which stokes up the worry all the more. These beliefs turn the whirlwind of worry into a hurricane or tornado. The worry rules provide the framework for the worry to happen in, and these beliefs 'soup it up' once it appears. People with GAD tend to believe that once they have started worrying their excessive worry will lead to a number of unpleasant and distressing outcomes. These are listed below.

---

### EXERCISE 11.10: BELIEFS THAT LEAD TO WORRY ABOUT WORRY

Stop for a moment and consider each belief in turn and ask which of them applies to you. You may want to rate them on the scale listed below. Reflect on these questions: which is the highest rated? Which beliefs fit most closely with your experience of worry?

*Worrying excessively means that . . .*    Not at all...................Totally true

*Tick the boxes that apply to you*    0%———————————100%

☐   I am out of control    ..............%
☐   I will be overwhelmed    ..............%
☐   I will go crazy    ..............%
☐   I will be unable to focus
     or work or perform    ..............%
☐   I will be condemned
     to a life of anxiety    ..............%

☐ I am on the downward
　　slide to depression　　　　　.............%
☐ I will become ill　　　　　　.............%
☐ I lack confidence　　　　　　.............%
☐ I am weak　　　　　　　　　.............%
☐ I will be stuck forever
　　in worry　　　　　　　　　.............%
☐ I am not in control　　　　　.............%

You may wish to ask yourself the following question to see if you can find out what thoughts might turbo-charge your worry.

## Questions to help uncover the turbo-charge (negative thoughts about activity of worrying)

What is the worst thing that could happen if you couldn't stop worrying?

What would it mean to you if you couldn't stop worrying?

If you continued to worry like this, what do you think would happen?

If you let yourself worry more and more, would anything bad happen?

In the next diagram we have added Tom's negative beliefs about worry or the turbo-charger. As you can see, once the worry has started, these beliefs emerge and they produce intense feelings of fear and panic because they feel so real and believable. One effect of this emotion is to boost the intensity of the worry, turning the whirlwind into a tornado or hurricane. In CBT the view that people have of their experiences is critical; the turbo-charger is an appraisal (or view) of the activity of worrying and it is this view of worry that can be challenged by using traditional ideas or techniques. These negative beliefs are likely to develop and persist as the worry takes hold and will lead on to counterproductive attempts to stop worrying. It is this that we turn our attention to in Chapter 12.

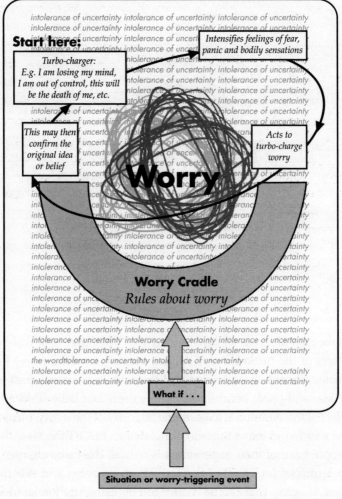

Figure 11.2. Tom's example continued: the turbo-charger of worry.

## Where have we got to so far?

So far, we have learned that worriers tend to be intolerant of
uncertainty; they will react to even tiny amounts of uncertainty,
which can be seen as the *fuel* for worry. We have learned how
uncertain situations can lead to *what if* type questions that then
spiral into the whirlwind of worry, generating further doubt
and uncertainty and fuelling more worry. The product of worry
is anxiety: this includes things like a strong sense of apprehension, muscular tension, being unable to relax, fatigue, irritability, sleep problems and difficulty in concentrating. The
longer-term products of worry are demoralization and exhaustion. We stopped to ask you to track a recent worry event using
this structure below. We discussed and assessed your themes
of worry and tried to help you see that you didn't worry about
everything. We also looked at the difference between *Real Event*
and *Hypothetical Event Worry*. You kept a diary to begin to spot
the differences.

**Trigger ⇨ What if ⇨ Worry ⇨ Anxiety ⇨ Demoralization & Exhaustion**

**Where ⇨ - leads to**

**Diagram of the story so far**

Next we looked more closely at how the intolerance of uncertainty was an essential ingredient that led us to worry. This
intolerance, coupled with the unavoidability of uncertainty, made
worry almost impossible to escape. Then we looked at the rules
and assumptions (*cradle of worry*) that influenced our tendency
to worry and how these rules maintained our worry. We looked

also at the *turbo-charger*, the negative appraisals of worry itself. We asked you to complete a rating scale to work out which of these appraisals you associated with your worry. Now it's time to see if you can change your worry rules.

**PIT STOP**

Let's stop and think about what you have just been reading. Can you summarize the key ideas you have taken on board? What is sticking in your mind? Maybe write them down. If you have any questions, jot these down too. You can return to them once you have had a chance to digest the information.

What is sticking in my mind from my reading so far?

1.

2.

3.

**12**

# Changing your worry rules

There are a number of ways of doing this. We hope that by becoming more aware of what leads you to worry, that worry will reduce. There are further exercises below to help you to think things through a little more. However, *thinking* is only one part of the learning cycle – we need to help you *do* things differently as well.

## Helping you to think things through

If your mind works best with images then the pie chart on page 263 might be useful for you. In its simplest form, this pie chart is a graphical way of representing *all* the ideas and factors that may come to bear on a thought or rule, and by so doing it may help to find other ways of seeing things or put things in perspective. This idea can be applied to most of the rules you will find in this book. But while we are focused on positive worry-promoting rules, let's take this rule as an example: *If I worry about my children every day, then this means that I am a good dad.* As we have suggested above, there may be better ways of showing that a father cares about his children than worrying.

In the heat of the moment, however, when the whirlwind is intense, it is often hard to see this. So it's important to take time to think through these new ideas not when you are worrying but before. In order to 'see' that there are better ways of showing that we care we can use the pie chart, which graphically represents the other things that can contribute and also their relative contributions.

### The steps

Once we have our rule on the table, written in words that feel right and tied into our everyday lives, we then need to rate how strongly we believe it, on a scale from 0–100 with 100 per cent being *I believe this absolutely*. We do this partly to make sure that it's worth spending time focusing on this rule (a very low score would suggest that this is not an issue) and partly to enable the worrier to get a sense of how important or influential the rule might be in their lives. For example.

If I worry about my children every day this shows that I care: belief rating = 75%

Next we want to make a list of all the things that the father does to show that he cares. This may be a little tricky. It could help if he steps away from himself and considers other dads. We may ask him to bring a caring father or mother to mind, someone he knows, and then ask him to think of all the things that this father does to demonstrate caring. We may also ask how his own parents or carers showed that they cared? We may ask him to think of 'caring' in general – what do people do to show they care? And so on. Here is our dad's example below:

**What do you do for the kids to show that you care?**
- Pick them up from school
- Make their breakfast and supper
- Wash their clothes
- Cuddle and kiss them
- Listen to them, pay them attention
- Give them my time
- Put them first
- Make sure they learn to look after themselves when I am not with them.

Next, we add worry as the final item. Then we ask the worrier to draw a pie which represents caring as a father, and ask them to divide up the pie to show how much of each of these 'slices' contributes towards showing that they care (they can divide up the pie into portions that represent the relative importance of each slice). Sometimes it is helpful to give a rough percentage to each slice to help with this. So, for example, how much does cuddling and kissing them show that you care? This *is not* a mathematical task – it doesn't matter if things don't add up perfectly. What is important is that the worrier begins to think about how important all the other things are that they do, and also seeing that worry is often either not there or a tiny part of what they do to show they care, even if the worry take hours and hours of their day. Look at our pie below. We have rated the example, lumping three together under 'practical stuff':

- Practical Stuff                                          5%
- Pick them up from school
- Make their breakfast and supper
- Wash their clothes
- Cuddle and kiss them                                    15%
- Listen to them, pay them attention                      22%
- Give them my time                                       24%
- Put them first                                          25%
- Make sure they learn to look afer themselves            13%
- Worry                                            Less than 1%

Once the pie has been drawn, we ask the worrier to step back and think about what the pie chart is telling them. Finally, we ask to them to re-rate their original belief and see what has happened to this. We can take it much further, and it is often helpful to follow up one example. For instance, if you spend hours and hours worrying, what does that take you away from? What could you do with that time if you had it? Maybe you could spend even more time with your children, or find something that you can enjoy together.

You may want to try this with one of your positive beliefs. For example, what else might motivate you other than worrying? And how influential might each of these strategies be to getting the *job done*? Could you try to do a little more of the others and a little less worrying? If you have found that worry shows that you care, then why not try this out with your rule?

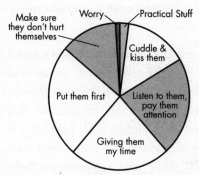

**Figure 12.1. Pie chart illustating ways that I show I care about my kids.**

## Surveys

In the flat world example in Chapter 7 we mentioned speaking to sailors to see if talking to others could provide more information to help us change our perspective. Thinking about what you have learned so far about your worry, what would you like to ask others? You could, for example, ask other people if worry motivates them, and what other things they do other than that. Finding out how other people do things can give us ideas about what we might try ourselves instead of worrying, such as building in small rewards or using the support of our friends to help us achieve our goals. Or you may want to ask others what they do with the thoughts that just pop into their head about tasks or jobs that need their attention (see Dawn's example above). Often, finding out that others have similar experiences can be helpful. Hearing that others have had the same thoughts about their worry makes us feel less lonely with it, but may help us feel less convinced by our worry – for example, asking others if they ever thought that their worry would get out of control.

## Getting active – behavioral experiments and other ideas

The rules you came up with will suggest ideas for behavioral experiments. Please find a list below of some ideas you may wish to try. Remember that you will feel anxious and will worry, but the important thing is that you are also doing something new and different to challenge your rules and beliefs. It may be worth reading the behavioral experiment section in the last chapter (pages 217–221), which gives some helpful advice on what to do if you are feeling anxious about these new and uncertain experiences.

| TABLE 12.1: BREAKING THE RULES | |
|---|---|
| Belief/Rule | Ideas to help you challenge your rules and beliefs |
| Worry will drive me insane | When was the last time you thought this? How did you stop yourself from going insane? If you used a safety behavior (e.g. counting, making sure you can still read, doing sums in your head, etc.), then could you drop this and find out what happens? Then focus on a smaller worry to start with and see if you can actually drive yourself insane (we wouldn't be suggesting this if we thought it might work!). You may want to do this first with someone around, but then do it alone. Then pick a larger worry and do the same. And so on. Be aware of anything you are doing to keep yourself from going insane. You need to find out for yourself that there is nothing to be frightened of. |

| | What might happen, how will we know that you have gone insane? What would you be doing? What is your personal prediction? |
|---|---|
| I will lose control if I do not keep my worry in check | When was the last time you felt this? How did you stop yourself from losing control? If you used a safety behavior (e.g. calming yourself, sitting alone or with someone, distraction, etc.), then could you drop this and find out what happens? Then focus on your worries, concentrate on them and try to lose control. Again, like the example above, start small and work up to a significant worry. But you must *really try* to lose control, dropping all your safety behaviors. You may feel strong emotions, but this does not mean you are out of control. Stay with it and see. By the way, what would happen if you were close to losing control of your worry, and the doorbell rang and a friend dropped in? Would you stop worrying? How does this work, if you were truly heading toward losing control or going insane? If the doorbell did stop insanity, then psychologists and others would be out of work and working in hardware stores. |
| I have no control over my worries | Delay your worry by writing them down and promising yourself that you can return to them later. Give yourself a good 20 minutes later in the day to have a good worry. What do you find? |

| Worry makes bad things happen | Let's start simple. Worry for 20 minutes a day about how awful it would be to win the jackpot in a lottery. You could win, but it's unlikely. What does that tell you? Now, try the same, but this time think about your toaster breaking. Move it on to bigger and more difficult things. What do you find? While you may read this and say *yeah, yeah, I know,* you really need to do it to learn that this rule is unhelpful. So do it. |
|---|---|
| Worry helps me to solve problems | With a small problem, for 20 minutes a day, each day for a week, focus on the problem. Write the problem down and break it into small chunks. Spend at least as long as you would worrying about the problem, but this time focus on finding a solution (see Chapter 16). What do you find? If you have solved it, have you done it any quicker than if you had just worried? If you have not solved it, then did you feel less stressed or tense? Again, increase the 'size of the problem' slowly, but make sure you trigger some anxiety. Is there a less costly way of solving problems? |
| Worry helps to motivate me | Use the pie chart and see what else might motivate you (also see section on approach goals). How did you feel when you worried to motivate yourself? Would you be prepared to be a little less anxious and a little more positive, if you used helpful motivational ideas rather than worry? Next time use strategies to motivate yourself rather than scare yourself. |

| I worry to prepare me for bad things happening | We cannot prepare ourselves for the unknown. Write down one or two specific examples of when you think this may have helped you. How effective was it – could this have been done any other way? Now think of all the times you have done this – would you prefer to follow the worry path or use one of these alternative ideas you have come up with? |
|---|---|
| I worry to prevent something bad from happening | The task here is to drop the worry and see what happens. Does the bad thing actually happen? Pick an easy situation first and slowly build up. Make a ladder of situations that are increasingly difficult. Sit with the uncertainty. Realistically, how could worrying stop something from happening? What else might be involved? (Design a pie chart.) What are the costs and benefits of doing this? |
| Worry shows I care | Is there a less costly way of showing this? What happened when you worried last – did it help or get in the way of you caring? Find other ways of caring and use these. (Pie chart?) |
| Rain on my parade: If I worry about good things they won't happen | Worry about a small nice thing that is going to happen (e.g. a cinema trip, meal out, meeting a friend for coffee) and see what happens. Do this again and again. What do you find? What other factors might influence good things happening or not (consider doing a pie chart to help you with this)? How important is worry? |

| | |
|---|---|
| Foreboding:<br>*If I worry about bad things happening, they will happen* | Think about a couple of specific examples of when this has happened in the past. Was your worry an accurate predictor of the future? How well did you do predicting the bad thing? Think about all the times this has happened and ask how good at forecasting the future is your worry. Let's test it out. Start by worrying about an inanimate object, your TV, car or MP3 player. What would happen if you thought about bad things happening to these? What do you find? Then move on to thinking about other things happening to you, and then to others. Make sure you write down clear predictions about what will happen, worry about it in detail and see if this works. |
| All thoughts are important:<br>*If I think of something, then it must be important* | Write down all the little things you have worried about in the last hour. Now apply the following criteria: the end of the world is coming in half an hour. Which of these things do you want to spend your time thinking about? Any, none, some? What does this tell you? |
| Tying up loose ends:<br>*If I think something I should think it through* | Think about a couple of specific examples of when you could not stop yourself from thinking something through to the end even though, at some level you knew it was unhelpful; how did it help? What were the costs of doing this? Did doing this make the outcome any better? Is this a strategy you would advise others to use? If not, why not? Pick a trivial worry that comes to mind, |

really push this, make sure and double check that you tie up *all* the loose ends. What happens? What happens when you think things through so completely? Are things clearer or less clear? Are thing more certain, or less certain? What, if you just left it hanging, is the worst thing that could happen? Make a prediction, leave it hanging and see if your prediction comes true.

| | |
|---|---|
| **Instant and perfect answers:** *I must resolve the issue, right now and perfectly* | What would happen if you did not try to resolve the worry and just waited? What's your prediction? In order to do this, we need a worry that has some kind of time limit so we know at the end of the day whether your prediction has come true – for example, worrying about missing a train, or worrying about meeting someone for lunch, something where you will know how things will turn out. When the issue appeared in your mind and you did not resolve it, what happened? Did your prediction come true? If it didn't, then what does that tell you? That you didn't need to find an instant and perfect answer? That you did need to worry? If it did happen, then what did you do? Would instant and perfect answers have made any difference? Try not to tie up the loose ends. Don't engage, don't worry. Alternatively, you could pick a less than perfect solution and see what happens if you go with this. |

## How does this worry rule work?

It is often helpful to sit with our beliefs and work out exactly how our worry might have an impact on events. Use diagrams to help you do this. For example, how exactly would worry about your finances stop them from getting out of control? How would worrying about something bad lead to it happening? Look at the diagram below.

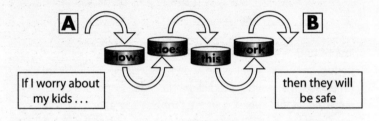

**Figure 12.2**

## What steps need to happen in order to make this work?

Think about how your worry might operate. Split the rule and see how you would get from A to B? If you think you find a way that it might work, then show it to someone else and see if they agree. Draw out your rules and see if you can make A link to B.

## Closing comments

Remember the Kolb learning cycle. *Doing* something new to challenge your worry is a very important part of getting better. Thinking, reflecting and developing an understanding are critically important, but *actions speak louder than words* and you need to experience new things to really understand at a deep level how things can be different. You will be anxious about this, and that is to be expected. But you can do this – you can 'turn down your worry dial' – but in order to do so you have to begin to do things differently.

## PIT STOP

It may be helpful to stop here and think about what you have just been reading. Can you summarize the key ideas you have taken on board? What things are sticking in your mind about uncertainty? Maybe write them down. If you have any questions, jot these down too. You can return to them once you have had a chance to digest the information.

What things are sticking in my mind from my reading so far?

1.

2.

3.

# More ideas to help spot your worry rules

If you have struggled to recognize the rules that make up your cradle of worry, or you want to make thing clearer for yourself, then you may find the following chapter helpful. It includes more information on rules, a questionnaire to help you spot which positive beliefs are most important to you and some worksheets to help you work with your worry and spot your rules.

## Spotting and re-evaluating rules

The first thing we need to work out is what rules make up your cradle of worry. This is not an easy task, and requires some thought and practice, but there are several exercises below to help you to work this out. Also, remember these rules are like bad habits that we may not really want to admit to. Think about the last time someone pointed out one of your bad habits: how did you feel? Did you want to believe them or did you tell them where to go? You may think, *No way! I don't believe it, this can't be true*. This might be a sign, however, to stop and have a good think about this rule. You may also want to check it out with someone you trust and who knows you well. As you read this, you may not be worrying or feeling anxious and the rules may feel remote and hazy; use a recent bout of worry to work with and then see if you can find the rules. Find a pen and paper and write the rule down as best you can. If it doesn't seem right, then play with the way it reads. Change the endings or the beginnings until it feels right to you. This is what we sometimes do in therapy sessions, 'playing' with the rules until they feel right. You could try swapping *I must* with *I must not*, or using *should* or *ought* instead. If your rule is an *if–then* rule, then change this around – for instance, *If I do this, then* . . . versus *If I don't do this, then* . . .; or, *If I worry about my decisions* versus *If I don't worry about my decisions*.

## The importance of personal rules

In order to re-evaluate your rules, it is important to uncover rules that are personal or specific to you. Trying to re-evaluate the broad categories, such as *worrying shows I care*, will not work. There are many reasons for this, but put most simply, 'off the peg' ideas are no substitute for those tailor-made for an individual. In addition, by trying to address these broad categories we might be overwhelmed with too much information; or, because it's not tied into a real experience, what we take from it might be woolly or hypothetical, making it hard to apply to day-to-day experiences. So, just as with setting goals (see Chapter 6) it is much better to have a specific rule to try to work with than a general one. For example, rather than the general *worrying shows I care*, your rule might be, *If I worry about my friends, then it shows that I care about them*. The way the second belief is written gives us many more avenues to explore: some of the ideas will result in concrete suggestions, like talking to your friends to find out if they agree with you. Finally, our rules tend to cross situations; so if we worry about our friends because it may show that we care, then we will probably have rules that if we worry about our family, our work, our dog and so on, then its because we care. So once you have found a rule that seems to fit, ask yourself in what other situations is this rule active.

In summary, try to uncover the specific rules that are active in a specific situation. If our efforts to re-evaluate how our positive worry rules are tied into detail, then they are more likely to be effective. This is why we need a rule that fits closely to *your experiences*. Although many people can and will share a common set of rules, there are always *house rules* or *local rules*, which are specific rules applied to a specific situation. For example, each local council has a different set of rules as to what can be recycled, when recycling happens and where.

### How do I spot my rules for worry?

First, review your worry diary together with the information that you have accumulated in the exercises on the pages above (you reflected on your worry rules in Chapter 11, on page 253). It's now time to play detective and see if you can spot the general categories that influenced each bout of worry. Remember that there may be both positive and negative worry promoting rules in action. The following questions may help you to think this through.

- Are there situations that reliably make you worry?
- What is it about that situation that leads you to worry?
- Supposing you didn't worry, what would this say about you?
- Supposing you didn't worry, what would this mean to you?

Second, it can be hard to spot our own rules, so we can also use the Why Worry II questionnaire to help us think about which category of *positive* rules apply to us (see below). The Why Worry II questionnaire can be broken down into the five categories of positive worry beliefs already mentioned. From this we can see which of the categories are most common for us. Third, you may wish to use the diary sheets below (Exercises 14.1 and 14.2) to help you. There is one worksheet for positive rules and one for negative and general rules. These worksheets will help you to spot the broad category first and then ask for your specific, personal rules in each case. Fourth, use Exercise 11.10 above to work out what beliefs add to your turbo-charger.

## WHY WORRY II QUESTIONNAIRE

Below are a series of statements that can be related to worry. Think back to times when you worried and indicate, by circling a number (0–5), to what extent these statements are true for you.

| Item number | Not at all true | Slightly true | Somewhat true | Very true | Absolutely true |
|---|---|---|---|---|---|
| 1. If I did not worry, I would be careless and irresponsible. | 1 | 2 | 3 | 4 | 5 |
| 2. If I worry, I will be less disturbed when unforeseen events occur. | 1 | 2 | 3 | 4 | 5 |

| | | | | |
|---|---|---|---|---|
| 3. I worry in order to know what to do. | 1    2    3    4    5 | | | |
| 4. If I worry in advance, I will be less disappointed if something serious occurs. | 1    2    3    4    5 | | | |
| 5. The fact that I worry helps me plan my actions to solve a problem. | 1    2    3    4    5 | | | |
| 6. The act of worrying itself can prevent mishaps from occurring. | 1    2    3    4    5 | | | |
| 7. If I did not worry, it would make me a negligent person. | 1    2    3    4    5 | | | |
| 8. It is by worrying that I finally undertake the work that I must do. | 1    2    3    4    5 | | | |
| 9. I worry because I think it can help me find a solution to my problem. | 1    2    3    4    5 | | | |

| 10. The fact that I worry shows that I am a person who takes care of their affairs. | 1 | 2 | 3 | 4 | 5 |
|---|---|---|---|---|---|
| 11. Thinking too much about positive things can prevent them from occurring. | 1 | 2 | 3 | 4 | 5 |
| 12. The fact that I worry confirms that I am a prudent person. | 1 | 2 | 3 | 4 | 5 |
| 13. If misfortune comes, I will feel less responsible if I have been worrying about it beforehand. | 1 | 2 | 3 | 4 | 5 |
| 14. By worrying, I can find a better way to do things. | 1 | 2 | 3 | 4 | 5 |
| 15. Worrying stimulates me and makes me more effective. | 1 | 2 | 3 | 4 | 5 |
| 16. The fact that I worry incites me to act. | 1 | 2 | 3 | 4 | 5 |

| | | | | | |
|---|---|---|---|---|---|
| 17. The act of worrying itself reduces the risk that something serious will occur. | 1 | 2 | 3 | 4 | 5 |
| 18. By worrying, I do certain things which I would not decide to do otherwise. | 1 | 2 | 3 | 4 | 5 |
| 19. The fact that I worry motivates me to do the things I must do. | 1 | 2 | 3 | 4 | 5 |
| 20. My worries can, by themselves, reduce the risks of danger. | 1 | 2 | 3 | 4 | 5 |
| 21. If I worry less, I decrease my chances of finding the best solution. | 1 | 2 | 3 | 4 | 5 |
| 22. The fact that I worry will allow me to feel less guilty if something serious occurs. | 1 | 2 | 3 | 4 | 5 |
| 23. If I worry, I will be less unhappy when a negative event occurs. | 1 | 2 | 3 | 4 | 5 |

| | | | | | |
|---|---|---|---|---|---|
| 24. By not worrying, one can attract misfortune. | 1 | 2 | 3 | 4 | 5 |
| 25. The fact that I worry shows that I am a good person. | 1 | 2 | 3 | 4 | 5 |

## SCORING THE WHY WORRY II QUESTIONNAIRE

There are five scales (A to E) on this questionnaire: the relevant item numbers that make up these scales appear below. To score in each scale, simply add up the numbers you have circled for each item on the Worry II Questionnaire. There are five items in each scale. Once you have done this plot your scores on the graph that appears below the questionnaire on page 281. Just looking at the profile will tell which of these scales applies most to you.

| Scales of positive belief group | Relevant item numbers | My score for each group |
|---|---|---|
| Scale A. Worry aids in problem-solving | 3, 5, 10, 14, 21 | |
| Scale B. Worry helps to motivate | 8, 15, 16, 18, 19 | |
| Scale C. Worry helps protect the individual from difficult emotions in the event of a negative outcome | 2, 4, 13, 22, 23 | |
| Scale D. The act of worrying itself prevents negative outcomes | 6, 11, 17, 20, 24 | |
| Scale E. Worry is a positive personality trait | 1, 7, 9, 12, 25 | |

Now plot your scores on the graph. Do any of these groups of worry stand out from the rest? Are you surprised by this? Do you agree with it? Can you review the information on each group above and see if this makes sense to you?

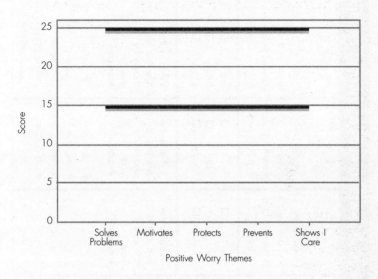

My scores on the Why Worry Questionnaire

INSTRUCTIONS FOR THE DIARY SHEETS

Briefly describe each worry in the left-hand column – just the gist of the worry rather than the detail. Then ask the questions posed in the boxes in the second row to find out which positive belief categories might be operating. Finally, using the phrases, *if–then, should, oughts* and *musts*, see if you can work out which of your own rules are active in each bout of worry – try to tie the rule to the situation where the worry happened. We have filled in the first sheet for you (the example diary sheet). Look at what we have written: does this make sense to you?

| EXAMPLE DIARY SHEET: SPOTTING THE POSITIVE RULES THAT MAKE UP YOUR WORRY CRADLE | | | | | |
|---|---|---|---|---|---|
| Describe worry briefly below | I worried to help solve a problem or to find a solution. | I worried to motivate myself to get something done. | I worried to prepare me for something bad happening. | I worried to prevent something bad from happening. | I worried because it showed I care. |
| Worry No. 1 | Yes ☐<br>No ☒<br>Maybe ☐ | Yes ☐<br>No ☒<br>Maybe ☐ | Yes ☐<br>No ☒<br>Maybe ☐ | Yes ☒<br>No ☐<br>Maybe ☐ | Yes ☒<br>No ☐<br>Maybe ☐ |
| My children were visiting their grandparents. I worried about whether they would be safe. | What is the rule that is shown by your example?* | What is the rule that is shown by your example?* | What is the rule that is shown by your example?* | What is the rule that is shown by your example?*<br><br>*If I did not worry, then something bad might happen.* | What is the rule that is shown by your example?*<br><br>*If I worry about my kids, then it shows I am a good parent.* |

**EXAMPLE CONTINUED:**

| Worry No. 2 | | | | | |
|---|---|---|---|---|---|
| I was worried about our finances and whether we could afford a holiday. | Yes ☒ No ☐ Maybe ☐ | Yes ☒ No ☐ Maybe ☐ | Yes ☐ No ☒ Maybe ☐ | Yes ☐ No ☒ Maybe ☐ | Yes ☐ No ☐ Maybe ☒ |
| | What is the rule that is shown by your example?* | What is the rule that is shown by your example?* | What is the rule that is shown by your example?* | What is the rule that is shown by your example?* | What is the rule that is shown by your example?* |
| | If I worry I will find a way of solving our money problems. | If I worry then I will stop spending so much. | | | If I worry it shows i care about my family |

## EXERCISE 13.1: DIARY SHEET 1. SPOTTING THE POSITIVE RULES THAT MAKE UP YOUR WORRY CRADLE

| | Solves problems | Motivates | Prepares | Prevents | Shows I care |
|---|---|---|---|---|---|
| Describe worry briefly below | I worried to help solve a problem or to find a solution. | I worried to motivate myself to get something done. | I worried to prepare me for something bad happening. | I worried to prevent something bad from happening. | I worried because it showed I care. |
| Worry No. 1 | Yes ☐ No ☐ Maybe ☐ What is the rule that is shown by your example?* | Yes ☐ No ☐ Maybe ☐ What is the rule that is shown by your example?* | Yes ☐ No ☐ Maybe ☐ What is the rule that is shown by your example?* | Yes ☐ No ☐ Maybe ☐ What is the rule that is shown by your example?* | Yes ☐ No ☐ Maybe ☐ What is the rule that is shown by your example?* |

## EXERCISE 13.1: DIARY SHEET 1. SPOTTING THE POSITIVE RULES THAT MAKE UP YOUR WORRY CRADLE

| Worry No. 2 | | | | | |
|---|---|---|---|---|---|
| | Yes ☐ No ☐ Maybe ☐ | Yes ☐ No ☐ Maybe ☐ | Yes ☐ No ☐ Maybe ☐ | Yes ☐ No ☐ Maybe ☐ | Yes ☐ No ☐ Maybe ☐ |
| | What is the rule that is shown by your example?* | What is the rule that is shown by your example?* | What is the rule that is shown by your example?* | What is the rule that is shown by your example?* | What is the rule that is shown by your example?* |

## EXERCISE 13.2: DIARY SHEET 2. SPOTTING THE NEGATIVE AND GENERAL RULES THAT MAKE UP YOUR WORRY CRADLE

| | Negative Rules | | | General Rules | | |
|---|---|---|---|---|---|---|
| | Foreboding | Rain on my Parade | All thoughts are important | Tying up loose ends | Instant and perfect answers | |
| Describe worry briefly below | I worried to help solve a problem or to find a solution. | I worried to motivate myself to get something done. | I worried to prepare me for something bad happening. | I worried to prevent something bad from happening. | I worried because it showed I care. |
| Worry No. 1 | Yes ☐ No ☐ Maybe ☐ | Yes ☐ No ☐ Maybe ☐ | Yes ☐ No ☐ Maybe ☐ | Yes ☐ No ☐ Maybe ☐ | Yes ☐ No ☐ Maybe ☐ |
| | What is the rule that is shown by your example?* | What is the rule that is shown by your example?* | What is the rule that is shown by your example?* | What is the rule that is shown by your example?* | What is the rule that is shown by your example?* |

## EXERCISE 13.2: DIARY SHEET 2. SPOTTING THE NEGATIVE AND GENERAL RULES THAT MAKE UP YOUR WORRY CRADLE

| Worry No. 2 | | | | | |
|---|---|---|---|---|---|
| | Yes ☐ No ☐ Maybe ☐ | Yes ☐ No ☐ Maybe ☐ | Yes ☐ No ☐ Maybe ☐ | Yes ☐ No ☐ Maybe ☐ | Yes ☐ No ☐ Maybe ☐ |
| | What is the rule that is shown by your example?* | What is the rule that is shown by your example?* | What is the rule that is shown by your example?* | What is the rule that is shown by your example?* | What is the rule that is shown by your example?* |

**PIT STOP**

Let's stop and think about what you have just been reading. Can you summarize the key ideas you have taken on board? What is sticking in your mind? Maybe write them down. If you have any questions, jot these down too. You can return to them once you have had a chance to digest the information.

What is sticking in my mind from my reading so far?

1.

2.

3.

# 14

# Doing something instead of worrying

In April 2006 *Time* magazine had a cover story on climate change with the headline 'Be worried, be very very worried'. What would you say if we proposed that the journalists at *Time* were suggesting that the best way to address the problem was through worrying? Do you think that if we *only simply* worried about climate change this would make any difference to the problem? Of course, this isn't sensible, but this slightly off-beat stance highlights one of the main issues for worriers – that worry is often used as the only strategy for dealing with life's problems. Unfortunately, it has a tendency to make them worse.

Needless to say, *Time* seemed to be suggesting that climate change is something we should be very concerned about, which many of us would agree with. So, if worry will not help us to address climate change, something else is needed to make a difference. Worry cannot be simply turned off like a tap; so what can we do instead of worrying? The simple answer is that we need to *act* in another way, replacing worry with something that can actually help us achieve our goal or solve a problem. Instead of continuing to worry about problems, we can try to solve them. In the example of climate change, actions might include, 'topping up' our loft insulation, turning down the heating in our homes, cycling rather than driving or lobbying our government for action. We need to learn to be active in the face of our worry rather than remain trapped by it. Worry should not be the only thing you do, but become a signal or sign for you to do something else. *Instead of worrying about some types of problems, we should try to solve them.*

## *Real Event* and *Hypothetical Event Worry*

In Chapter 5 we discussed the idea that there are two broad types of worry. Some of the problems we worry about exist; these worries are called *Real Event Worry*. And there are worries about problems that *may* exist, otherwise known as *Hypothetical Event Worries*. This second type of worry may never exist in the way that we imagine it; even so, it is like a terrible daydream and is often set in the future and includes all sorts of highly unlikely events. By comparison, *Real Event Worry* is about problems that exist, and so it is possible to do something about it by problem-solving – even if you are not quite sure how to go about it, or you are not confident that you will succeed. Indeed, one's own ability is one more thing to worry about! In fact, worriers are rarely confident about their true abilities. On the other hand, *Hypothetical Event Worries* are, by their very nature, not yet real and are also highly unlikely and usually so far in the future that problem-solving will *never* work. So, when faced with worry, we need to think carefully about what kind of worry it is we are trying to address. *Real Event Worry is about problems that exist, and so it is possible to do something about it by problem-solving.*

Another key issue is that worriers tend to confuse worrying with solving problems. Worry is exhausting; after a bout of worry we often feel tired and drained. Yet all the activity involved does not amount to change, since we are usually left with the problems that triggered the worry in the first place. While it sometimes feels as if we are doing something about our problems by worrying about them, in reality worry itself can never consistently solve the problems – *worrying is not problem-solving*.

If we repeatedly fail to address problems, this can have a serious impact on how we feel about ourselves, leaving us feeling anxious, disheartened and less sure of ourselves. Failing to act might also lead to a sense of powerlessness and helplessness, and seriously undermine our confidence to cope. If we continue to worry rather than address our problems, then the problems usually get worse and we worry all the more. Finding another way to act rather than just worrying can help with these strong feelings. For example, a friend who was very concerned about the environment said that, while he knew there were major problems, when he was active in doing something about them he felt empowered and hopeful rather than powerless and demoralized. Even though many of the environmental problems remained, he felt much better because he felt he was doing something to address them.

So far we have suggested that worry will not consistently solve life's problems and that we need to find other things to do instead. One of the most powerful solutions to *Real Event Worry* is to solve the problems that trigger the worry in the first place. We also learned that worrying was not the same as problem-solving, and, finally, the longer-term emotional consequences of continuing to worry and failing to act to solve problems result in powerful negative feelings about oneself. So the next chapters will enable you to become better at solving problems and dealing with *Real Event Worry*. In the chapter on facing our fears (Chapter 17), we will turn our attention to dealing with the other type of worry, namely *Hypothetical Event Worry* – but one step at a time.

## Approaching problems

With climate change, as with the traffic metaphor, in order to begin to solve the problems we have to engage with them. Unfortunately, worriers tend to have an unhelpful *attitude* towards problems, which makes this harder to do. Typically, they see problems as threatening, they doubt their ability to cope with problems, and even if they try to engage in problem-solving they are pessimistic about the outcome. This means that overall they tend to have *an unhelpful approach to problems*, which has a dramatic effect on their capacity to solve them. It's like trying to do everyday tasks while wearing boxing gloves; imagine trying to do up your buttons or zips in the morning. How would you use your phone, drive, write, type or prepare food? The boxing gloves prevent us from using our hands efficiently, our dexterity is lost and ultimately tasks become fevered and frustrating. We might feel very demoralized and irritated, useless and pessimistic about things to come. But there is an important positive message within this metaphor, which is supported by research, namely that, although worriers might have an unhelpful approach to problem-solving, once this has been addressed their problem-solving skills are found to be as good as those of non-worriers. In other words, if we remove the gloves then we discover that we have the skills to do all these tasks; the boxing gloves kept us from finding this out.

There are two main components in learning better problem-solving skills. The first is our approach to problems. This includes what we think when faced with problems, what we think of our skills in solving them and finally our expectations about how well we might do (taking off the boxing gloves). The second component involves the skills we have for solving problems. This refers to our ability to define problems, generate alternatives, choose solutions, put the plan into action and assess how well we did (or, exercising to improve our dexterity).

Before going on please stop for a moment and use the table below reflect on these two components. Can you 'see' the distinction?

## TABLE 14.1: THE TWO COMPONENTS OF PROBLEM-SOLVING

| Unhelpful approach to problems | Problem-solving skills |
| --- | --- |
| How do I approach problems? | How good am I at solving problems? What skills do I have? |
| What goes through my mind when faced with everyday problems? How do I feel when faced with everyday problems? | Which of the following can I do even if I do not feel confident about doing them? Defining problems Generating alternatives Choosing solutions Putting plans into action Assessing how well I did |

In order to help you overcome worry, you will need to learn to adjust your approach to problems, remind yourself that you have or can develop the capacity to solve problems successfully, and use these skills rather than engage in worry. Before looking into this further, we will look at what we mean when we talk about problems.

## What is a problem?

While this may be obvious, it is worth spending some time reminding ourselves of what exactly a problem is. This is because, without knowing, we are dealing with problems virtually all the time, and this fact challenges the idea that we have difficulty solving them. When we think of problems our mind may naturally jump to serious issues or experiences such as unemployment, losing a job, depression, death, serious illnesses, and so on. Like most things, however, problems appear on a scale, from everyday events or situations, such as forgetting to charge your mobile phone, or not having the right change for a parking meter, to major life events such as death, serious illness or unemployment. Problems can also be repetitive or persistent, like those we face in relationships, or with health, or with our finances – for example, when the money going out of our bank account is always slightly more than the money coming in, or continuing to avoid talking about a difficult issue in your relationship. The diagram below helps us to consider all the possible problems we may encounter. It does not tell us about how much a particular problem should bother us – this will vary from person to person – but is there to remind us that when we are referring to problems we mean all life's problems and not just the 'heavy' or serious end of things.

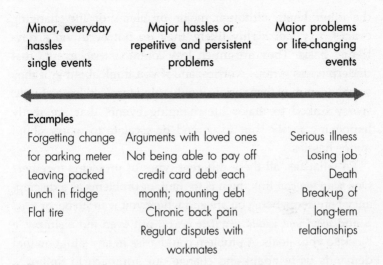

| Minor, everyday hassles single events | Major hassles or repetitive and persistent problems | Major problems or life-changing events |
| --- | --- | --- |

**Examples**

| | | |
| --- | --- | --- |
| Forgetting change for parking meter | Arguments with loved ones | Serious illness |
| Leaving packed lunch in fridge | Not being able to pay off credit card debt each month; mounting debt | Losing job |
| Flat tire | | Death |
| | Chronic back pain | Break-up of |
| | Regular disputes with workmates | long-term relationships |

**Figure 14.1. Problems on a scale of importance.**

What makes a problem serious depends on a number of things. Critically, cognitive therapy suggests that the issue it is not *what* the problem is but *our view of it*. So what is a problem for one person may not be a problem for another, since their view might be different (remember the example of someone losing their job in Chapter 4). In other words, one person's mountain is another's molehill and vice versa. However, there are other influences: for instance, a flat tyre outside your home on a Saturday morning may not be as problematic as a flat tyre in the early hours of the morning in the middle of winter in a remote area. A flat tyre is an 'everyday' event; but it has a beginning, middle and an end. The consequences are limited. Expert worriers though do worry about these things happening, but their worry often escalates into major hassles and even into major, life-changing events as their *worry moves* from left to right in the diagram above (remember the express elevator). On the other hand, although major problems or life-changing events may feel highly likely, they do not occur on a day-to-day basis. They are much less common than events that underpin less serious worries; and if you think about it, if they were as common then society would grind to a halt! Interestingly, worry linked to major life-changing events that are really happening rarely shift focus and de-escalate to worry about minor hassles.

So what ties all these different types of problems together? One way we can link them is to think of problems as a discrepancy between where you are and where you want to be, or *what is* and *what you would like it to be*, or, put even more simply, a block to your goals. A problem could arise in any situation that demands us to adapt and change our approach to finding a solution. In problematic situations, there is generally no obvious solution that jumps out. This might be because the obstacles are more noticeable than their solutions; this 'blocks' the solutions from view. When this happens our progress towards our goals are blocked and we have a problem.

## Problems are a normal part of life

As you will have seen from the diagram above, problems are a normal part of life, and, like uncertainty, directing time and energy into avoiding them is pointless. It's like trying to live life without gravity having an impact. Think about this for a moment. How much time and energy do you put into trying to avoid the unavoidable (life's problems)? Remember, in life most people have to deal with hundreds or even thousands of minor hassles, tens to hundreds of major hassles and far fewer life-changing events. Worriers on the other hand don't keep worry for the big occasion, they use it for the hundreds to thousands of minor hassles.

You can see from the diagram above that problems take many shapes and forms and are a constant feature of life for all. This is important, since if you think that problems happen to you because it is something about you that causes them, or if you think that having problems is abnormal in some way, then you are more likely to feel upset and distressed when problems appear. This is a little like blaming ourselves for the sun setting – it happens everyday without fail, so how can we take personal responsibility for it?

Where are you on this line? Do you see problems as normal or abnormal? Put a cross that shows where you are now. Put a second cross where you would like to be.
What beliefs might you need to think through in more detail? What is one thing that you could do to move you along the line?

| Problems are normal | Problems are abnormal |
| --- | --- |

| Typical beliefs | Typical beliefs |
| --- | --- |
| Everyone has them | Only I have them |
| It's not about me, it's about life | There is something about me that causes them |
| I'm a human and I have problems | I'm abnormal and I have problems |

**Figure 14.2. Are problems normal?**

As problems are everywhere, like gravity, then simply living means that we are overcoming them everyday – we just may not notice that we are. We face and solve problems without even knowing it. For example, to get to a meeting on time, I may need to plan my journey, take what I need for the meeting, get the right train, follow the directions I have been given, and then be on time. Each stage can be broken into a mini-goal, and within this example there are many, many more mini-goals that we have not outlined. My goals might be to pack my bag the night before, set my alarm, find the quickest way of getting to the city, take my laptop, phone and files, get the 7.45 train from platform 3 and to walk to the venue in 15 minutes.

When moving from one place to another, there will be a number of things that might get in the way at any stage. Furthermore, things are much more likely to get in the way if we have not engaged with the problem and broken it down into practical steps. This is something we often do without thinking, and we may not even think of this as 'problem-solving', but it is! We also may not think of this as goal-setting, but again it is – *There is something I want to do tomorrow, my goal is to* . . . In the example above obstacles could include no quick way of getting to the city, forgetting my laptop or charging my phone, having no reception on my phone, cancellation of the 7.45 and inaccurate directions. So, now we have a series of problems that need to be dealt with. Each is an obstacle between the current situation and the desired situation, or each is an obstacle to my achieving my goals. As we have suggested, problems demand that we adapt and change to overcome them. So if my train has been cancelled, what do I do now? Get the bus? Phone ahead and warn my clients? Find out when the next train is and get on that one? Order a taxi or cab? Head for the waiting-room and get some work done? Go home? Buy a coffee and read the paper? There are many possible solutions, and the eventual solution will depend on many things, such as how important the meeting is, how central is my role in the meeting, how much money I have, how bothered I am about missing the meeting – and so forth. This everyday example shows that in order to get by in life we are solving problem all the time and we may not even realize it.

If you are encountering problems all the time without knowing it, you are successfully solving them. Can you think of a problem that you have already solved today or this week? Did you run out of milk this morning? Did you have the right change for the bus? Did you forget your mobile phone? Did you encounter traffic or delays? Did your children forget their packed lunch for school? Did you spill coffee on your work shirt or blouse? What problems have you already encountered and dealt with today?

This presents an interesting question? Why might some everyday problems get solved and dealt with while others become the subject for worry? The answer to this is not clear, but we know that worry tends to run on themes, with each worrier worrying about a different set of concerns. So it might be worth asking yourself this question, *Why do I worry about these problems and not others that I take in my stride?*

## Intolerance of uncertainty and problem-solving

As we discussed in Chapter 9, the situations that worriers tend to avoid usually contain some element of uncertainty. Problems are typically 'dripping' with uncertainty; it is hard to predict what will become a problem; once the problems appear they are still unpredictable; the worrier doubts their ability to solve or cope with them; and as you would expect, the outcome is usually unclear or tricky to predict. So it will be no surprise that when facing problems worriers tend to worry and try to avoid facing and dealing with them. Worriers find it hard to put plans into action because they can't be sure that their plans will work or the slightest hint of things not going to plan may stop them in their tracks. So it is also not surprising that in people who suffer with excessive worry or GAD tend to have an unhelpful approach to problems. As you know, worriers tend to be acutely aware of even the merest hint of uncertainty – remember that all you need is a *splinter of doubt* to stoke up worry. So, when faced with a problem, worriers tend to 'examine' the problem from this perspective. It's almost as if they are wearing special glasses that enable them to see the uncertainty in any situation. When we defined what a problem is, we noted that a problem was something that did not have a clear or immediate solution; in other words, the outcome is uncertain. So as you learn to tolerate uncertainty you will be more able to tolerate the uncertainty found within problem-solving. In fact, you can begin to treat problems as another way of overcoming your intolerance of uncertainty. However, there are other ways forward, not least challenging the ideas that underpin the unhelpful approach to problems. It is to these ideas that we will turn next.

## Fitting this into the diagram of worry

As you will have read, the main outcome of poor problem-solving is to increase the level of uncertainty and thus worry in the system. We will now return to Tom who is waiting at the train station. Track the example through: we have included all the details so far.

Tom has a really important meeting today and is waiting for his train. His train is late and he wonders, *What if I am late for work?* This thought opens up doubt and uncertainty and he starts to worry. He starts to *feel* anxious, tense and restless and he looks about nervously.

Rather than worry, Tom could have done something else about his train being late. He could have tried to find another way of getting to work, or find out from the station attendant when his train would actually arrive, or remind himself that he was only 5 minutes late, or phoned work and explained what had happened. As he was standing at the platform these solutions flashed through his mind, but all they did was trigger more worry. With each solution arrived a whole new set of worries. He worried that if he got a taxi he would get snarled up in traffic, and that if he asked the platform attendant he would get annoyed with him for wasting his time. He tried to calm himself down saying quietly, *It's only 5 minutes Tom, pull yourself together*, but when he looked at his watch, he realized he was now 6 minutes late. He started to feel irritated with himself. He put off contacting work because he wasn't sure how they would react and because of how he was feeling he didn't think that he could cope with that as well. Tom believed that if he tried to solve his problems he would just make everything worse. Convinced that there was nothing he could do, and convinced that he was going to lose his job, he worried all the more. Lost in his worry, he nearly missed his train.

Unfortunately, Tom has an unhelpful approach to problems; he thinks he's not good at solving them; he's fairly pessimistic about the outcome and is sure that he will make this worse. When his train is late he faces a new problem, and he comes up with several potential solutions, but each solution arrives with more worry and uncertainty. He thinks about calling a taxi, but then worries that he might get caught up in traffic, and that if he doesn't do this, then his employers might be annoyed with him for not taking the initiative. If he took the initiative, then he might end up being disciplined for spending company money without authorization – and so on. He is paralysed by choices and the worry that comes with each new solution. At this moment, 'every silver lining has a cloud'; as he finds a potential way out, his worry interferes and brings to mind several new awful outcomes. Not surprisingly, he avoids trying to do anything about the problem; it's almost as if it is much safer to sit perfectly still and hope that things work out.

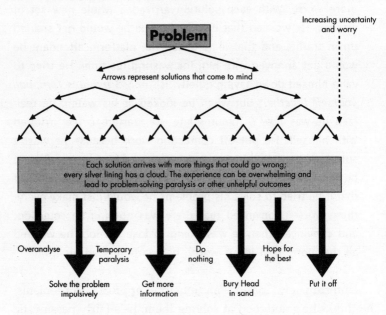

Figure 14.3. Every silver lining has a cloud.

As he continues to sit with his problem, the problem slowly gets worse (it is getting later and later), confirming to him that he cannot solve problems. Then he starts to worry all the more (notice the arrival of more *what if* statements triggered by his failure to act, leading to more worry). His worry generates more anxiety, making it much harder for him to try to solve the problem he faces. Like many people who are feeling anxious, he starts to notice all the things that could go wrong, which leads him to worry more, pushing him further away from solving the problem and confirming to him that he is no good at solving problems. Follow this through on the diagram below.

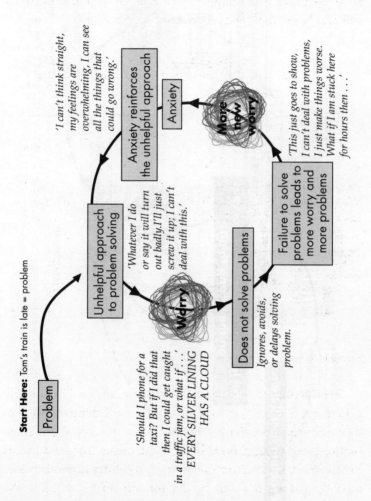

**Figure 14.4. Unhelpful approaches to problem-solving – a typical vicious circle.**

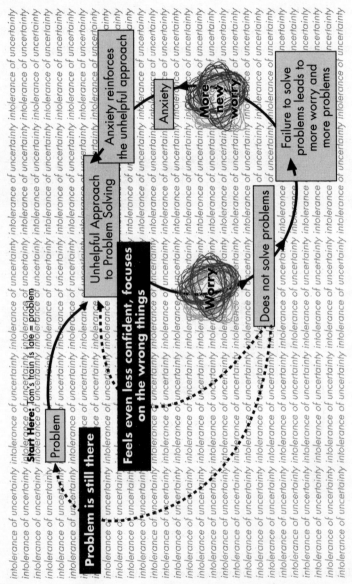

Figure 14.5. Adding in the intolerance of uncertainty and other things that maintain our unhelpful approach to worry.

In Figure 14.5 we added some dotted arrows to show other patterns that can appear when worriers are faced with problems. The worrier's lack of success in dealing with the problem in the first place reinforces the *beliefs* that support their unhelpful approach to problems in at *least* two ways. First, the problem remains unsolved and as a result may get bigger and more problematic. Second, the lack of success erodes the worrier's confidence and leads them to deploy other unhelpful ways of trying to address the problem, which may also fail. Examples of these include ignoring, delaying, focusing on the wrong thing, partially engaging with, or impulsively solving, the problem. These lead to poor solutions, or make the problem worse, which in turn serves to confirm the starting point, i.e that the worrier has an unhelpful approach to problems. Both of these reinforce the idea that the worrier *can't solve problems* or that *attempts to solve problems never seem to work,* and so the unhelpful approach to problems is maintained.

Can you think of an example where your worry about a problem has meant that you did not solve it, so that it became a self-fulfilling prophecy such as, *I think I am no good at solving problems, my worry gets in the way of me solving them, and then this confirms that I must be bad at solving problems.*

There are many more arrows we could have added, but these are important ones. Track the new patterns on the diagram above and see if it makes sense to you. Again, remember that we are talking about your unhelpful approach to problems, and not your problem-solving skills, which research tells us are as good as anybody's – we are describing the boxing gloves.

Next let's turn our attention to the intolerance of uncertainty, which appears in the diagram as a backdrop. It is presented like this because uncertainty is everywhere and it influences all the elements of the pattern above. In particular, and as we have already mentioned, problems are 'dripping' with uncertainty at all stages. To begin with, it is hard to predict what will become a problem; once the problems appears, the worrier doubts their ability to solve or cope with them; and, as you would expect, the outcome is usually unclear or tricky to predict. In fact, problems arise when there is no obvious solution, in other words, when there is no certainty about the outcome. So, given that worriers are intolerant of uncertainty, it makes absolute sense that problems are experienced as very threatening. So there is a direct relationship between an unhelpful approach to solving problems and an intolerance of uncertainty.

In the diagram on page 302 we showed the way problems seem to 'fan out' as each new solution arrives with its own set of uncertainties and worry, which we have called 'every silver lining has a cloud'. At this stage each new solution presents more uncertainty and triggers more worry, generating more uncertainty, severe anxiety and powerful physical sensations (e.g. stomach churning, tension, etc.). Very quickly the worrier is overcome by the worry generated by the solutions they bring to mind. This is made worse by the often intense, physical and emotional experience that accompany them, which leads to a state of momentary paralysis, as the worrier feels unable, as their thoughts race, to think things through or make decisions.

Reading the above may leave you feeling on edge and frightened. We want to describe what happens when worriers are faced with problems because understanding how things work gives us better ideas about what to do to make things better. To become better at solving problems the first step is to really understand what you are doing now. For example, a garage mechanic will spend time trying to work out what the problem is before taking an engine to pieces. Working out what the problem is helps them to decide where to start and what to do. It would be a little disconcerting (and very expensive) to drive into a garage and for them to start to take your engine apart without working out what needs to be done. We should not do this with worry. In our clinical work, one of the implicit ideas within CBT is that, while people arrive with problems, they also arrive with many of the solutions, but these are often hidden or hard to access. Part of our role in treating people with worry is to help them realize what skills and abilities they have. So, while you may bring problems, you will also carry the solutions.

With this mind, it may be helpful to spend a few moments drawing out your problem-solving pattern. There is no right or wrong way of doing this and there are more ideas about how we get stuck with problem-solving later in this chapter. But have a go – again, resist the urge to find the perfect solution. If worry interferes then wait for it to pass and ask yourself, *What was I doing before I started to worry?* and then return to it.

The following questions may help. They trace the diagram above:

- Can you think of a recent problem you faced?
- What went through your mind when you faced this problem?
- How did it leave you feeling?
- What was it about the problem that might have led you to feel uncertain?
- Can you recognize the *what if* statements that appeared when you faced this problem?
- What were the themes of your worry?

- What did you do to deal with the problem (avoid, delay, put off, etc.)?
- What happened as a consequence?
- When this happened, how did it influence your worry?
- When you started to worry, how did it make you feel about your ability to solve problems?
- How might this influence your approach to problems in the future?
- How certain did you feel about your capacity to solve problems well?

Next, we need to add this pattern to the diagram we have been developing throughout the book. To summarize, the anxiety caused by worry makes it very hard to do anything about the problems we face. Because we feel so wound up by our worry, we may find it very hard to organize our thoughts, and because we are feeling anxious we are more likely to think anxious thoughts. We can be so convinced that none of our solutions will work that we don't even try to put them into action. This leads to more worry, because the problem remains unsolved as time ticks by. This is how an unhelpful approach to solving problems keeps worry alive. Notice that the diagram does not suggest that worriers lack problem-solving skills. In Tom's story above, this was clearly not the case – he came up with a number of possible solutions. The problem for Tom was that he saw the late train as a threat, he doubted his ability to solve his problem and he didn't think his solutions would work, even if he tried. The diagram below is growing more complex, but we hope that each element is familiar to you.

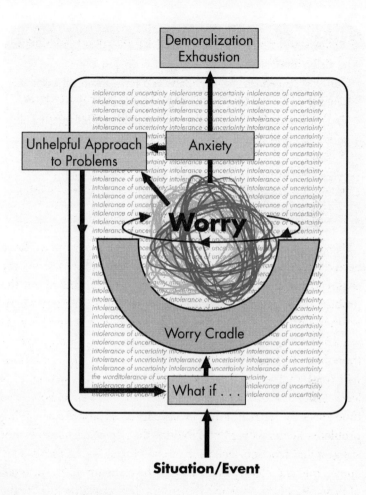

Figure 14.6. Building the picture: the unhelpful approaches to problem-solving.

**PIT STOP**

Let's stop and think about what you have just been reading. Can you summarize the key ideas you have taken on board? What is sticking in your mind? Maybe write them down. If you have any questions, jot these down too. You can return to them once you have had a chance to digest the information.

What is sticking in my mind from my reading so far?

1.

2.

3.

# 15

# Getting better at approaching problems

As you may have learned above, there are two main components in learning better problem-solving skills. The first is our approach to problems, which includes what we think when faced with problems, what we think of our skills in solving them and finally our expectations about how well we might do. The second component is the skills we have for solving problems. This is our ability to define problems, generate alternatives, choose solutions, put the plan into action and assess how well we have done.

Before enabling you to develop a more helpful approach to problems, first we want you to develop a better understanding of your approach to problems and of what makes your approach unhelpful. There are four sections in this chapter to help you get better at approaching problems:

- Section A focuses on helping you to develop a better understanding of how you approach problems.
- Section B looks at eight typical patterns that worriers fall into when faced with problems.

- Section C begins to help you to start thinking differently about how to approach problems.
- Section D returns to behavioral experiments and things you can do to challenge your approach to problems.

## Section A: Understanding how you approach problems

While we discuss this idea, it would be helpful for you to think about what fits with your experiences and what reminds you of the way you approach problems. As you read, there may be solutions that bubble up when you think this through. As always, have a pen and a notebook to write down your reflections.

In this section there are three main ways to help you learn more about how you approach problems. The first uses a questionnaire to show you what beliefs might contribute to your unhelpful approach to problems. The second is an exercise to help you understand more about how these beliefs might impact on your actions, your ability to solve problems and your worry. Finally, we return to rules, to see if we can uncover any that might influence your approach to problems.

At the end of the section is a space to reflect and write down the rules and beliefs that influence your approach to problems. The rules, as always, help suggest ways to change – by bending, adjusting or breaking them we can learn something new. As with the other chapters, you will need to think about how you can do things differently to challenge your approach to problems.

## A questionnaire to develop your understanding

The first task is to complete the questionnaire called the NPOQ. This was developed by a team of researchers from Canada who wanted to find a way of assessing the unhelpful approach to problem-solving that worriers tended to have. They called it the NPOQ, which stands for the Negative Problem Orientation Questionnaire. You can use this questionnaire in two ways, either as a checklist to help you think about the ideas that influence your approach to problems, or as a tool for measuring change. At the moment, as this questionnaire is still being developed – there are no hard and fast rules about how to interpret it. As a rule of thumb, however, if you score 3 or more on any question, then you probably need to spend some time working on the issue it raises. Completing the questionnaire will help you to develop a profile of your unhelpful approach to problems.

People react in different ways when faced with problems in their daily lives (health problems, arguments, lack of time, etc.). Use the scale overleaf to indicate to what extent you react or think when confronted with a problem. Circle the number that best corresponds to you for each item.

| NEGATIVE PROBLEM ORIENTATION QUESTIONNAIRE (ASSESSES UNHELPFUL APPROACH TO PROBLEMS) | Not at all true of me | Slightly true of me | Moderately true of me | Very true of me | Extremely true of me |
|---|---|---|---|---|---|
| 1. I see problems as a threat to my wellbeing. | 1 | 2 | 3 | 4 | 5 |
| 2. I often doubt my capacity to solve problems. | 1 | 2 | 3 | 4 | 5 |
| 3. Often before even trying to find a solution I tell myself that it is difficult to solve problems. | 1 | 2 | 3 | 4 | 5 |
| 4. My problems often seem insurmountable. | 1 | 2 | 3 | 4 | 5 |
| 5. When I attempt to solve a problem I often question my abilities. | 1 | 2 | 3 | 4 | 5 |
| 6. I often have the impression that my problems cannot be solved. | 1 | 2 | 3 | 4 | 5 |
| 7. Even if I manage to find some solutions to my problems, I doubt that they will be easily resolved. | 1 | 2 | 3 | 4 | 5 |
| 8. I have a tendency to see problems as a danger. | 1 | 2 | 3 | 4 | 5 |
| 9. My first reaction when faced with a problem is to question my abilities. | 1 | 2 | 3 | 4 | 5 |
| 10. I often see my problems as bigger than they really are. | 1 | 2 | 3 | 4 | 5 |
| 11. Even if I have looked at a problem from all possible angles, I still wonder if the solution I decided on will be effective. | 1 | 2 | 3 | 4 | 5 |
| 12. I consider problems to be obstacles that interfere with my functioning. | 1 | 2 | 3 | 4 | 5 |

Source: M. Robichaud and M.J. Dugas, 'Negative problem orientation (Part I): Psychometric properties of a new measure', *Behavior Research and Therapy*, in press. With permission from Elsevier.

When reviewing the questionnaire, think about how each item might influence how you approach problems. What impact might it have on your actions? What problems does this belief give you? For example, if you often doubt your capacity to solve problems, then what problems does this give you? Think of real-life examples – think of the last time that this belief was active. What might these beliefs stop you doing? What do you avoid because of them? What do you do to keep yourself safe when confronted with problems?

You can also use the questionnaire to begin to think about how you might begin to see or do things differently. For example, if you thought that, *When I attempt to solve a problem, I often question my abilities*, then you could ask, *How often have I thought this and then managed?* Or, *How does thinking this help me to solve the problems, what might I think instead?* Or, *What kinds of things would a friend say to me if they knew I was thinking this?* What facts or proof do you have that this is true? What does this belief motivate you to do? The idea is to challenge each belief by asking questions that bring other perspectives to mind. You may want to turn the questionnaire on its head. For example, *If I did not see problems as a threat to my wellbeing how would I do things differently? What would I do instead? How might I feel?* And so on.

## Developing my understanding

There are three main groups of ideas that conspire to lead people towards an unhelpful approach to problem-solving. These are:

- Seeing problems as a menacing or threatening
- Doubting our ability to solve problems successfully
- Making negative predictions about the outcome of problem-solving.

The exercise below helps you to understand the impact on you of each of these strands that contribute towards our approach to worry.

## EXERCISE 15.1: THE IMPACT OF AN UNHELPFUL APPROACH TO WORRY

### If you saw problems as menacing or threatening

| | |
|---|---|
| What would go through your mind when faced with a problem? | |
| What feelings might be generated? | |
| What might you feel like doing? | |
| What impact might all of the above have on worry? | |
| What impact might all of the above have on solving the problem? | |
| What rule might be operating here?<br>i.e. If–then, shoulds, oughts, musts*. | |

### If you doubted your ability to solve problems successfully

| | |
|---|---|
| What would go through your mind when faced with a problem? | |
| What feelings might be generated? | |
| What might you feel like doing? | |

| What impact might all of the above have on worry? | |
| --- | --- |
| What impact might all of the above have on solving the problem? | |
| What rule might be operating here? *i.e. If–then, shoulds, oughts, musts\**. | |

**If you held negative predictions about the outcome of your problem-solving**

| What would go through your mind when faced with a problem? | |
| --- | --- |
| What feelings might be generated? | |
| What might you feel like doing? | |
| What impact might all of the above have on worry? | |
| What impact might all of the above have on solving the problem? | |
| What rule might be operating here? *i.e. If–then, shoulds, oughts, musts\**. | |

\* For a reminder of how to spot rules, please see Chapter 7.

## Focusing on rules to develop my understanding

In the previous exercise we included a space for you to consider the rules that might underpin your approach to problems. To help you to elaborate these rules further we have included several common rules. As you read it is important that you begin to think about what specific rules might be in operation for you. Remember, when faced with a problem, worriers will often experience strong feelings of anxiety, frustration and irritability, which arise because our rules have been challenged. Usually it is these feelings that the worriers spot: they rarely notice the underlying beliefs that motivate them. Our first task is to bring these underlying ideas to the surface.

### EXERCISE 15.2: EXPLORING MY APPROACH TO PROBLEMS

Circle the number most appropriate to you.

| Unhelpful approach to problems | Problem-solving rules (examples) | Not like me | | | | Very much like me | | |
|---|---|---|---|---|---|---|---|---|
| Seeing problems as a menacing or threatening | Problems are dangerous and should be avoided | 1 | 2 | 3 | 4 | 5 | 6 | 7 |
| | If I have problems then I am abnormal | 1 | 2 | 3 | 4 | 5 | 6 | 7 |
| | I attract problems | 1 | 2 | 3 | 4 | 5 | 6 | 7 |
| My rule is ...................................... | | 1 | 2 | 3 | 4 | 5 | 6 | 7 |

| Doubting our ability to solve problems successfully | If I try to solve a problem, I will fail | 1 | 2 | 3 | 4 | 5 | 6 | 7 |
| | I should always ask others to solve problems for me | 1 | 2 | 3 | 4 | 5 | 6 | 7 |
| | I should always ask for help or reassurance when solving a problem | 1 | 2 | 3 | 4 | 5 | 6 | 7 |

My rule is ........................................ 1　2　3　4　5　6　7

| Making negative predictions about the outcome of problem-solving | If I try to solve a problem, it will go wrong | 1 | 2 | 3 | 4 | 5 | 6 | 7 |
| | If I try to solve a problem, I will make it worse | 1 | 2 | 3 | 4 | 5 | 6 | 7 |
| | Whatever I do, things always turn out badly | 1 | 2 | 3 | 4 | 5 | 6 | 7 |

My rule is ........................................ 1　2　3　4　5　6　7

**PIT STOP**

Let's stop and think about what you have just been reading. Can you summarize the key ideas you have taken on board? What is sticking in your mind? Maybe write them down. If you have any questions, jot these down too. You can return to them once you have had a chance to digest the information.

What is sticking in my mind from my reading so far?

1.

2.

3.

## Section B: Dealing with typical unhelpful patterns in problem-solving

There are many ways in which the rules and beliefs that make up an unhelpful approach to solving problems make the problems much worse. In this section we have identified eight common patterns. Like a dog chasing its tail, each pattern or strategy adds more uncertainty, worry and anxiety, which makes it much harder for us to solve problems. This in turn leads on to more worry, anxiety and uncertainty, strengthening the unhelpful approach to problems. We will outline some of the main mechanisms below. As with your worry rules, it is important that you begin to recognize which strategies are typical for you and understand how this makes your problems worse. After each description there is a mini-questionnaire to help you decide what are the main things that you do to maintain an unhelpful approach to problems. Each mini-questionnaire also asks you to think about what you need to do in order to challenge these strategies. Later we help you understand how to do this in more detail, but a simple sentence to capture the essence of what you need to do will be helpful. We have offered some hints for each pattern, but there is nothing better than a solution that works with the problem pattern you bring. When developing your answers, it might be worth thinking of these as goals. Use the SMART-COPER ideas in the goal-setting chapter (Chapter 6) to help you develop these.

## Pattern 1. Avoiding or delaying the problem-solving

Worriers can tend to avoid or delay solving problems. As a result, what could be a minor problem becomes progressively worse, leading to more severe problems and stimulating even more worry (e.g. avoiding paying credit card bills, leading to charges and increasing debt). In addition to the problems getting worse, this strategy then influences how we think about problems. If many of the problems we face 'snowball' and get worse, it is not surprising that when new problems appear we start to get nervous, making catastrophic predictions about what could happen. In this way this strategy maintains our unhelpful approach to problems.

## EXERCISE 15.3: AVOIDING OR RELAYING

How typical or characteristic is this strategy for you?

None   A little   Some extent   Moderately   Somewhat   Mostly   Completely

  0        1          2             3           4          5          6

Can you think of an example of when you have avoided or delayed solving a problem?

What impact did it have on the problem? What impact did this have on your worry?

What could you do to challenge this way of approaching problems?

*Hint: By facing the problem, things are likely to get better. Ask yourself, What is the worst thing that could happen if I faced my problems? Write your answer down and then have a go. Does your answer fit with what happened?*

## Pattern 2. Trying not to think about it – putting it to the back of your mind

As we discovered in the chapter on positive beliefs about worry, trying not to think about something has the unfortunate effect of making it jump into our minds all the more often. These intrusive thoughts can be regarded as a sign of unfinished business, which our mind is trying hard to get us to deal with. So, as long as the problem is still a problem, it will butt in until we deal with it. This usually happens when we are reminded of the problem by something else, or it can just appear in the way other things might do (e.g. remembering to return a phone call). When the problem appears, it does so with a 'mental flinch' followed by a stream of worry, and because the problem appears frequently and regularly, it tends to trigger more worry – again ending up making us more concerned about problems when they appear in the future.

## EXERCISE 15.4: DON'T THINK ABOUT IT

How typical or characteristic is this group of rules for you?

| None | A little | Some extent | Moderately | Somewhat | Mostly | Completely |
|------|----------|-------------|------------|----------|--------|------------|
| 0 | 1 | 2 | 3 | 4 | 5 | 6 |

Can you think of an example when you tried to push a problem to the back of your mind?

What impact did pushing the problem to the back of your mind have? What impact did this have on your worry? What impact does it have on the problem?

What do you need to do to address this problem?

*Hint: Trying to push a thought out of our minds never works – the problem only pops up all the more often. So, face the problem in your mind – doing so will not make it any worse. Write the problem down. It may help you see what you need to do to solve it.*

## Pattern 3. Asking others to solve the problem

If we continually ask others to solve problems for us, we are denying ourselves the opportunity of finding out that we could manage the problem for ourselves. This keeps the idea alive that we cannot deal with problems, or that if we try to solve them they will go wrong. In doing this we maintain our unhelpful approach to problems.

### EXERCISE 15.5: ASKING OTHERS

How typical or characteristic is this strategy for you?

| None | A little | Some extent | Moderately | Somewhat | Mostly | Completely |
|------|----------|-------------|------------|----------|--------|------------|
| 0 | 1 | 2 | 3 | 4 | 5 | 6 |

Can you think of an example of when you have asked others to solve a problem rather than deal with it yourself?

What impact did this have on how you think you deal with problems and on your confidence? What impact did it have on the problem? What impact does it have on your worry?

What do you need to do to develop confidence in managing problems for yourself?

*Hint: Start with smaller problems first. Deal with them without asking for reassurance and once you are starting to feel more confident move on to the bigger problems. Ask yourself, What is the worst thing that could happen if I make a decision without asking for reassurance?*

## Pattern 4. Solving the problem impulsively

Another way of dealing with problems is to respond impulsively to them, without thinking things through. Attempts to solve problems in this way often lead to hurried or incomplete solutions, or solutions that make the problem worse. As you can imagine, these kinds of solutions then lead to more problems and ultimately to more worry. While the intolerance of uncertainty is an important factor in all problem-solving, it has a key role to play in this type of attempted problem-solving. It is often this intolerance that motivates people to make decisions quickly so they can defuse the sense of uncertainty. As we have mentioned above, this kind of response will work well from time to time, and it is this irregular nature of the rewards (i.e. things working out once in a while) that encourages us to adopt this strategy. But this strategy is like rolling a dice to make decisions; if we did it continually we would never learn to trust our own judgment. We would also continue to doubt our ability to solve problems and would believe that luck was the most important factor in solving problems, which simply is not true.

### EXERCISE 15.6: IMPULSIVE PROBLEM SOLVING

How typical or characteristic is this strategy for you?

| None | A little | Some extent | Moderately | Somewhat | Mostly | Completely |
|------|----------|-------------|------------|----------|--------|------------|
| 0 | 1 | 2 | 3 | 4 | 5 | 6 |

Can you think of an example of when you solved a problem impulsively?

What other problems did this cause you? What impact does it have on the problem? What impact does it have on your worry?

What do you need to do to overcome this type of impulsive problem-solving?

*Hint: If you jump in without thinking, you need to make sure you give yourself time to think. Give yourself at least 10 minutes to come to a conclusion or even better sleep on it; this really helps. Ask yourself, What's the worse thing that could happen if I delayed solving the problem for 15 minutes?*

## Pattern 5. Trying to solve everything at once

Worry has the tendency to multiply and expand, and this pattern has echoes in problem-solving. Often worriers will partially engage in trying to solve one problem, and then flip-flop between this and other problems. As their attention is divided, this can mean that nothing gets done and all problems are in a semi-unsolved state. In this state the problems actually provoke more uncertainty and worry, making focusing and completing the tasks much harder. This confirms to the worrier that they are no good at solving problems and their multi-attempts produce poor, incomplete outcomes; this reinforces the belief that efforts to solve problems will only result in negative outcomes.

## EXERCISE 15.7: DOING IT ALL AT ONCE

How typical or characteristic is this strategy for you?

| None | A little | Some extent | Moderately | Somewhat | Mostly | Completely |
|------|----------|-------------|------------|----------|--------|------------|
| 0 | 1 | 2 | 3 | 4 | 5 | 6 |

Can you think of an example when you tried to solve too many problems all at once?

What impact does trying to solve too many problems at once have on you? What impact does this have on your worry? What impact does it have on the problem?

What do you need to do to address this problem?

*Hint: Remember, one thing at a time. Resist the urge to start a new problem. If there are several stacked up that need to be dealt with, choose the one that needs to be solved first. You can't land all the aircraft at Heathrow Airport at once; you have to bring them down one at a time. Ask yourself, What might be the advantages of solving one problem at a time?*

### Pattern 6. Approach–avoiding flip-flop

This is another common kind of pattern that worriers unwittingly fall into. They approach a problem and then flip-flop between trying to solve the problem by doing something purposeful and then flip to avoiding the problem. With this strategy, worriers are partially engaged in trying to solve the problem – it's like trying to clean the loo while at the same time trying not to look into the bowl too closely, or smell, or think. To the do the job well you need to look and see what needs to be cleaned. This 'avoidance' leads to a less than clean loo! This is closely related to the pattern above. Problems are solved poorly and take much longer, and the resultant uncertainty triggers more worry.

## EXERCISE 15.8: FLIP-FLOPPING

How typical or characteristic is this strategy for you?

| None | A little | Some extent | Moderately | Somewhat | Mostly | Completely |
|------|----------|-------------|------------|----------|--------|------------|
| 0 | 1 | 2 | 3 | 4 | 5 | 6 |

Can you think of an example when you flip-flopped between trying to solve a problem and avoiding it?

What impact does this pattern have on you? What impact does this pattern have on your worry? What impact does it have on the problem?

What do you need to do to address this problem?

*Hint: Keep focused on one problem at a time; solve this before moving on to deal with another. Learn to spot when you change from dealing with the problem to flipping or avoiding, then catch this early, and without beating yourself up bring your attention compassionately back to the problem (don't give yourself a hard time for flipping or avoiding, just say, 'back to it'). Ask yourself, If I solved one problem at a time on a regular basis how might this help me?*

## Pattern 7. Prejudging the outcome of our efforts

Often, worriers will think that whatever they do the problem will turn out badly; they are in essence prejudging themselves. Understandably, having this view makes them less likely to engage with problems. This can be captured in the following statement: *If I try to solve it, it will go wrong and then I'll pay, so best do nothing.* This stance motivates worriers to stand back and avoid getting involved in solving the problem. This can apply even if they know that not doing anything will make the problem worse. If the idea that *any attempt at problem-solving leads to catastrophe* is never challenged, then it makes perfect sense to avoid trying to solve problems. But if we avoid solving problems, they never go away, nor does the worry triggered by the problems. By using this strategy, the unhelpful approach to worry is strengthened since it supports the idea that problems are threatening, that we do not have the ability to cope, and we are defiantly pessimistic about the outcomes of our problem-solving.

---

**EXERCISE 15.9: PRE-JUDGING**

How typical or characteristic is this strategy for you?

| None | A little | Some extent | Moderately | Somewhat | Mostly | Completely |
|------|----------|-------------|------------|----------|--------|------------|
| 0 | 1 | 2 | 3 | 4 | 5 | 6 |

Can you think of an example of when you have avoided or delayed solving a problem?

What impact does this have on how you think about your ability to solve problems? What impact does this pattern have on your

worry? What impact does it have on the problem?
How could you find out that your predictions about your efforts are not true?

*Hint: Before you start to solve the problem, write down what you think will happen – the full catastrophe version. Then have a go. Was your prediction accurate? Was it as bad as you thought?*

## Pattern 8. Overanalysis

Since problems lead to anxiety, the worrier might be motivated to try to reduce their anxiety by trying to think of all the possible ways that the problem could be solved and of the outcomes of each solution: each solution then generates more problems, which require more solutions, which generate more problems, and so on. A worrier may think and rethink alternative solutions, and in doing so get lost within the labyrinth of alternatives, never solving the problems. Each solution brings more worry and uncertainty, which leads to more anxiety, making problem-solving all the more difficult. By overanalysis our minds tend to turn molehills into mountains, or benign problems into demons, so that the idea problems are threatening is maintained.

**EXERCISE 15.10: OVERANALYSING**

How typical or characteristic is it of you to overanalyse problems?

| None | A little | Some extent | Moderately | Somewhat | Mostly | Completely |
|------|----------|-------------|------------|----------|--------|------------|
| 0 | 1 | 2 | 3 | 4 | 5 | 6 |

Can you think of an example of when you have overanalysed a problem?

What impact does this have on how you think about your ability to solve problems? What impact does this pattern have on your worry about this situation? What impact does it have on the problem?

What could you do to reduce the degree to which you over-analyse problems?

*Hint: Give yourself a time limit. What's the worse thing that could happen if you made a less than perfect decision? Ask yourself, How long do you need to make the perfect decision (to infinity and beyond!)?*

**SUMMARY BOX**

What ideas have you come up with to change the way you approach problems?

- 
- 
- 
- 
- 
- 

## Bringing it all together

By now you will have an idea about what rules and beliefs combine to make up your unhelpful approach to worry. You will also have a better idea of the type of unhelpful patterns that are typical for you. These rules and the patterns are linked. For example, doubting my ability to solve problems may make me more likely to ask others to solve them for me. Believing that problems are actually bigger than they actually are might lead me to put off dealing with them. If I thought that I attracted problems, then I might stick to a safe routine and not take risks because breaking my routine would lead to more problems.

So, as we showed earlier in this chapter, these approaches to problems can have the unfortunate side-effect of making the problem worse. This then confirms to us the idea that we are no good at solving problems. In order to overcome your worry you need to begin to engage with everyday problems in a more helpful way – but to do this requires you to take risks and do things differently.

At this point you may wish to return to the problem-solving diagram on pages 303–04. With the new information you have about your approach to problems, about your rules concerning problem-solving and about the patterns of behavior that are key to you, can you draw up your own vicious cycle? If you can, then what does this suggest that you need to do?

In Sections C and D, we will focus on some ideas to help you get better at approaching problems differently. We start with the transforming your approach to problems, we then try to help you spot problems sooner rather than later, and finally we return to the idea of behavioral experiments to challenge the rules that underpin your approach to worry.

## Section C: Problems as opportunities

One way of working towards challenging an unhelpful approach to problems is to turn your approach to them on its head. To do this we have to begin to think of problems as coming with both opportunities and threats. This makes sense if you consider the idea that personal growth or development usually takes place outside our comfort zone.

The Taijitu (above) is a traditional Chinese symbol that represents the forces of yin and yang. It can be thought of as a plan or formulation of how things work. It shows how one part cannot exist without the other – indeed, each part is needed to define the other. It is non-judgmental: neither part is considered better than the other. Consequently, the symbol does not 'instruct' us to eliminate one side or another to make things better. The symbol conveys the dynamic interaction between the two parts as they wax and wane, eternally moving towards and away from harmony or balance. So, dark exists with light, order with chaos, anxiety with comfort and problems with opportunities. It reminds us that there are usually two sides (or more) to every story and that we should spend time finding out what else might be going on before accepting just one side. It can be helpful to keep this symbol in mind when we are facing problems because, when problems appear, they also come with opportunities, but these need to be 'looked for' as they are not clear at first glance. It may sound trite, but in part you have to make friends with problems, moving towards them and learning to accept them for what they are, 'warts and all'.

Let's return to Tom at the train station. His initial reaction to his train being late is to worry: each solution he comes up with triggers more worry – he is going to be late for an important meeting and he believes his job is under threat because of this. But if Tom could begin to see the opportunities in his situation, then this might help him to feel better. So, he could ask, *What are the opportunities in this situation?* He could tell himself that he has more time to prepare his notes, he could learn about a new way of getting to work (bus?), he could use the time to have a good cup of coffee and a muffin; he could also phone in and show he is responsible. By changing his approach to problems, Tom could start to feel less stressed by his problem. None of these approaches actually change the problem (he is still late for an important meeting), but this more helpful approach adds a new way of thinking, which ultimately will reduce worry.

If every time a problem appears you see it as *entirely* threatening, it is not surprising that you find it hard to solve. Worse still, this perspective allows you to see only the negative aspects of the problem, which offers only a restricted viewpoint. Indeed, because of this, it makes absolute sense to avoid them at all costs. Seeing problems as threatening or menacing generally means that worriers fail to recognize that there are both positive and negative aspects to problems. As we have mentioned above, problems appear on a scale and to see them all as inhabiting either end of the pole is unhelpful and unrealistic. Rarely are problems entirely threatening or loaded with opportunities.

## EXERCISE 15.11: PROBLEMS – THREATS VS OPPORTUNITIES

Problems are completely threatening

Problems are opportunities

←——————————————————————————————→

### Balance:
### problems come with both threats and opportunities

Where are you on this line? Do you see problems as completely threatening? Put a cross that shows where you are now. Put a second cross where you would like to be.

What do you need to do to change your views about problems?

We know that problems come with a sense of threat, but they also come with opportunities. We return in a new way to the saying 'every cloud has a silver lining'. Opportunities might include personal growth, bettering relationships, learning new skills, developing existing skills or simply having new experiences. We are not suggesting that you suddenly develop a fatalistic approach, or just give in to problems, but we are suggesting that you begin to recognize the threat and then seek out the opportunity; look for both sides of the story before making up your mind. As we have said earlier, it is our firm belief that when people arrive with problems, they also carry with them the solutions; these are simply hidden from view.

**Questions that feed this idea include**
- What is the threat in this problem/situation?
- What could I learn from this problem/situation?
- What can I get out of this situation?
- What's in it for me?
- What new experience might I gain from it?
- How could facing this problem/situation help me to grow?
- What is the opportunity that this problem/situation is offering me?
- What advantages might there be?

Using some of these questions, we will work through the following problem:

John faced a meeting with his boss because he made a potentially serious but accidental mistake. Believing that his job was under threat, he worried a great deal. Then he started to think through his approach to the problem. He thought that he might be able to get something from the experience. First, he knew that he would never make the same mistake again. Second, it had made him much more aware in general and so less likely to make other mistakes. He also realized that he genuinely cared about the consequences of his actions, which made him see that, despite making a mistake, he cared about his job and how he did it. He thought that the meeting with his boss might offer him the opportunity to apologize and let his boss know that this would make him a better employee. While there was no doubt he had made the mistake, and he still had a difficult meeting with his boss to get through (his problem still existed), he now had some ideas about what to say and felt better because he could see that his work was important to him and his mistake was only a small part of him. Although John's boss was not happy with the mistake, his opinion of John was strengthened because he could see how John felt about his job, saw the importance of his mistake and wanted to learn from it.

If John had not been able to shift to a helpful approach to his problem, then in all probability he would have worried much, much more and he wouldn't have been able to think things through in the way that he did. But being able to see that his problem came with 'hidden' opportunities helped him to feel better. This approach is reminiscent of the saying 'all is grist for the mill', which means that everything can be of some benefit or profit. John was not simply thinking positively and hoping that things would turn out OK; his approach made him stand back and think things through – it enabled him to 'open his mind'. The problem remained, as did the threat, but he felt better able to deal with it.

Can you think of a problem you are currently facing that you could start to investigate using these questions?

## Learning to recognize problems sooner

Everyday we are confronted with new problems, and, like uncertainty, problems are everywhere – that's why trying to avoid them is pointless, a little like trying to avoid raindrops. A by-product of an unhelpful approach to problem-solving is the tendency to ignore problems when they first appear, 'sweeping them under the carpet', or 'pretending' not to have noticed them. Failing to recognize and deal with problems early on leads to their becoming more serious and complex as they 'snowball'. And, not surprisingly, as this happens we worry more, making it harder to solve the problems – and so on. For this reason the first few steps in improving your problem-solving is to become better at recognizing when problems first appear and then to get better at defining what exactly the problem is. When excessive worry is around, however, it is often very hard to *see the wood for the trees*; so it is important to think this through when your worry is less troublesome.

### What tells us that there is a problem afoot?

As everyday hassles and problems are everywhere and we face them constantly some people will not need to think too hard about this question, but others will. If problems are 'dripping' with uncertainty, then the same things that trigger worry (remember the splinter of doubt) might also tell us that there is a problem to deal with. So what can you do to help you learn to spot problems sooner? We can use a number of signs that a problem is around namely our; diaries, emotions, actions, bodily sensations and statements or thoughts.

The first thing you can do is use your worry awareness diary to help you think about the type of problems that triggered your worry? We will suggest other alternatives below, but you already have this information and sitting down with your diary with 'problems' in mind might glean some answers. Again, a notebook and pen are essential.

---

**SUGGESTION FOR YOUR WORRY DIARY**

With each bout of worry, ask the following questions:

Was there a problem that triggered this worry?
What was your worry helping you to do in this case?
Was your worry a way of trying to deal with the problem?

---

The second idea is for us to become more aware of our feelings when we face problems and learn to use them as an early-warning signal that there is problem we need to attend to.
In their excellent book called *Solving Life's Problems: A 5-Stage Step Guide to Enhanced Wellbeing*, Arthur Nezu, Christine Maguth Nezu and Thomas D'Zurilla remind us that feelings are a signal that a problem exists; but *the feelings, however, are not the problem*. Their book is well worth a read and many of the ideas that are found in this chapter are based on their work.

Our actions can also provide clues about when problems are afoot – this is the third idea to help us spot problems sooner. Is there anything you know that you do when you are struggling with a problem? Worry will no doubt be top of your list, but is there anything else that will help you to spot problems? Is there something you do habitually as a sign that there is something going on for you? This might be working longer hours, drinking more alcohol, smoking more cigarettes, avoiding work, people, places or things that remind you of the problem, sleeping badly, biting your nails, pacing the room and so on. What are your signs that there is a problem? Remember that these actions are not the problem, but are a *sign* that there is a problem. For example, it might be that you know you have to have a difficult conversation with your partner, so rather than deal with this you stay later and later at work. Or you notice your bills are piling up in the hallway, but you decide to clean the house from top to bottom rather than opening the bills to find out what you owe. Do any of these sound familiar?

Fourth, we can use the experience of our body to tell us that there is a problem around. For some, feeling as if we need the loo, or headaches, or stomach upsets may be a sign that there is a problem. Often we trust our gut instinct, which can be a good way of making a decision, but must not be the only way, since solving problems in this fashion might lead us to avoid actually thinking it through. Fifth, there may be telltale thoughts or statements that habitually fly through our minds or that we mutter under our breath. These are important because they may be the very first sign of a problem. For example, in the film *Four Weddings and a Funeral*, Hugh Grant's character would habitually swear when a problem appeared (see the first scene for example). You may know the sorts of words that appear for you – write them down. We can turn these habitual statements into early warning signs, and these may enable us to become more aware of the problems as they appear.

## Becoming more tuned in to problems in our lives

Another strategy is to begin to record and review our problems – you can use the worksheet Exercise 16.1 on page 364. This helps you to review your current life and think about what problems arise. When you come up with a problem, then take the problem a little further and ask, *What problems does this cause?* This is particularly useful if you come up with emotions, or single statements, like *I'm stressed, I'm too busy, my life is chaos.* Asking this question will help to break down your problems into smaller parts, as you can see from the example below.

When reflecting on this question, Eva just noted that she felt stressed.

In this example, we can quickly see that there is a vicious cycle at work, which makes it difficult for Eva to solve her problems. Her problem is that worry interferes with doing tasks, which means that she only half-heartedly engages with them. This in turn means that the solutions are incomplete, the problems remain and they may even get worse as a consequence. The partially solved problems stack up, leading to more stress and more problems. Imagine what it would be like to start several jobs in the home and then stop halfway through to attend to other problems: the house quickly fills with tools strewn around, paperwork on tables, washing in the sink and on the drainer, the Hoover is out and plugged in with half the floors done, water is boiling on the hob without any rice – and so on. This adds stress and worry. Eva's problem exists, and there is in all probability something she can do about it. The problem is repetitive. She can see that she needs to begin to recognize sooner when the problems appear, and she then needs to complete one problem before moving on to the next. While this may feel slower in the short term, it avoids the pitfalls of half-finished problems and breaks the cycle of worry.

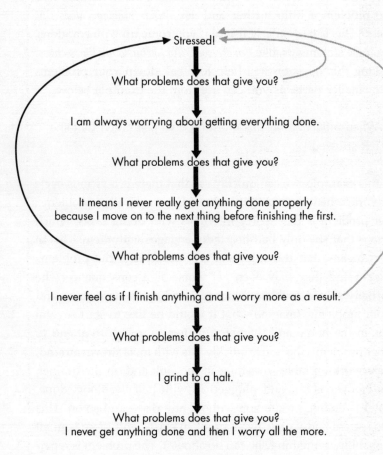

Figure 15.1. What problems does this cause?

## EXERCISE 15.12

Note as many problems as you can think of for each category and then answer the questions for each one.

| Problem category | 1. What comes to mind when I think of . . . 2. Write a sentence to describe the problem. 3. How does this cause me problems? | Do the problems exist? | Is there a solution that comes to mind? If so what is it? Do you need to take this problem through problem-solving? See page 348. | Does this problem appear again and again? Is it a repetitive problem? |
|---|---|---|---|---|
| Emotional problems | | | | |
| Relationship problems | | | | |
| Work-related problems | | | | |
| Health/illness problems | | | | |
| Family problems | | | | |
| Financial problems | | | | |
| Housing | | | | |
| Others | | | | |

**PIT STOP**

Let's stop and think about what you have just been reading. Can you summarize the key ideas you have taken on board? What is sticking in your mind? Maybe write them down. If you have any questions, jot these down too. You can return to them once you have had a chance to digest the information.

What is sticking in my mind from my reading so far?

1.

2.

3.

## Section D: Behavioral experiments and problem-solving

It will be of no surprise by now to know that we need to help you to challenge your unhelpful approach to problems. We hope that the information contained in the problem-solving chapters is beginning to erode some of the strongly held ideas that underpin your approach to problems – for example, the idea that problems only happen to you, or that problems are entirely negative experiences. All this information may shake the foundation of your beliefs, but it does not rebuild them. In order to do this you need to begin to do things differently, in a practical way.

We will now follow the steps necessary for developing a behavioral experiment focused on a rule that underpins the unhelpful approach to problems. Our example follows the steps laid out in Chapter 7 on planning behavioral experiments.

Let's take one of the general rules such as *I should always ask for reassurance when I have solved a problem*. In this case, the first thing we have to do is to make this generic, 'off the peg' rule, real for us. (But you may not have to do this if the rule is already nested in the real world – look at the language: is it tied to a particular event or situation?) So, imagine you believed this rule very strongly, what might it lead you to do? And then write down the rule as it appears in your life.

For example, if a light bulb blows (problem) then the rule starts to operate. *When I have changed a light bulb I always ask my partner, did I do it right?* So the rule becomes, *If I change a light bulb, I should always check it out with my partner afterwards*. There is a silent consequence hanging within this statement, and a really helpful question is, *Supposing that I didn't seek reassurance, then what might happen?* Here we are getting at the hidden consequences. The person might then say, *Well something terrible might happen*, and being curious, we might ask. *And what might that be?* So we might end up with a rule that looks something like this: *If I don't get my partner to check the bulbs after I have changed them, then they might get electrocuted when they switch the lights on*. For a moment stop and reflect on how this rule fits with the rule that we came in with. The same overall pattern remains: *If I try to solve a problem then seek reassurance – or else!* So now we have a prediction or forecast about what will happen if they break their rule, namely electrocution, and you could try to break the rule at this stage. If this is too hard at this stage, then we will need to 'ferret around' for other perspectives. We could ask, *Has anyone been electrocuted before? What happens when your partner is away and a bulb blows? What exactly could you do wrong to lead to electrocution? What are the advantages of holding this belief and what are the disadvantages? Have you always done this, if not, then how did you manage before? Are there times when you haven't done this? What was different then?* And so on. The answers to these questions gently rock the belief, making it more flexible and amenable to change. So can we now think of an alternative? *If I don't get my partner to reassure me that I have not done something wrong, then I will feel jumpy, but this does not mean that someone will be electrocuted.*

We also need to consider safety behaviors: what might they look like in this situation? A safety behavior is something we do to keep ourselves or others safe from our awful prediction. It might be, *I will only change the bulbs when my partner is wearing rubber soled shoes*, or *I will flick the light switch on and off several times afterward with a stick to see it's OK.* It is important to abandon their safety behaviors to find out what could happen when we try out something new (remember the rope to shore for the flat world brigade?) Then we rate their new belief. And we get them to do it. We review how things went, and then think of how to take it even further. The rule we came in with is a very general one and will apply in many situations. You may want to use the exercise sheet in Chapter 7 to help you to plan your behavioral experiment.

What rules have you uncovered that support your unhelpful approach to problems? Which of these rules might be an easier one to start to work with?

In the suggestion box is a series of beliefs and some ideas for experiments. As always, these are 'off the peg' versions: creating your own is going to be much more useful.

For some of the behavioral experiments you actually need to work on some problems, but it's important to choose the right sort of problem for this type of experiment. There are some hints in the problem-solving box that follows in the next section.

Some ideas for experiments.

| Rules | Possible behavioral experiments |
| --- | --- |
| I attract problems | Make a survey of your friends and family and make a list of everyday problems that you have: see how many of them have these as well. This belief would suggest that you predict that you will be the only one with problems. Let's see. |
| If I have problems, then this means I am abnormal | Again, make a survey of friends and family, but this time you might want to ask a question and ask people to rate it. Do you think people are abnormal if they have problems? If not why not? If so, why? |
| If I try to solve a problem, then I will fail | Pick a problem, predict what will happen, have a go. Is it as bad as you first thought? |
| Problems are dangerous and trying to solve them should be avoided | How might they be dangerous? What would happen if you didn't avoid them? Make a prediction, solve the problem and see if your prediction was correct. |
| I should always ask for help or reassurance when solving problems | Pick a problem that does not involve others. Predict how you would feel if you did it in a) your usual way with others' help and b) by yourself. Have a go. What happened? How did you do? |

## Change through understanding

The other thing to bear in mind is that you could simply try to understand how your thoughts, feelings and actions relate to one another and how they might end up creating a vicious cycle. For example, if I believe that my problems are insurmountable, I may feel hopeless, which may drive me to give up on trying, which then confirms the original belief that my problems are insurmountable. The pattern to follow is thoughts leading to feelings, motivating actions, which then serve to maintain the original thought. When we do this, we can see clearly that there is nothing to lose in trying to solve problems, because not trying is not solving them either.

This may then lead us to consider the advantages and disadvantages of solving a problem rather than avoiding it.

Use these points below as a quick memory guide to problem-solving.

> **Quick problem-solving**
> - What's the problem?
>   - Choose a problem that is not life-changing (i.e. relatively simple and small)
>   - Not involving or depending on others
>   - One where you can see the result quickly.
> - Break it down into mini-steps.
> - What is the first step in the sequence? What is the first thing you need to do? Don't get ahead of yourself.
> - At this point, what are the options?
> - Out of all the possibilities, identify two or three that feel OK but are not perfect.
> - Spend a bit of time thinking about each of these solutions or options.
> - Choose the one that seems *slightly better* than the others.

*Slightly better* in this case means, real, the simplest, most likely to succeed, with minimum cost (time, effort, money, etc.) and with a good result.

- Act on it.
- What happened?
- Was the outcome at least OK?
- What happened to your worry about this problem?
- How does it feel to be one small step closer?

*Don't get ahead of yourself:* spend time reflecting on what has been achieved. Yes, there is a lot left to do, but don't look up, look down. You have made some progress, that's great. Now what's the next step? . . . Back to the top.

## PIT STOP

Let's stop and think about what you have just been reading. Can you summarize the key ideas you have taken on board? Make a note of any new ideas that are sticking in your mind. What have you taken from this chapter? If you were to print your learning on a t-shirt, what would the slogan be? If you have any questions, jot these down too. You can return to them once you have had a chance to digest the information.

1.

2.

3.

# 16

# Problem-solving skills

This chapter is about problem-solving skills. It is a detailed, step-by-step account of how to find better solutions and make better decisions. However, you need to think about how you currently approach problems and decide whether this chapter will be of use to you. For example, some worriers are impulsive decision-makers (to avoid uncertainty), and this chapter will probably help them to slow down and think things through. Others will be perfectionists, and want to explore every avenue and idea to the limit. If this is the way you approach problems, then while you may find this chapter interesting, it may only reinforce your ideas about the best way of solving problems. There is a more 'punchy', pared down version of problem-solving towards the end of Chapter 15 (see page 348). If may be useful to think about the eight patterns of unhelpful problem-solving in the last chapter. If you overanalyse, then a less detailed approach will be useful; if you avoid or flip flop, then the structure of this chapter may be of use. So think for a moment about how you generally solve problems. Do you need to slow down and consider each step because you usually rush through, or do you need to speed up and come to decisions more quickly?

Whatever your approach, it might be useful to familiarize your-self with the content of this chapter, but keep this in mind: *one size does not fit all*, and you have to tailor the information to suit you. You may ask yourself, *What if I get it wrong?* Well, make a prediction – what's the worst thing that could happen? Turn it into a behavioral experiment and see how it pans out.

## Developing your skills

Research tells us that people who worry excessively possess problem-solving skills; in fact, their skills are as good as any one else's. Unfortunately, in the population as a whole, the general level of skill in problem-solving is not as good as it could be, and most people would benefit from learning these skills. Consequently, like most people, and depending on your problem-solving style, it will probably be beneficial to spend time focused on developing your problem-solving skills.

What follows is based on a program of problem-solving developed in the United States by Professors Thomas D'Zurilla and Arthur Nezu. Together with Professor Christine Maguth Nezu they wrote an excellent self-help book on solving life's problems. They offer a wealth of experience in working with problem-solving that stretches over many decades. If you would like to read a more detailed account of problem-solving, their book is listed in Further Reading.

### Stages of problem-solving skills

We will outline each stage in detail, but first here is a brief run through of the different stages. The first stage is defining the problem. The second stage, setting goals and considering road-blocks, will be familiar (see Chapter 6). The third stage is generating as many different solutions as you can think of. The fourth is choosing a solution. The fifth is putting your ideas into practice and, finally, reviewing how you did. Remembering and stepping though these steps is very important.

Write these important steps on a credit card-sized piece of paper and carry it with you.

> **Problem-solving stages – key questions to ask**
> 1. What is the problem?
> 2. What am I trying to achieve? What is getting in the way of me achieving this? How can I navigate through the roadblocks or overcome them?
> 3. Given the above what could I do about this? (Generate as many ideas a possible.)
> 4. Which solution could work best?
> **5. Do it!**
> 6. How did I do?

## Stages 1 and 2. Defining problems and setting goals

### Sketching out the problem – what is the problem?

Working out what your problem is can take you a very long way to actually solving it. Problems often appear as statements – *I'm stressed; I hate my job; The children are doing my head in; I never have enough money*. We talked about defining goals in Chapter 6: these are like those 'headline' goals that tell us very little about what we need to do to improve things. So, defining a problem is a little like 'panning for gold': we have to filter and sieve lots of material before we are left with the 'nugget' that lies at the heart of our problem. By doing this we are breaking down large unwieldy problems into smaller, well-defined and manageable chunks. On pages 342 and 343 we mentioned two exercises that might lead you towards a more clearly defined problem. One was a question exercise where the question, 'What problems does that give you?' was repeatedly asked. This questioning helps us to understand the impact of problems, and helps to further define them. There was also a worksheet, where you were asked to think of problems in a number of different areas of your life. We will now focus on helping you to define your problems.

## Arthur's example

Let's use the following example: Arthur is worried, and that's about all he can say. To help him sift more detail he drew the following diagram, his problem porcupine. He first added in the areas of his life where he thought stress might be having an impact. He then asked himself, *What problems does my worry cause me in this part of my life?* Look at his diagram below.

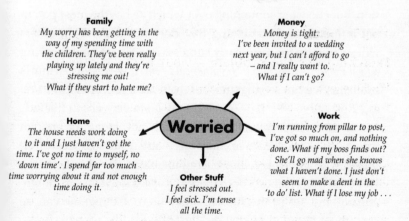

**Family**
*My worry has been getting in the way of my spending time with the children. They've been really playing up lately and they're stressing me out! What if they start to hate me?*

**Money**
*Money is tight. I've been invited to a wedding next year, but I can't afford to go – and I really want to. What if I can't go?*

**Home**
*The house needs work doing to it and I just haven't got the time. I've got no time to myself, no 'down time'. I spend far too much time worrying about it and not enough time doing it.*

**Worried**

**Work**
*I'm running from pillar to post, I've got so much on, and nothing done. What if my boss finds out? She'll go mad when she knows what I haven't done. I just don't seem to make a dent in the 'to do' list. What if I lose my job . . .*

**Other Stuff**
*I feel stressed out. I feel sick. I'm tense all the time.*

**Figure 16.1. Arthur's problem porcupine.**

This is Arthur's first attempt at defining his problem and it needs more work, but, critically, he is beginning to *put pen to paper* to try to address his problems rather than avoiding thinking about them or repeatedly circling around *all* of them without doing something about *one* of them. Even on its own it's better than the starting point he had of just feeling generally worried. He even began to see the relationships between some of his problems – for instance, he wondered if his absence from home was contributing towards his children being difficult. This enabled him to stand back and feel less upset by them. As a rule of thumb, writing things down is a useful thing to do: amongst other things, it puts the problems 'out there' so that you can step back from them and think them through.

So what might he need to do to sift his problems out further?

## Choosing a problem to work on

The first thing that Arthur needs to do is to work out which problem he would like to work on. This can be a difficult decision, but choosing something over which he has the most potential influence and something that does not depend on others will set him up for some early success. This also means choosing a *Real Event* rather than a *Hypothetical Event*. If we review Arthur's problems we can see that most of them are a mix of *Hypothetical and Real Event Worries* – for example, his worry about his kids hating him (*Hypothetical*) coupled with not spending enough time with them (*Real*); or, his worry about his finances (*Real*) linked with his worry about being unable to afford to go to the wedding (*Hypothetical*). Both these *Hypothetical* events are 'downstream' and set in the future – they are not things he can do something about immediately – so we would be wise to choose something at the *Real* end of the spectrum. The others seem to offer a little of each; but, crucially, he needs the problem to be

*Real enough* to be able to *actually* do something about them. So, he could choose work, working on the house or finding time to spend with the kids.

Our problems are often linked and we may have to work on one problem before another. Arthur can see that his children's difficult behavior and his worry about their rejecting him might be because he's not spending very much time with them, so freeing up some spare time by focusing elsewhere could help. Also, some problems are more central, and focusing on these can improve other areas. Arthur might realize that work is the main problem for him and he might try to focus on this first. If he chooses work, he would still be wise to choose an area over which he has the most potential influence, which does not involve other people and which is a *Real Event*. However, within the work group there are several problems within this category as well. For example, he is becoming unhappy at work, he worries that he has too much to do, he is worried about talking with his boss, and he is struggling to focus. Whatever idea he uses, the important thing is that he starts to actually do something about his problems, working through them one at a time.

## Describe the problem in clear and concrete language

In order to take his problem further, Arthur needs to *slow down* to get to the detail of the situation and then focus on the *facts*. When we are feeling upset or worried the language we use reflects this. Arthur has said he is 'running from pillar to post' and we get a sense of what the problem is for him. But here we have an example of language that tells us very little about the specifics of Arthur's situation. So we have to explore this further by asking him to tell us more about what this means. He might mean that he is having to juggle lots of different tasks, or it might literally mean that he is driving from one meeting to the other across great distances. In order to get to clear language we have to find a way of describing what is going on that leaves nothing to the imagination. This means that we make no assumptions about what we think is going on, we only report what we actually know to be true. It's a bit like being a scientist and reporting only the facts without speculating or assuming. As a general rule of thumb, facts are what others would agree on, assumptions are more our personal viewpoint, opinion or beliefs. This is critically true of worriers, as worries can often feel very real and so are accepted as fact without question. Can you spot any assumptions in Arthur's description? It seems as if he is assuming (worrying) that his boss will 'go mad' at him (*What if my boss goes mad?*). There is an assumption about what his boss will do; also, he is using vague language – what does 'go mad' actually mean? There are other silent assumptions that Arthur is making; he is ignoring other important facts, for example the work he has *actually* done. He is also taking the problem very personally and blaming himself, without considering all the other things that may be influencing his problem (see thinking chutes section below).

The following will help you to refine your problems and focus on facts:

- Is it a worry? Is it *Real* or *Hypothetical?*
- Who is involved?
- What is going on that bothers you?
- Where and when is it happening?
- What was going through your mind?
- How did you feel?
- What did you do as a consequence?

## Thinking-chutes

The assumptions we make are to a large extent necessary and normal, and they help us to make quick decisions about problems we face. They are, in a sense, mental short cuts. However, for some people they become habitual and are used repeatedly like a reflex, irrespective of whether the assumption fits the problem or not. So these thinking styles become set and people may become reliant on them in an unhelpful way. Imagine these assumptions or thinking styles are like a mental laundry chute or a slide: once in them it is very hard to change direction. This means that once our thoughts are taken down a particular chute we tend not to consider other information that lies outside the chute. If our thinking is boxed in or constrained in this way, it will have a very strong influence on *what* we are able to think about. So, spotting these thinking chutes is very important to problem-solving, because if we are trying to solve problems based on unfair, wrong or misleading information generated by these assumptions, then the problem-solving will be much, much harder.

For example, if a worrier always blames himself for problems, then this quickly takes him down the self-blame chute, leaving him feeling distressed by his problem. The self-blame chute doesn't give him a chance to think about who else may be involved, or what other factors may be influencing the problem. The chute moves him quickly towards a conclusion, which is accepted because no other ideas or viewpoints are given a chance to influence the outcome. This is another reason why we have to *slow everything down* to look at the things that influence what we think and begin to work out which thinking chutes or slides that we use habitually.

There is an ancient Indian (some say a Hindu) tale of a group of people who were presented with an elephant in a dark room.

Each was presented with a different part of the elephant and then asked to say what they believed that elephant part to be. None had ever seen one. One, touching the broad side of the elephant, concluded that the elephant was a wall; another, touching the trunk, that it was like a snake; another, touching the leg, that it was like a tree; and another, who touched the ears, thought that the elephant was like a fan. Knowing what we know about elephants, we can see why each of these people came to their conclusions, but we also know that each of them, while partly right, was actually wrong. They were wrong because they did not have access to *all* the information or evidence. Thinking chutes limit what information we can 'see', and this strongly influences what we are then able to think, just as each person's view of the elephant was biased by what they could feel. This story also reminds us of the importance of perspective in emotional problems.

Our language gives us clues to the presence of these thinking chutes or slides, words like *should*, *mustn't*, *always*, *never* are often used. Once we have identified them, we need to find ways of challenging them. In the table below is a list of thinking chutes with descriptions, and then questions to help you challenge them.

## TABLE 16.1 THINKING-CHUTES AND OTHER ROUTES

| Thinking-chutes | Questions to help spot your thinking chute | Question to help challenge your conclusions |
|---|---|---|
| All or nothing | Am I seeing this problem in all-or-nothing terms? | Is it that clear-cut? Is there a way I can see this which is less all or nothing? |
| Mixing feelings and facts | Am I feeling strong emotions – what are they telling me? | What do I know to be true and what do I feel? |
| Sweeping statements (generalization) | Am I thinking that this problem is the same as many others? Or am I making a sweeping generalization on the basis of a single event or single piece of information about this problem? | Is it true that this problem is the same as others? What may be unique or different about this problem? |
| Focusing on the negatives | Am I overly focused on the negative or upsetting aspects of this problem? | What I am ignoring in this situation or event? |
| Destroying the positives | Am I 'shooting down' anything positive that I have contributed to solving this problem? | What have I 'shot down'? Make a list. Was I fair on myself? |
| Jumping to conclusions | With this problem in mind, am I jumping to conclusions without considering all the evidence? | What is *all* the evidence? What am I ignoring? |

| Mind-reading | Am I mind-reading? That is, am I thinking that I know what others are thinking about this problem, or do I feel like I know what is behind their actions? | Could I ask them to find out? |
|---|---|---|
| Fortune-telling | Am I predicting how this problem will turn out before even starting to solve it? | How often are my your predictions right? |
| Magnifying or minimizing the problem? | Am I exaggerating any aspect of this problem? Am I minimizing any aspects? | If I am exaggerating then what am I playing down? If I am minimizing, then what I am ignoring? |
| Putting others on a pedestal | Am I putting others on a pedestal (*they could solve this, but I can't*)? Or am I putting myself down to put them there (*I can't solve this, but they could*)? | Do I have experience of solving other similar problems? Is it true that others are better at solving problems? What does this style do for me? |
| Snowballing or catastrophizing | Am I focused on the worst possible outcome for this problem? | How often have my worst possible outcomes come true? What other outcomes might there be? Do I need to adjust my imagined catastrophe? |

| Pressurizing | Am I focusing on what I think I should or ought to do with this problem, rather than on what I can actually do? | What actually can I do? |
| Personalizing | Am I always blaming myself for problems? Am I taking this personally? | Who else is involved? What other things are influencing this situation? |

Focus on a recent problem – a real event that you worried about that you needed to *do* something about. It may be helpful to think through this situation and your worry in the light of the above table. What thinking chutes might you have taken?

You will no doubt recognize catastrophizing as a pattern, but what other patterns are typical in your worry? If you can spot the patterns then you will be in a much better position to stand outside your worry rather than being in it. Also, recognizing these patterns may help to interrupt the flow of worry.

On the next page you find a worksheet outlining how Arthur worked through his problem. There is a blank version of this for you to try out for yourself on the following page.

## TABLE 16.2: DEFINING YOUR PROBLEMS: ARTHUR'S WORKSHEET

| First pass at defining problem | Facts and assumptions (see list of questions on page 356) | Redefining the problem in clear and concrete terms | Which of the problems in the last column should I work on first? |
|---|---|---|---|
| **I am worried** **Worry at work** I'm running from pillar to post, I've got so much on and nothing done. What if my boss finds out? She'll go mad when she knows what I have not been able to do. I just don't seem to make a dent in the 'to do' list. I'm beginning to hate my job. | **Facts** Most of this is real, but I can see some hypothetical stuff too. In my office yesterday, I was finding it difficult to concentrate because I had too many projects on the go. The telephone kept ringing and I had fifty e-mails to read and respond to, I worked late to catch up. | There is usually more than one problem: sift out each one I can't concentrate I have too many projects to manage. The emails are time-consuming. I'm working late. I'm feeling frustrated. I'm avoiding some work because I'm too busy. I don't have enough time to work on each project thoroughly. | Is the problem a *real* problem? Yes. What is the central problem? I can't concentrate at work because the telephone interrupts my concentration and I have too many emails to respond to. What is my goal for this problem? (see Chapter 6) I want to focus on these projects and finish them. SMART-COPER GOAL I want to complete one project by the end of the week. |

## TABLE 16.2: CONTINUED

| | | |
|---|---|---|
| I felt frustrated, I wanted to do a good job, but couldn't give each task the time it needed. I have avoided some jobs because I can't face dealing with them. | | |
| **Assumptions or thinking-chutes** | **Thinking-chutes** | **Turn this into a 'how can I' question.** |
| My boss may not be angry with me; she has been fair in the past. I'm just worrying about it. There are other influences on this problem such as deadlines and other people missing their deadlines. I guess it's not all down to me. | I'm taking things personally. Other people also have responsibility. I have not met with my boss for several weeks. I'm jumping to conclusions without any real evidence for this. I'll talk to my boss to discuss this and find out what she thinks. | How can I complete one project by the end of the week? |

## EXERCISE 16.1: WORKSHEET A – DEFINING YOUR PROBLEMS

| First pass at defining problem | Facts and assumptions (see list of questions on page 356) | Redefining the problem in clear and concrete terms | Which of the problems in the last column should I work on first? |
|---|---|---|---|
| | Facts | There is usually more than one problem: sift out each one | Is the problem a *real* problem? circle Yes/No<br>What is the central problem? |
| | Assumptions or thinking-chutes | Thinking-chutes | What is my goal for this problem? (see Chapter 6) |
| | | | SMART-COPER GOAL |
| | | | Turn this into a *How can I* question. |

## Summary of the steps so far

First, we drew a problem porcupine; in Arthur's case this illustrated his feeling of worry. Second, we added the areas where his problem appeared, including home, work, money and so on, and outlined the problems in each area. This activity already started to help define the problem. But as we are 'panning for gold' we needed to sift and sort more. Third, we decided on which of these areas to work on first, using the criteria of *Real vs Hypothetical*, the easiest first, self-reliant and with the best guarantee of success; Arthur chose work. Fourth, we wrote out the problem in clear and concrete terms. Fifth, we reviewed the information and had to separate out assumptions from facts (these appear separately in the worksheet above, but only to help you see the difference more clearly). Where we found assumptions we looked for the information that underpinned them and asked questions to challenge them. Sixth, we developed a new problem list, breaking the old one into as many problems as we could see. Seventh, we then further sifted and sorted out which of problems we could then focus on. This led us to a problem of being unable to concentrate because of telephones and other disturbances.

The eighth stage is *goal-setting*, which we have discussed in detail in Chapter 6. In Arthur's example, we considered where he is and where he wanted to be, or what his goal was with regard to this problem. So, remember it is helpful if our goals follow the SMART-COPER guidelines. Arthur's goal was *I want to focus on these projects and finish them*: his new goal, using the SMART-COPER guidelines, is *I want to complete one project by the end of the week*.

The last thing we did was to turn his goal into a question to lead us into the next stage of problem-solving, namely generating as many solutions as possible. So, in the ninth stage we turned the problem into a *How can I* question, namely, *How can I complete one project by the end of the week?*

## Spotting the roadblocks

Now that we have a goal in mind, the tenth step is to ask what obstacles or roadblocks are stopping us from reaching our goal. What makes this a problem for us? Look at the exercise below. Arthur could ask what is stopping him from completing his project right now, or what needs to happen to make it possible, and what roadblocks are currently in the way. We already have some clues from his description, such as competing demands on his time, tiredness, interruptions and so forth. Working out what the blocks are will help to further define the problem and thus to outline the pathway to solving it.

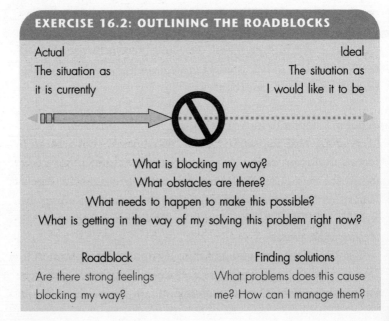

**EXERCISE 16.2: OUTLINING THE ROADBLOCKS**

| Actual | Ideal |
|---|---|
| The situation as it is currently | The situation as I would like it to be |

What is blocking my way?
What obstacles are there?
What needs to happen to make this possible?
What is getting in the way of my solving this problem right now?

| Roadblock | Finding solutions |
|---|---|
| Are there strong feelings blocking my way? | What problems does this cause me? How can I manage them? |

| | |
|---|---|
| Are other's expectations conflicting with my own? | Who can I talk to? How can I work this out? |
| Do I have the skills or resources? | Where can I learn them? Where can I get them? |
| Is uncertainty or perfectionism stopping me in my tracks? | If so, then act. All problems are uncertain, do not expect to feel certain. No solution is perfect, expect both advantages and disadvantages. |
| Is the situation too complex and knotty? | Do I need to break things down further? How can I break things down into smaller and more manageable chunks? |

## Note of caution – finding the perfect solution

The intolerance of uncertainty will also influence how you work on your problem-solving skills. How will it do so? As we have said, problems are 'dripping with uncertainty', each stage of the problem-solving process will trigger uncertainty and you may want to feel certain about one stage before moving on to the next. However, *resist the urge to find the perfect solution* as this is probably a way of trying to attain the impossible. Don't try to wrestle certainty from the jaws of uncertainty. Perfect solutions simply do not exist and all solutions are trade-offs between competing demands. The only certainty in life is uncertainty. This problem-solving chapter is another opportunity to challenge uncertainty, by taking risks. It can be considered as a series of behavioral experiments (see Chapter 7) to challenge both your intolerance of uncertainty and your beliefs about problem-solving. We will return to this below, but, for now, recognize when uncertainty appears and ask, *If I put this solution into place right now, then what am I afraid of happening?* Or, *What is the worst thing that could happen?* Write down your predictions and see if they come true.

Stages one to six are all focused on defining the problem, and we cannot stress enough how important it is to take time to do this. Understanding the problem is more than halfway to solving it. So don't rush this stage. At any point you can stop yourself and adjust what you are trying to do, nothing is set and again we remind you that problem-solving is a skill, and practice will make you better at doing it. When you try this for yourself, be aware of perfectionism and keep in mind the idea that as well as learning to solve problems you are also challenging the uncertainty that comes with doing this. If uncertainty is drawing you into playing it safe, into avoiding something, or is keeping you stuck at one stage, then ask, *What am I afraid that might happen if I went ahead?* Write your prediction down and then see if this comes true in the way you imagined.

**General helpful tips**
- Write things down
- Use diagrams and pictures to help you
- Take your time and slow down (depending on your approach to problems)
- Separate facts from assumptions and spell out the thinking chutes

- Break big problems into smaller more manageable chunks
- Set clear SMART-COPER goals

## Stage 3. Generating as many solutions as possible

During this stage you should aim to think up as many different solutions to your problems as you can. To do this, there are three things to bear in mind. First, you must try to *suspend judgment* about the usefulness or otherwise of each solution you come up with. Second, by being non-judgmental about your solutions you will generate as many possible solutions as you can, or increase the *quantity* of solutions available. The third idea is to come up with a *variety* of solutions and not the same solution masquerading in different guises. So, for example, the goal of getting fitter may lead to solutions such as running, weight training or cycling. These are all similar solutions that live within the same family of solutions – doing exercise to get fitter. You can use the variety idea to trigger to help find more solutions. In this case thinking about eating healthy foods, going out for a coffee rather than a beer, taking the stairs and not the lift, getting more restful sleep and so on. These solutions offer some variety. Research tells us that, if we use these three ideas to guide us when looking for solutions, we are more likely to come up with more effective solutions. Frankly, the more solutions you have to choose from the better chance you have of picking a good one.

Generating as many ideas a possible is a both a creative exercise and a skill, and like all skills it needs practice. Every new idea or solution you come up with should be thought of as a positive step, even if it seems a little 'off the wall'. Often we 'shoot the idea down' even before we finish thinking it. If you notice your mind thinking *that will never work*, or *that's silly* or *that's stupid* or just a plain *nah*, with a mental shake of the head, then remind yourself that all ideas are valid at this stage. We need you to put your ideas on the table and leave them there. The ideas that you come up with will probably be coated in doubt, but that's OK, so long as you leave them on the table. Write down all the ideas: take a sheet of paper and write *Solutions* at the top and numbers one to ten down the page. For each problem find at least ten solutions. Remember not to judge, think broadly or 'outside the box'. Use humour if that helps – turn the problem on its head. If you were solving this for someone else, then what would you suggest? If a 10 year old were solving this problem how would they solve it? If the 'A' Team, Lara Croft, Marg Simpson, or Elvis or Bob Marley were solving this problem, how would they solve it? What ideas might they suggest? Or think about people you know – what ideas might they come up with?

This is not easy, but with a little time and practice, then you will be able to get to the magic number ten. Try the exercise below, with a notebook and pen see if you can come up with ten solutions while at the same time suspending judgment on each. Review them and see if you have families of solutions: have you come up with some variety?

Here is a list of common problems. Have a go at generating ten solutions for each, keeping in mind the three ideas above.

I want to read more

I want to lose weight

I want to spend more time with my family

I want to work more efficiently

I'm bored with my cooking, I want to make more adventurous food

HERE IS A SOLUTION LIST FOR *I WANT TO MAKE MORE ADVENTUROUS FOOD*

1. Search the Internet 2. Buy a book 3. Go to a different supermarket 4. Go to the local shops 5. Change where I shop 6. Invite friends around for supper 7. Get my partner involved 8. Buy a good quality frying pan 9. Choose a country and cook recipes from there 10. Ban processed foods.

[Some of these solutions look like family solutions. e.g. 1 and 2 are about getting more information; 3, 4 and 5 are about shopping differently. We may need to add a few more solutions]. 11. Read a recipe book before shopping and make a list 12. Choose one night a week to have adventurous food. 13. Take a night class.

## Habitual solutions

Have you noticed any patterns in your problem-solving? Are there solutions you use regularly or habitually, apart from worrying? These regular solutions can often help, but sometimes we go straight to them, even when the problem doesn't fit. So, to manage stress or to feel better we may go for a run to clear our head, but going for a run won't sort out the bills or fix a leaking tap. What happens when our habitual solutions are taken away (for example by injury, so that you can't run)? It is important not to put all our eggs in one basket. If habitual solutions appear when you are developing your list, you must not judge them, just write them down along with the rest. In the next stage we will learn how to sift and sort out the solutions we come up with.

## Review your list

Once you have a list of ten solutions it's time to review them. You may want to do this using the ideas found in the goal-setting chapter. For example, if I am feeling stressed by work then going for a relaxing sauna is a great solution – it's very clear, concrete and practical; it's obvious what will happen. But what about things like improving my time-keeping? This needs specifying. How could you improve your time-keeping? What do you need to do to achieve this? These kinds of questions will look for more concrete, practical solutions. I may come up with several more solutions to add to my list, such as 'Buy a good alarm clock', 'Get a diary', 'Teach the kids to make their own sandwiches', etc. If you combined some of these solutions, would that make a better solution?

## Interlude – why am I doing this?

The thought that this is a chore might go through your mind. So let's review why these processes might help. They will add structure, which will demand that you take new mental paths to come to solutions rather than the well-worn routes of worry. They take your mind and thoughts away from worry and give them back to you. When we see the detail spelt out in black and white on the page it can help us to stand back and see things differently. Problem-solving is a skill and skills can be a chore to learn, but once we have grasped them we can go though the steps much more quickly. Think about learning to drive, where each skill is introduced one by one – knowing where to look or which gear to use requires a great deal of thought, but after a few months of driving they become second nature. So keep at it and you will reap the rewards.

You may also be having the reaction *I know this already*, and indeed you do probably know much or all of this. If this is the case, the question may be why aren't you being successful in consistently applying these ideas? The most likely reason is your approach to solving problems. In which case you may want to go back to Chapter 15 and pay particular attention to your responses to Table 15.1, or the Negative Problem Orientation questionnaire on page 314. You may like to reflect on these and work out what ideas or thoughts might influence your ability to engage in solving problems. On the other hand, it may be that you get through the first steps each time and then get stuck in choosing the necessary solutions and action. In this case you may want to keep going through this chapter.

## Stage 4. Decision-making

Now that you have ten solutions to your problem it's time to decide which one will be the best solution. As you know all too well, trying to make decisions can trigger worry, as they are a step into the unknown and into uncertainty. So here is another opportunity to challenge uncertainty. Also be on the alert for perfectionism – trying too hard to get it right or delaying choosing. Remember to take one step at a time. If your worry gets the better of you, then once it has passed return to the task, and if it happens again, then again bring your mind back when you can. But do so compassionately and without *beating yourself up* – this only adds to the problem and doesn't help in any way. Making decisions for yourself will develop your self-confidence and challenge the idea of uncertainty.

In this stage it's time to lift the ban on suspending judgment and bring your critical mind to bear on each solution. To help you with the sifting and sorting there is a series of questions below (page 375) and a worksheet (page 377).

### Throw out the lame ducks

In the first sweep of the ten solutions we need to see if there are any real 'lame ducks'. Are there solutions that would be impossible to put into action? Are there solutions that will obviously lead to overly negative outcomes? Review your ten and decide which of them you should put aside. Draw a line through them. Are there two or three that look like possible solutions? Try to order these with the most preferable solution first. If you feel like acting on this solution now, then do so; in coming this far you have already 'sifted and panned' for your solution. If you see 'gold' then go for it, but remember to stop and review how things went. If later you find out that your solution didn't quite work out then, you may want to take the next problem into the next stage and hold off on acting on a solution until you have done so. It's OK to take small risks, and learn from them.

## PIT STOP

Let's stop and think about what you have just been reading. Can you summarize the key ideas you have taken on board? Make a note of any new ideas that are sticking in your mind. What have you taken from this chapter? If you were to print your learning on a t-shirt, what would the slogan be? If you have any questions, jot these down too. You can return to them once you have had a chance to digest the information.

1.

2.

3.

## Evaluating solutions in detail – using the worksheet

The worksheets on the next pages will take you through the steps needed to assess a solution in detail. You will need to use a sheet for each of your solutions: if there is not enough space to fill in all the details, write them down in your notebook. The worksheets try to show on a couple of pages all the steps needed for evaluating a solution. There are eleven types of question in total. Some of these you will be able to answer very quickly, others may need more thought and time.

Worksheet 1 starts with a space for you to outline your problem and the solution you want to think through. Notice it asks for a number for the solution, as you may be working through several. In other words, this worksheet tries to help you to decide if a solution is a potential candidate for further investigation. It includes questions focused on the 'fit' of the solution to your problem, the practicality of the solution, the roadblocks or obstacles, and finally it asks you to rate how well this solution addresses your problem on a scale from – 5 to + 5.

### EXERCISE 16.3, WORKSHEET B: SUITABILITY, PRACTICAL ISSUES AND NEGOTIATING ROADBLOCKS

Write out or circle the most appropriate answer in each case.

**Problem**

_____

**Solution number____**

1. If I use this solution will it help me to solve my problem?
Yes / No / Maybe

**2.** Is this solution practical? What practical steps are required to put this solution into action? Do I have the time and energy to put this solution into action? Do I have the resources?

Yes / No / Maybe

**3.** What might stop me from using this solution? What are the roadblocks? List them here:

**4.** Can I navigate a way through these roadblocks?

Yes / No / Maybe

**5.** Considering your responses so far; how well might this solution address your problem?

Does not address                                          Addresses it
it at all                                                          completely

$- 5 - 4 - 3 - 2 - 1\ 0 + 1 + 2 + 3 + 4 + 5$

**6.** Is this solution good enough to go onto the next step in the problem-solving process?

Yes / No / Maybe

On the next page you will find the advantage and disadvantages worksheet (and you will find a simplified version of this table in Appendix 4). The second worksheet takes you through the advantages and disadvantages both to you and others, and over two time frames, namely in the shorter and longer terms. This worksheet goes through specific advantages and disadvantages and ends with a more global rating of the advantages and disadvantages of a particular solution.

The final task is to try to put these two worksheets together. This means considering practical issues, roadblocks and the general advantages and disadvantages in a final assessment of the solution. The worksheet is structured like a funnel; it is wide and includes as much detail as possible to start, it then narrows, asking you to make choices and rate the information gathered. The stages are numbered to help you order your thinking. Have a look through the worksheet now and see if this makes sense to you. Considering the long and short term can be very helpful. For example, we may feel very anxious about a particular solution in the first few hours, but making our own choices enables us to develop confidence in the longer term.

## EXERCISE 16.4, WORKSHEET C: ADVANTAGES AND DISADVANTAGES

*You may find it helpful to reflect on the following questions for this exercise:*

7. Questions about you: How will this leave me feeling? How much time and energy will I need to use this solution? Will this have an impact on my health? Will it make me feel better about myself? Will it make me feel more or less worried, anxious or low? Will it have an impact on me financially? What might I learn from this solution?

Questions about others: Will I be stepping on others' toes? How might my partner, friend, lover, work colleague, etc., feel about this? How might I be seen by others if I use this solution?

| For me | | For others | |
| --- | --- | --- | --- |
| Short term | Long term | Short term | Long term |
| What advantages might it have today and in the next few days? | What advantages might it have in the next week or months and beyond? | What advantages might it have today and in the next few days? | What advantages might it have in the next week or months and beyond |
| What disadvantages might it have today and in the next few days? | What disadvantages might it have in the next week or months and beyond? | What disadvantages might it have today and in the next few days? | What disadvantages might it have in the next week or months and beyond |
| Thinking of the short-term advantages and disadvantages, is this solution an overall advantage or disadvantage for you? | Thinking of the long-term advantages and disadvantages, is this solution an overall advantage or disadvantage for you? | Thinking of the short-term advantages and disadvantages, is this solution an overall advantage or disadvantage for others? | Thinking of the long-term advantages and disadvantages, is this solution an overall advantage or disadvantage for others? |

*Using the scale below, rate each of the following:*

Mostly
disadvantageous

Mostly
advantageous

$-5 \quad -4 \quad -3 \quad -2 \quad -1 \quad 0 \quad +1 \quad +2 \quad +3 \quad +4 \quad +5$

*Insert
number* ____

*Insert
number* ____

*Insert
number* ____

*Insert
number* ____

**8.** Considering all the above advantages an disadvantages for me, where does the balance lie for **me**? *(please circle)*

**9.** Considering all of the above advantages and disadvantages for others, where does the balance lie for **others**? *(please circle)*

Mostly
disadvantageous

Mostly
advantageous

$-5-4-3-2-1\ 0+1+2+3+4+5$

Mostly
disadvantageous

Mostly
advantageous

$-5-4-3-2-1\ 0+1+2+3+4+5$

**10.** Where does the overall balance lie between advantages and disadvantages?

Mostly
disadvantageous

Mostly
advantageous

$-5 \quad -4 \quad -3 \quad -2 \quad -1 \quad 0 \quad +1 \quad +2 \quad +3 \quad +4 \quad +5$

## Summary box

The final task is to try to put all this information together in a summary box. When completing this you will need to include both the suitability of the solution, its practicality, the roadblocks and the overall sense of the advantages and disadvantages.

---

Problem

_____

Solution number____

11. Considering all your responses so far; how well might this solution address your problem?

Does not address it at all                                Solves the problem

*(please circle the most appropriate number)*

$- 5 - 4 - 3 - 2 - 1 \quad 0 + 1 + 2 + 3 + 4 + 5$

---

When you have gone through these steps once, then it's time to take the other solutions through them as well. As we said, these steps will add structure; they will demand that you take new mental paths to come to solutions rather than the well-worn routes of worry. Over time you will internalize the questions and the steps will become automatic, just like driving. Consequently, it is very important not to simply dodge this, since in taking this step-by-step approach you will be laying down new mental paths, enabling you to overcome your worry.

## Choosing a solution

By now you will have evaluated several solutions in detail. The best solution will be the one with the highest ratings. If you have several of equal rating, then write those solutions on pieces of paper and try to order them with the best or most preferable at the top and the least preferable at the bottom. Which solutions offer the best fit to your problem? Which are easier to get on and do now? Which might be better left for later? The bottom line at this stage is that no solution is perfect. As you will have noticed from the advantages and disadvantages worksheet, no solution is wholly advantageous or wholly disadvantageous. You will never find the *perfect* solution. So choose the one that fits best. When you look at the solutions, is there one that needs to happen first? Can you arrange them like stepping stones?

Sometimes the ratings are mostly negative: this might tell us a number of things. First, the problem may not actually be solvable. If this happens then you will need to think about how you can best manage your emotional response to the problem rather than trying to solve an insolvable problem. Second, you may need to go back and redefine your goal. It might be that your goal is set too high or is impossible to reach. Third, you may need to find more information about the problem, to see if this helps to find a better solution. If this is a strategy you use to manage uncertainty and worry, then guard against it. It is better to take a risk than remain stuck within the endless activity of information gathering. Fourth, your mood or your approach to problems may be interfering with how you have rated the solutions. Are your ratings influenced by the view you are taking rather than by considering the evidence? Could you have a chat with someone about your decision-making and see what they think? Fifth, are you trying to find the perfect solution? If you are, you will never find one – all solutions have advantages and disadvantages. Again, better to take a risk than get stuck within the endless search for perfection. Sixth, are you putting off making a decision because you are worried about moving on and putting the solution into action? If so, be kind to yourself and compassionate, but also remind yourself that to overcome your worry you need to take risks.

## Stage 5.  Putting your solution into practice – doing!

One of the central messages so far is the need to keep a realistic idea of how things will turn out. No solution is perfect! This is always a difficult step because up until now the work you have been doing has been mostly in your mind. In Chapter 2 we talked about the Kolbian learning cycle (see page 23).

Professor Kolb believed that in order to learn we should go through four types of experience. These include engaging in new experiences; learning to observe our own experience; creating ideas to explain what we are seeing; and testing out these ideas by making new decisions or solving problems, leading back to new experiences, and so on. The stage you are at now is the moment before gaining concrete experience by doing something new. Now is the time to remind yourself of why you are trying to overcome your worry. In the chapter on goals we asked you to write down on a postcard why you wanted to overcome your worry and also to list the ideas that will keep you engaged with your goals. Think about how life will be when you are keeping worry for the big occasions and not for every situation or event.

Newcastle-upon-Tyne is on the east coast of the UK. The North Sea, even in summer, can be a chilly place, to say the least. Change is like going swimming in the North Sea. When you first get in, the cold and shivering tells you to get out. But after a while your body adapts and you can swim and enjoy yourself – really! So, in putting your solutions into action, we have to expect some uncomfortable feelings, but these will pass as you get more accustomed to the new experience.

Once you start acting on your solutions you will quickly find out much more about the roadblocks that lie in the path of your goal. This is to be expected; we are now in the world of experience and doing, and we will get much better information about how things really are when we are active in this way – there is simply no substitute for real-life experience. Just return to the earlier stages and add this new information: this is now 'grist for the mill'. Like other stages, if you are feeling uncertain and worried, then sit with it. Problem-solving is a challenge to the intolerance of uncertainty, and, like a school bully, it will want to 'up the ante' before leaving you alone. As far as you can, stay with the feelings and keep on track.

## Planning

What practical steps do you need to take to put your solution into practice? What needs to happen first, and what logically follows on from this? Write your plan down. Remind yourself of the SMART goals: keep your goal concrete and keep it specific. Setting up some way of measuring the outcome of your solution is very, very useful. This is one of the best ways of telling us that our solutions have worked – for example, noticing that it takes less time to do a particular task (measure how long it takes), or that you are spending more time out of your comfort zone (how many minutes or hours, the type of places you are going), or that you are feeling less worried or low (using the questionnaires found in this book).

**Questions to help you develop your plan**
- What is my goal?
- What is my solution?
- How can I put my solution into place?
- What steps do I need to take?
- Make a list of the things you may need to do.

- Draw out a series of steps leading to your goal. What needs to happen to get you to your goal using this solution?
- What will tell you that you are on track to reach your goal using this particular solution?
- What could tell you that the solution isn't working? Again, we should not be dependent on our feelings as guide, but focus on the facts.

## Stage 6. So how did you do?

It is important after all this hard work to sit down and think about how you have done. What did you do well, what did you learn, what could you do differently next time? Were your fears confirmed, were your predictions about how things will turn out accurate? Are you feeling better since you put your plans into action? What have you noticed as a side-effect of doing so? Were there any unexpected benefits or otherwise? You may want to walk back through the steps you have taken to define your solution and see if there are new ideas that come to mind.

## What next?

We are drawing to the end of the problem-solving chapter. Now you have the idea in mind about what you need to do, the next stage is turning to solve more of your problems rather than worrying about them. Return to your Worry Diary: what other problems do you need to take though this process? *Practise, practise, practise.* There are no short cuts or magic cures; the more you do, the better you will become at problem-solving and the more you will internalize the processes we have discussed. And you will develop mental pathways when faced with problems other than worrying.

This chapter has looked at the steps involved in solving problems. There were six stages. The first was defining the problem. The second was setting goals and considering roadblocks. The third was generating as many different solutions as possible. The fourth was choosing a solution. The fifth was putting solutions into action and the sixth was reviewing how you did. One size does not fit all and what you need to do, in terms of problemsolving, depends to a large extent on how you currently solve them.

### PIT STOP

Let's stop and think about what you have just been reading. Can you summarize the key ideas you have taken on board? Make a note of any new ideas that are sticking in your mind. What have you taken from this chapter? If you were to print your learning on a t-shirt, what would the slogan be? If you have any questions, jot these down too. You can return to them once you have had a chance to digest the information.

1.

2.

3.

**17**

# Learning to face your *Hypothetical Event Worry*

As you may have learned above, there are broadly speaking two different types of worry. Some of the problems we worry about actually exist: these we have called *Real Event Worries*. We learned that we can deal with this type of worry by problem-solving. But other worries are problems that could possibly exist, otherwise known as *Hypothetical Event Worries*. This second type of worries may never exist at all or may not exist in the sense that the worries are imagined by an individual, but they can feel very real, just as a nightmare feels real. This type of worry is often set in the distant future and is usually very unlikely to happen, so trying to problem-solve this type of worry is impossible. This chapter is about helping you to deal more effectively with this kind of worry.

In Chapter 5 we showed that most of the time *Real Event Worry* is about daily hassles or ongoing problems where there is actually something that can be done to solve them. There are indeed occasions when people worry about real events that are life-changing, but in these situations everyone will worry, not just worriers. However, as we have shown, worry often telescopes so that *Real Event Worry* about everyday hassles telescopes into *Hypothetical Event Worry*, which is almost always about potentially life-changing events at some point in the future.

In our clinical experience, we see many people for example who start to worry about the knocking noise in their washing machine, which then leads on to worrying about whether the machine is about to break down and needs fixing. But it is interesting that they don't then go on to worry, *What if this time next year, the washing machine is still making this noise and it still needs fixing*? It is far more likely that the worry about the noise will telescope into thoughts and 'flashes' of the house flooding, the leaks damaging the electrics and great damage occurring to their home; or how they will not be able to do the 'mountains of washing' when the washing machine has completely died and they cannot fix it or buy a new one, and then how others might judge them for not being able to send the kids to school in clean clothes. As you know, worry is not static, it spirals, moving on in both time and place while circulating around particular themes. There are no limits on where your worry will take you; it is bounded only by your imagination. Usually there are key themes or tracks that the worry takes, and the worry 'improvises' on and around these themes, much like a guitar solo that improvises around a chord or scale of notes.

So *Hypothetical Event Worry* almost always turns into 'horror stories', with images that are vivid, upsetting and seem very real at the time (remember the mirage analogy in Chapter 1). Indeed, if these scenarios were to happen, they would indeed be upsetting and may be very difficult to deal with. But they are *not happening yet* and may never happen; yet our emotional reactions to them are *as if* they were happening right now.

A critical message is that *Hypothetical Event Worry* is a stream of thoughts. These thoughts do not describe real events: they are not facts, they are thoughts. Though they can be powerful and influential, because of the feelings they generate, they are products of your imagination, spinning around things that are important to you. So, *Hypothetical Event Worry* ends up being about potentially life changing-events (that have not happened yet) and can involve themes of loss of loved ones, rejection by others, breakdown of important relationships, loss of financial security, illness and suffering and inability to face or cope with any of these. They can also be seen as threats to meeting one's goals or ambitions. In the washing machine example above, the goal may be to have a secure home or be an organized and respected parent and member of the community.

**PIT STOP**

For a moment return to your Worry Diary and think about the things that you worry about. Do you recognize what we are describing? Is it familiar to you? Make a note of some of the Hypothetical Event Worries that you have had. What themes have been emerging within your hypothetical worry? What things are sticking in your mind from the above? Write them down here.

1.

2.

3.

## Developing our understanding of worry – what lies at the heart of worry?

At the heart of worry lie our dreams and aspirations, our ambitions and goals. All of us are afraid when the things we value are threatened. For worriers, the thing that threatens these ambitions and goals arrives in the form of worry, and usually in the form of *Hypothetical Event Worry*. Because our goals and ambitions are set in the future, and the future is uncertain, there is uncertainty as to whether our ambitions and goals will be realized. These *splinters of doubt* trigger worry about threats to our hopes and aspirations. In the diagram below we have added this extra part, which now sits at the heart of worry: the *beating heart* of worry and the emotional core. The heart of worry may contain our goals and ambitions and at the same time contain strong visual images or powerful ideas about threats to the world we hold dear.

**Figure 17.1. The emotional core of worry.**

Let's take a 'concrete' example. Many of us will have the ambition of wanting a safe and secure home to live in. Think about the last time you sat looking at the wall. With the idea of a safe and secure home in mind, what's the first thing that goes through your mind when you first notice a small crack in the plaster? *What if . . .?* Where does your worry take you both in time and in place? If the first crack is followed by others, or widens, then the worry could telescope first to more redecoration and then spiral to thoughts of major and costly repairs – and a house that's impossible to sell. And the minor cosmetic cracks could be a sign of major structural problems and the possible collapse of the house, leading to our loved ones being trapped in the rubble with serious injuries. To reiterate, this would of course be terrible if it happened, but can you see how the emotional experience of the nightmare vision spirals from the tiny crack? The cracks in the plaster are like the doubts about whether our goals and ambitions will be realized. The doubts, like cracks, can spread and are elaborated until worry spirals from them. *Hypothetical Event Worry* is wholly out of proportion to the starting point. However, as it telescopes into the nightmare scenario while you are looking at your wall, sat in an armchair, you may experience some of the powerful feelings that you might have if indeed the house were at the point of falling down around you.

## Worry and upsetting emotional material

When we think about the experience of worry, we know that worry spreads out and hops around from one worry to the next. So we may start off by worrying about one thing and end up worrying about something completely different. It's important to ask why this happens, and why we move between worries so easily. It appears that worriers don't tend to settle on a worry for long enough to actually deal with it, either as a problem that can be solved in a practical way or as an upsetting emotional experience that can also be dealt with. Thus, with *Real Event Worry*, worriers find it difficult to get on and solve the problems (see Chapter 4), and with *Hypothetical Event Worry* they find it difficult to deal with the thoughts and feelings about terrible events that haven't happened yet (and probably never will happen). So *Hypothetical Event Worry* is about dealing with *the thought* of such things happening. Even though it is just a thought, let's not forget that these worries can feel awful and be terribly upsetting, like worrying about the death of a loved one, not succeeding in doing something that is really important, or being disgusted with oneself for being unable to cope. What is interesting is that worriers will experience an emotional rollercoaster as their worry plays out, and the feelings that the worry generates are very real. But, at the same time as their worry plays out they are often doing their level best to avoid *really seeing* the nightmares. It's a little like watching a film through your hands, or watching *Dr Who* from behind a sofa. It makes it much more frightening than if we simply watched from *on* the sofa or without our hands in front of our faces.

## How this keeps our worry alive

First, as we have said above, worriers 'allow' themselves to experience only some of the nightmare. They protect themselves from the worst moments by moving away quickly using worry as a 'get-away car'. They may also fast-forward through painful bits, or they may avoid focusing on the painful parts and focus instead on something less bothersome. Therapists call this cognitive avoidance. The overall effect is to see the worry out of focus, which means avoiding the painful and upsetting details. This part of the treatment means slowing down our *Hypothetical Event Worry* and bringing it into sharp focus to *see* what it contains. By doing this we can learn that we can handle it, and that we have nothing to fear from it. Second, it is no surprise that worriers want to move on and away from these difficult emotional ideas as quickly as possible. As they do this or avoid them the worrier discovers a way of managing them by making themselves feel less upset (*If I avoid it then I feel less upset; this works, so next time this happens I will avoid and so on . . .*). In this way their avoidance is reinforced. Third, they never learn that they may be able to cope or deal with the emotions or experiences that appear in their worry (the out of focus stuff mentioned above). Fourth, by not inspecting them in detail, they never get the opportunity to see if the nightmare is really likely to happen if this is really likely to happen – the glimpse of a nightmare scenario feels real, so it feels likely. Fifth, the other important thing that happens is that we are left with unfinished business; this might be a problem we have not resolved, or an idea about ourselves that we cannot face. Unfinished business tends to stick in our mind and demand attention; our minds are built this way. It helps us to remember what we need to remember and forget the rest. Imagine what it would be like if you remembered every detail and every moment – it would be overwhelming. So problems that have been solved or faced do not demand our attention: they get filed away and do not pop up out of the blue in the way that unfinished business does.

The idea that worry is used as a way of avoiding dealing with or facing painful emotional material was first developed from the 1980s onwards by Professor Tom Borkovec from Pennsylvania State University in the United States. Professor Borkovec was a pioneer in the exploration of worry; his ideas have influenced many other researchers and the treatment program that we are outlining was strongly influenced by his ideas.

## What is the emotional core?

Worry seems to revolve around the 'emotional core'. This is made up of the things that are fundamentally important to us, the things that we value in our lives. In a sense it is how you want your bit of the world to be – for example, wanting to be a good parent, having good health, being a valued colleague at work, becoming a thoughtful and caring person, providing for and protecting your loved ones and wanting to have the corner of the world you live in to be safe, predictable and certain.

The bad things that worriers tend to worry about in *Hypothetical Event Worry* tend to be things that threaten all that is important to them (such as being a good parent, financial security, their health, their relationships, their family and so on). In our washing machine example above, the important things might have been to have a safe and secure home and to be seen as a competent parent and an upstanding member of the community. These are ambitions that many of us would share. But when the washing machine started to make knocking noises, the worrier's sensitivity to uncertainty triggered worry: *What if the machine breaks? Then the things that I value may be taken away from me*. Their worry paints a picture and shows how their ambitions and goals might be thwarted. For example, their goal of a safe home is threatened by the worry that telescopes into thoughts and 'flashes' of the house flooding, the leaks damaging the electrics and so on. Can you see how this hypothetical worry threatens their ambition of a safe home? Their other ambition, to be seen as a competent parent by their neighbours, is threatened by the worry that *the washing machine has completely died and I cannot fix it or buy a new one, and then others will judge me for not being able to send the kids to school in clean clothes*. Can you see how this worry threatens the ambition of being a competent parent?

This is how an everyday happening that is a minor event in the great scheme of things can trigger feelings of uncertainty, especially among those who are particularly sensitive or intolerant of uncertainty. This leads to worry, which then telescopes, creating worries about threats to important ambitions or aspirations that the worrier holds.

As we have said, worriers are very sensitive to uncertainty, and in this example the *splinter of doubt* arrives in the form of a knocking in the washing machine. Worry is triggered by mundane, commonplace and everyday things. Our minds turn the uncertainty we find into nightmares, which are then felt to threaten all that we hold dear. Can you think about other examples where fairly innocuous things have triggered you to worry in this way? Think about noises you hear in the home, or comments people have made, or smells while travelling, or as yet unexplained pains in your body, or the slowness of a cash point, or juddering on a train, or loved ones who are feeling unwell. What kind of *Hypothetical Worry* did you have? How might this be related to something you hold dear, or an ambition that you might have or a goal that you may hold? Later we will use an exercise to help you to 'chase the rabbit' and follow this idea up. It is called the 'Downward Arrow Technique'.

## Flip-flopping – in and out of worry

Worry moves around and from emotionally powerful flashes and images into words, which may seem less emotionally powerful. The worrier is caught between wanting to look out for possible threats to their ambitions and aspirations and not wanting to look at the glimpses of potential disaster that threaten these. Within the emotional core are things that are fundamentally important to them, such as *being a certain type of person, or family, friends and community, or a safe and predictable world.* These are the things that they *value* – it's how they *want* their world to be.

However, worriers also tend to see their idealized world going horribly wrong. Thus, *Hypothetical Event Worry* involves glimpses of the potential for things to go wrong, of the threats to their worldview. It leads to uncertainty and to images of the end of their world, which flash through their mind; this is terrible and uncomfortable and quite naturally they do not want to think about it and this leads to other spirals of worry. The emotional core can also be thought of as having its own gravity, which is made up of what is important and valuable to us. This pulls the worrier back in towards it, but, again, the flashes of things going wrong repels and moves the worry away and on to a different worry, though the core pulls again, and away the worry moves now on to something else. This activity is repeated and repeated.

## Worry as a sign of hope?

It may seem an odd thing to say, but it can be very helpful for worriers to understand that worry is a sign of hope. For most worriers the problem is not that they believe they are inherently weak, worthless or incompetent, but that they *fear* this *may* be true. These fears threaten their sense of who they would like to be and the things that they would like to be able to do for themselves and others, leading them to feel anxious. In fact, worriers are in a strange way inherently optimistic in that they continue to aspire, they want to achieve things for themselves and others and better their situation. As bizarre as it may seem, they have hope; their worry tells us this. Put simply, if they did not have hope they would be very unlikely to worry. This does not mean that one must worry to have hope. It is the intolerance of uncertainty, together with the rules that people hold, that leads from hope to worry. So, most worriers have not *given up*. They continue to strive to achieve their goals and aspirations while worrying that they may fail; but they have not reached the conclusion that they *are* a failure. As we said in Chapter 1, worry is a burden, and worriers tend to get on and try to cope with life, worrying all the time but rarely giving in. This continual struggle might ring a bell for you when you think about your past, either your childhood or the period of your life before you started to notice that your worry was getting out of hand. Were you pursuing something important, or trying to meet multiple demands, and, although fearing that you may not succeed, continuing your efforts and striving (and worrying)?

The low mood that comes from worrying is linked to exhaustion and an erosion of self-efficacy. It has been described as demoralization and tends not to be about a stable and fundamental sense that the worrier is a failure and that the world is hopeless; but, rather, the worrier is concerned that this *may happen* and they *may feel helpless*. This they experience as a *threat* to the core sense of who they are, who they would like to be and the corner of the world that they want to live in with the people who are important to them.

## Worry in words and pictures

The other aspect of worry that hints at its role in avoiding painful emotional material is the relative lack of visual images found in worry. Worry is often experienced in words and tends not to have many clear pictures, although we may experiences flashes or images throughout our worry. Mental pictures or images are thought to make a much bigger emotional impact than those thoughts that are expressed in words. Mental images are known to trigger strong bodily sensations and experiences and lead to immediate behavioral reactions such as fight, flight or freeze. Because these mental pictures are so upsetting, the worrier has learned to use word-based worry as way of getting away from them. Worry almost becomes a 'get-away car' from the terrible images of what could happen to important people, goals or projects that lie with the emotional core of worry. We will come back to this idea later in this chapter.

There may also be other reasons why this switch away from images to thoughts occurs. As we mentioned in Chapter 3 regarding the evolutionary perspective to worry, when we worry there is an increase in brain activity in that area of the brain associated with planning type activities. If we do get fearful glimpses of what could go wrong in the future, it would be helpful in evolutionary terms (to the extent that this thing is likely to happen) to try to do something to counter this, such as planning and problem-solving. There would be no value in having the limbic system overactivated and staying in fear mode, trying to react with the immediate responses of fight, flight, or freeze, for something that could possibly happen in the future but is definitely not happening now. So, even the ability to have some images and glimpses of things going wrong in the future can have some value if they are realistic enough, and so would the observed switch away from these upsetting images to worry-like activity. Once again, it is a question of how much and how often, and then keeping worry for the big occasion rather than using it dozens of times a day for everyday hassles that tele-scope and then masquerade as life-changing events of great potential threat but low probability of occurring.

So, for the worrier *Hypothetical Event Worry* cannot lead to useful problem-solving because the problem is not imminent enough to define and so solve. This, together with intolerance of uncertainty and the tendency to see that every silver lining has a cloud, means that worrying will lead to a greater sense of threat with more glimpses of more things that could go wrong. If we experience painful and upsetting emotions about our future aspirations being thwarted, it not surprising that we avoid them as much as we can. This is especially true if we think we are unable to cope or deal with strong emotions. In the next section we will explore some of the subtle things we may do to avoid difficult emotional experiences. We will start with fear and think about how fear motivates avoidance, which in turn keeps our fear alive.

---

**PIT STOP**

Let's stop and think about what you have just been reading. Can you summarize the key ideas you have taken on board? Make a note of any new ideas that are sticking in your mind. What have you taken from this chapter? If you were to print your learning on a t-shirt, what would the slogan be? If you have any questions, jot these down too. You can return to them once you have had a chance to digest the information.

1.

2.

3.

---

## Fear keeps us safe and motivates avoidance

For a moment, let's think about when we were children. Like us, you may have believed that there were 'monsters' or other terrible things under the bed. If this is familiar to you, think about what you remember, using the following questions.

What things did you do to keep yourself safe from the monster? What things went through your mind as you lay in bed? Did pictures flash into your mind, which then kicked off worry – for instance, *What if it gets me? What if no one hears? What if I'm, taken off to a far away place?* And when these worries arrived, how did that leave you feeling? Did you try to push the thoughts of the monster away? Did you try to think about nice things instead? Did you count sheep, or focus on the wall-paper, rather than think about the monster? And did you ever flatly refuse to go to bed or make other excuses like, *Just a few more minutes and then I'll go to bed, promise*! Did you ever ask someone to check under the bed or did you run from the door and leap into bed? If you were like us, you may have made sure that you slept with your arms and legs tucked in, 'Just in case'. You might have scanned the room for noises, holding your breath so you could hear better, hearing your heart thumping and analysing every scratch, creak and knock, asking yourself, *What was that? What's happening? Who's there?* Your mind may have turned the noises into pictures, which flashed through your mind only to disappear into the pea soup. The images triggered thoughts and worries as in your imagination you 'saw' what was going on under the bed – big sharp, teeth, dripping jaws, menacing face, which pushed you further under the duvet and triggered much more worry. You may have tried listening out for the things that lurked there, but heard nothing, or started singing to yourself to block out the 'terrible pres-ence', but kept stopping just in case you had missed something. You may have tried to block the monster out of your mind by thinking nice thoughts, but the thought of the monster kept returning, more and more often, or the monster appeared in your daydream, popping up unexpectedly. You may have held a teddy much more tightly, because you hoped that the teddy would keep you safe. You may have avoided looking under the bed for fear of discovering the awful things that lurked there. From time to time, you may have worked up the courage to look but done so very quickly; and by only snatching a glance you never really got a good look at what was there. You might have seen shadows or strange forms, which your mind then built into signs of the monster, which kicked off more worry. *What if he's moved? He might be crawling up the leg of the bed . . .*

Does this sound familiar? There are two main things we would like to draw your attention to. The first is that the overriding pattern within this story is avoidance of anything to do with the horrible thing that lies at the heart of the fear (the monster). The second is the way that our avoidance actually makes the problem much worse. Later we will spell out the ways the different layers of avoidance keep the fear alive. But this is like the layers on an onion; each layer keeps us from the awful things that lie at the heart of our fear. Helping a child or an adult to overcome their fear usually involves getting them to face whatever lies at the heart of their fear. This is usually best done in a stepwise way, starting off with the easier thing and moving towards the final fear. In our clinical experience, our minds seem to always make things much worse than they actually are; our mind is both our greatest asset and our greatest foe when it comes to fearful situations.

Before we go on, because you are now familiar with many of the strategies that are used to manage worry, and the way that our thoughts, feelings and actions keep problems going, it might be worth rereading the monster under the bed example and see if you can spot the things that keep the problem going (by the way, we have been told quite categorically by Hannah, aged 3, that these days there are no monsters that live under beds. Most have now retired to Florida, where they play golf, relive their glory days and leave alligators to stray under beds to scare the locals).

With your notebook and pen, review the monster under the bed example and see if you can begin to work out what might keep the fear alive. Use the following questions to help you:

- What actions might serve to keep the fear of the monster alive? How might this work using thoughts, feelings and behaviors?
- How might worry act as an avoidance strategy?
- Are there strategies that we have discussed in previous chapters that appear here as well? How might these keep the fear alive?
- Can you spot any safety behaviors?

If this exercise proves tricky, read the following section on avoidance strategies and come back to it. It's helpful to see the patterns in something other than your own worry, and this will help you to spot the patterns in your worry.

## Avoidance strategies

### Strategy 1. Suppression

One of the ways that worriers try to avoid worrying thoughts and images is to try to push the difficult images or powerful feelings to the back of their minds or by trying not to think about them. Unfortunately, this rarely works for long and there are good reasons why this approach fails. Before we go on, try the following exercise.

## PINK ELEPHANT EXERCISE

Take a blank piece of paper with a pencil. For the next minute or so, choose a subject that you want to think about and let your mind roam around this subject. As you are doing so, we would like you to do one thing; *do not think about a pink elephant*. Do not think about the pink elephant either in words, thoughts, pictures or images. Now put the book down, close your eyes and spend a few moments thinking about whatever you want to. With your pencil make a mark every time the elephant comes to mind.

Before you read on just reflect for a moment on what happens when you try *not* to think about the pink elephant. For most people, the act of trying not to think about the elephant means that they end up thinking about it even more. The thought, *I must not think about a pink elephant* reminds us about the pink elephant. Even if we are successful at blocking the elephant out, it often appears in another way, peaking out from behind whatever it is we have used to push it out with. The colour pink may appear in our thoughts, or the fact that our mind is full of something else we have purposely put in the way of the elephant means that once this leaves our mind the elephant will pop up again. Or we may know that there is something behind the thoughts we are trying to ignore; it's like pushing a balloon under the water – it always wants to resurface. *So, trying not to think about something seems to make us think about it all the more.* Can you see how this might apply to your worry or the pictures that might flash into your mind? What happens when you try to push worrying thoughts or images out of your mind?

With worry it takes a lot of effort and energy to hold our thoughts 'under the surface', but unfortunately this does nothing to make them go away and, like the balloon, they eventually resurface. How much energy and effort do you put into trying to push your worries out? Is the amount of effort you put in worthwhile? Often, the worries resurface at the worst times, when we can do very little about them, such as in the early hours of the morning or when our attention is demanded by something else.

With the pink elephant experiment you may find the pink elephant popping up in your mind later or in your dreams in the coming days. This is called the *rebound effect*, where things we have tried to ignore pop up spontaneously even when we have given up trying not to think about them. Again can you see how this might apply to your worry or to the images that flash through your mind?

So what should we do instead? The simple answer is that we should try not to push our thoughts below the surface. While this may not make our worries any less worrying or actually stop them from happening, it may have at least two important influences. First, you will spend less energy and effort trying to push these thoughts out of your mind. Second, you may in this way reduce the amount of worry by breaking a vicious cycle where trying to push the worries out makes you worry all the more. This reduces the amount of worry.

**EXERCISE 17.1: SUPPRESSION**

How typical or characteristic is this strategy for you?

| Not like me at all | A little like me | Somewhat like me | Moderately like me | Mostly like me | Nearly like me | Completely like me |
|---|---|---|---|---|---|---|
| 0 | 1 | 2 | 3 | 4 | 5 | 6 |

Can you think of a specific worry or image where you tried to push it to the back of your mind or tried to suppress it?

In this example, what impact did doing this have on your worry?

What do can you do to address this?

*Hint: Rather than trying to push the images or your worry away, allow them to surface. Hold it in your mind, and if you find yourself pushing it out, bring it back to the front of your mind.*

## Strategy 2. Distraction

This is another way of avoiding facing an issue, but rather than trying to push a thought out we choose to try to think of or do something else instead. This means that we give ourselves tasks so that we don't have the 'space' to worry – for example, you might choose to watch TV, read, clean the house or put things in order (grocery cupboards, toolboxes, sock draw and so on). Sometimes worriers do two or three of these at once as a 'belts and braces' approach to ensure that they do not have the mental space to worry. Distraction can also take the form of mental activity, such as doing sums in your head or imagining some beautiful deserted beach with palm trees and so forth. Unfortunately, however, distraction rarely works: slowly the worry will creep back in since it is more than likely linked to some unfinished business that will keep demanding your attention until we deal with it. Another of the problems worriers face is that the product of worry, namely anxiety, is accompanied by strong bodily sensations. While the worrier's mind might be able to focus on something other than their worry, the butterflies in their stomach or the muscular tension act to remind them of their worry. For example, if a worrier was using a daydream to distract themselves, at the back of their mind they might notice the feeling of butterflies and incorporate this into their daydream. Slowly this will be followed by other thoughts and worries, which dissolve the daydream and bring them back to the reality of their worry. Try as we might, it is impossible to run away from the things in our minds. While the thought of doing so might be scary, the critical message is that, rather than avoiding these painful and difficult worries, we need to face them.

## EXERCISE 17.2: DISTRACTION

How typical or characteristic is this strategy for you?

| Not like me at all | A little like me | Somewhat like me | Moderately like me | Mostly like me | Nearly like me | Completely like me |
|---|---|---|---|---|---|---|
| 0 | 1 | 2 | 3 | 4 | 5 | 6 |

Can you think of a personal example where you might have tried to distract yourself from a worry? How did you do this?

In this example, what impact did doing this have on your worry?

What can you do to address this?

*Hint: Rather than trying to find other things to do, bring your worry to mind on purpose. Notice what happens when you face your worry rather than distract yourself from it.*

## Strategy 3. Avoidance of mental pictures in worry

As we have mentioned above, worry is interesting because of the relative lack of pictures or images that make up the whirlwind of worry. Research has found that worry is a predominantly word-based experience, meaning that we mostly worry in words not pictures. Stop for a moment and think about this: how do you experience the whirlwind? Is it mostly in pictures or mostly in thoughts or words?

When images do appear in worry, they tend to 'pop up' or flash into our minds, appearing and disappearing very quickly. As we have mentioned above, our worry can be thought of as a get-away car – it helps us to escape from these mental pictures. Why would we want to escape them? Mainly we want to escape them because of what they show, namely awful and horrible things that no one would want to dwell on. But we also want to avoid them because of the strong emotions and bodily experiences that they provoke. By comparison to word-based worry, images provoke much stronger emotions and bodily sensations. Imagine a thick slice of chocolate cake. Picture it in your mind's eye: think of the texture of the icing, the soft, moist sponge and the way the light is caught by the icing. Then *see* yourself taking a bite, see the crumbs falling, and 'picture' the taste exploding in your mouth. See yourself licking your lips as you taste the chocolate. What happens? What sensation do you notice?

Images are packed with information and you may have noticed that using your 'mind's eye' to imagine the chocolate cake-triggered salivation may have also triggered a desire for chocolate cake. Worrying predominantly in words seems to help us to avoid the sharp and painful experiences that come with these images. Strangely enough, worry can have a kind of soothing quality, since it transports the worrier away from the painful images that might flash through their mind. Images or mental pictures provoke stronger reactions in our bodies and trigger stronger emotions, and so if we worry in words we are less likely to be upset or physiologically aroused. Thus we can understand why worry is used as the get-away car from these often apocalyptic images.

## EXERCISE 17.3: AVOIDANCE OF MENTAL PICTURES IN WORRY

How much of your worry is in words and how much is in pictures?

Write down an estimate.

Words _____%

Pictures _____%

Are there images that you know you avoid thinking about or that flash into your mind and are then quickly pushed away? If so what are they? If you can, write down a description of them. What feelings and sensations do you experience when you have these images?

Can you think of a personal example where you might have had an image followed by a worry stream? What was the image and what worry followed this?

What impact did the image have on your worry?

What can you do to address this?

*Hint:* Rather than moving away form the image, move towards it. Describe it: close you eyes and picture it. What do you see? Draw it.

## Strategy 4. Mental gymnastics – changing the detail of our worry

There are many seemingly small and insignificant things that people do to manage the images found in their hypothetical worry. As the term mental gymnastics suggests, these are ways of twisting and turning around the images in our worry to avoid them. For example, we may avoid the worst parts by 'fast forwarding'. When discussing their nightmare images with others, a worrier may talk in general terms about them but never talk about the detail. They may fear telling others about their experiences because, if they did, then they might fear that the worry was more likely to happen, or that telling someone about their thoughts might lead them to think us odd or strange. We may try to neutralize the anxiety we experience by thinking of something else, replacing negative images or thoughts with positive ones. Many worry rules (see Chapter 11) might be active at this level, such as, *If I think it, then it could happen.* The overall impact of all these gymnastic movements is that the worrier fails to face their fear head on, which, as you will now understand, maintains their fear.

In the monsters under the bed metaphor above, in order to overcome the fear, the bottom line was that the child needed to face its fear to learn that there was nothing under the bed. This would also mean stopping mental gymnastics, like running from the door to the bed, or asking others to check or only snatching glances under the bed. Of course, these are easier said than done, as the feelings of fear are very real. In order to overcome their fear, they needed to challenge the underlying idea that there was a monster under their bed. This is also true for facing the fearful images that appear in *Hypothetical Event Worry*. In the case of the distressing images and streams of worry, we need to turn our attention to the images and face them 'square on'.

## EXERCISE 17.4: MENTAL GYMNASTICS

In general, thinking about how you manage the difficult images in *Hypothetical Event Worry*, how typical are the ideas mentioned above to you?

| Not like me at all | A little like me | Somewhat like me | Moderately like me | Mostly like me | Nearly like me | Completely like me |
|---|---|---|---|---|---|---|
| 0 | 1 | 2 | 3 | 4 | 5 | 6 |

Which of the gymnastics do you use? Write them down here. What images or worrying thoughts were you trying to avoid? If you can, write these down too.

What can you do to address this?

*Hint: What would happen if, rather than trying to avoid the worst moments, you faced them? What if you slowed things down, or focused on the images? What would happen if you did not try to think of nice things to counter the negative? Can you think of an experiment to test this out?*

### Strategy 5. Avoidance of situations

As we have mentioned in previous chapters, worriers may avoid situations that they know are likely to trigger worry (i.e. uncertain situations). The avoidance that links to the emotional core of worry has a different flavour. The worrier is trying to avoid situations or events that match closely with what they imagine in their *Hypothetical Event Worry*. In these cases the worrier doesn't have to telescope their worry; the material is already there and because it's familiar they are already primed to feel terrible. So, if a worrier had awful images of a loved one being involved in a car crash, they may avoid watching TV programs where car accidents may feature because they know that they will feel terrible if their worry is triggered. So the *real*-world situations almost hotwire the worry and the feelings that come with it. The links between real situations and *Hypothetical Event Worry* can be less clear, when there are themes that bridge between them. For instance, if a worrier's goals and ambitions were about staying healthy and well for their children, then a film or book about a person who suddenly succumbs to illness and dies might well go to the heart of their worry. Sometimes this is present in the language that people use, *'Don't talk about that, you'll get me going'* or *'If I do that, then I know where that will take me.'* If there is any agreement between the things they 'see' in their *Hypothetical Event Worry* and the things they experience in the real world, then this is taken as a sign that they are right to be worried, because what they fear actually happens. However, some of the evidence for this is found in drama and movies, which need things to happen in order to create the tension and the gripping yet perfect finale. Think about news programs: they will often finish with a nice happy human-interest story such as the skate-boarding dog from Stevenage, or the budgie in Bristol that can salsa. The rest of the news is almost uniformly 'bad news', with reports of multiple pile-ups, train and plane crashes, or near misses, the horrific crime, the big financial scandal, none of which really represents a true picture of life. The millions of safe journeys by cars, planes, trains and other modes of transport, the millions of evenings out that did not end in murder, the billions of financial trans-actions that have been fairly and honestly conducted and so on are never reported. The 'bad news' stories are indeed terrible – this is why they are reported – but this does not mean that they are likely or imminent in most people's lives on a day-to-day basis. But their upsetting nature does make them seem more real.

So, worriers avoid situations for many reasons, but some-times the avoidance is about the links between what they worry about in their minds and what appears in the world for real. The boundary can feel blurred between what is real and what is imagined, but again this tells us the best way forward is to face the worry and see, once and for all, what is really going on.

Uncertainty also plays its part in *Hypothetical Event Worry*: for instance, a parent may make sure they arrive home after the rest of their family because they know that waiting for them will trigger all sorts of dark thoughts about things that could go wrong. Some worriers may avoid meeting the financial adviser at their local bank because they know they will be asked to make choices, and the uncertainty around these decisions provokes worry. In this case, hypothetical worry might be about the potential loss of their home, or struggling on the bread line in their retirement as they have made bad financial decisions. As you will understand, avoiding dealing with these issues means that they continue to worry and they never learn to manage their worry in a new way. Also, remember that worry is an awful, fatiguing, exhausting preoccupation, and the cost of worrying is very high. Learning to face your worry and deal with it might in the short term make you feel more anxious and upset, but in the longer term you will move towards overcoming it.

## EXERCISE 17.6: AVOIDING SITUATIONS

How typical or characteristic is this strategy for you?

| Not like me at all | A little like me | Somewhat like me | Moderately like me | Mostly like me | Nearly like me | Completely like me |
|---|---|---|---|---|---|---|
| 0 | 1 | 2 | 3 | 4 | 5 | 6 |

Can you think of a personal example where you avoided a situation because you knew that it matched with some of the things that appeared in your hypothetical worry? What was the situation, and what was the worry that you were trying to avoid thinking about?

In this example, what impact did doing this have on your worry?

What can you do to address this?

*Hint: Make a list of the situations that you avoid because they are linked with what you 'see' or think in your Hypothetical Event Worry. Chose an easier one to work on first, and expose yourself to the situation. How does the situation link with your worry? What do you notice by doing this?*

## Assessing the degree to which you avoid

The cognitive avoidance questionnaire that follows will help you to assess which type of avoidance you use most often. It measures suppression of thoughts, swapping negative thoughts for good thoughts, distraction, avoiding situations or actions that might lead to worry, and it also tries to measure how much a worrier might transform a distressing image into words. There are two possible uses for this questionnaire. The first is to help you get a snap shot of the things that you might do to avoid thinking about your worry. The second is that it might be a helpful tool to assess change. So, complete it early on and return to it once you have had a chance to use some of the ideas in this chapter.

## COGNITIVE AVOIDANCE QUESTIONNAIRE

People react differently to certain types of thoughts. Using the following scale, indicate to what extent each of the following statements is typical of the way that you respond to certain thoughts. Circle the appropriate number (1 to 5).

| Item number | Not at all typical | A little typical | Somewhat typical | Very typical | Completely typical |
|---|---|---|---|---|---|
| 1. There are things that I would rather not think about. | 1 | 2 | 3 | 4 | 5 |
| 2. I avoid certain situations that lead me to pay attention to things I don't want to think about. | 1 | 2 | 3 | 4 | 5 |
| 3. I replace threatening mental images with things I say to myself in my mind. | 1 | 2 | 3 | 4 | 5 |
| 4. I think about things that concern me as if they were occurring to someone else. | 1 | 2 | 3 | 4 | 5 |
| 5. I have thoughts that I try to avoid. | 1 | 2 | 3 | 4 | 5 |
| 6. I try not to think about the most upsetting aspects of some situations so as not to be too afraid. | 1 | 2 | 3 | 4 | 5 |

7. I sometimes avoid objects that can trigger upsetting thoughts.

  1     2     3     4     5

8. I distract myself to avoid thinking about certain disturbing subjects.

  1     2     3     4     5

9. I avoid people who make me think about things I don't want to think about.

  1     2     3     4     5

10. I often do things to distract myself from my thoughts.

  1     2     3     4     5

11. I think about trivial details so as not to think about important subjects that worry me.

  1     2     3     4     5

12. Sometimes I throw myself into an activity so as not to think about certain things.

  1     2     3     4     5

13. To avoid thinking about subjects that upset me I force myself to think about something else.

  1     2     3     4     5

14. There are things I try not to think about.

  1     2     3     4     5

15. I keep saying things to myself in my head to avoid visualizing scenarios (a series of mental images) that frighten me.

  1     2     3     4     5

| | | | | |
|---|---|---|---|---|
| 16. Sometimes I avoid places that make me think about things I would prefer not to think about. | 1 | 2 | 3 | 4 | 5 |
| 17. I think about past events so as not to think about future events that make me feel insecure. | 1 | 2 | 3 | 4 | 5 |
| 18. I avoid actions that remind me of things I do not want to think about. | 1 | 2 | 3 | 4 | 5 |
| 19. When I have mental images that are upsetting, I say things to myself in my head to replace the images. | 1 | 2 | 3 | 4 | 5 |
| 20. I think about many little things so as not to think about more important matters. | 1 | 2 | 3 | 4 | 5 |
| 21. Sometimes I keep myself occupied just to prevent thoughts from popping up in my mind. | 1 | 2 | 3 | 4 | 5 |
| 22. I avoid situations that involve people who make me think about unpleasant things. | 1 | 2 | 3 | 4 | 5 |

23. Rather than having images of upsetting events form in my mind, I try to describe the events using an internal monologue (things that I say to myself in my head).

1    2    3    4    5

24. I push away the mental images related to a threatening situation by trying to describe the situation using an internal monologue.

1    2    3    4    5

25. I think about things that are worrying other people rather than thinking about my own worries.

1    2    3    4    5

Source: © 2006 Taylor & Francis Group LLC. P. Gosselin, F. Langlois, M. H. Freeston, R. Ladouceur, M. J. Dugas and O. Pelletier, 'Le Questionnaire d'Evitement Cognitif (QEC): Développement et validation auprès d'adultes et d'adolescents', *Journal de thérapie comportementale et cognitive*, 12 (2002). Reproduced with permission of Taylor & Francis Group LLC.

| Type of avoidance | Items | My score |
|---|---|---|
| Suppressing worrisome thoughts | 4, 11, 17, 20, 25 | |
| Substituting neutral or positive thoughts for worries | 3, 15, 19, 23, 24 | |
| Using distraction as a way to interrupt worrying | 8, 10, 12, 13, 21 | |
| Avoiding action/situations that can lead to worrisome thoughts | 7, 9, 16, 18, 22 | |
| Transforming mental images into thoughts as words | 1, 2, 5, 6, 14 | |

Add up your score for each subscale. Which subscale stands out the most? Which do you score most highly on? It might be worth plotting your score out on a graph (see page 281 for an idea of what this might look like).

## Learning to face our fears

As we mentioned above, this chapter is focused on helping you to deal with *Hypothetical Event Worry*. We have highlighted the role of suppressing our thoughts, distracting ourselves, avoiding situations that trigger worry and the subtle mental gymnastics that we use to help us manage these awful experiences. In the monsters under the bed example, we learnt that we needed to face our fears, and this is no different for our worry. So what does this mean? It means confronting the thing that frightens us. It means focusing on our *Hypothetical Event Worry*, and slowing it down and exploring in detail the images that flash through our minds.

## Discovering the themes of *Hypothetical Event Worry*

For many reasons it may be helpful to be able to spot the themes that underpin your worry. By recognizing the themes, you may be able to interrupt the flow much more readily by spotting these well-worn paths. It will also help to remind you that, while your worry moves and shifts, it does so around themes: usually there are between one and three of these. It also helps to understand more about who you are and what's important to you, or what you value. This last issue is important, because knowing this will help you to understand more about why you worry about the things you do. For instance, in *Hypothetical Event Worry* a worrier may see images of their children being abducted, or being seriously injured in car crashes, or ending up on the streets and on drugs, and so on. It's *not* that the worrier wants these things to happen at some unconscious level; rather, it tells us categorically that one of their main goals is to look after and protect their children. Their worry spirals because of the possible threats to their goal, triggered by uncertainty in everyday situations such as the children walking home from school, a school bus trip or an argument at home.

In order to help you to spot the themes that underpin your worry we will provide you with some examples so that you can track your worry back to its core. And then you will need to pick one of your own worries and see if you can do the same.

## Spotting underlying themes

Worry tends to follow themes that are linked to what is important to us. So, if my ambition or goal is to be financially secure, then often the hypothetical worries will revolve around the things that threaten this goal. There is a powerful technique that we can use to help you to find out what the central themes are: this is called the *downward arrow* technique. This is a method of chaining worries together and following the links to the core of our worry. The key questions that are repeated are, *Supposing that were true, what would happen next?* and *Supposing that were true, what would be so bad about that?*

The first step is to find a hypothetical worry to work on. In the example above this might be, *What if my finances get out of control?* We then link the worry by asking the 'supposing' questions to see where they take us. The examples below are from a worrier.

**TABLE 17.1**

| What if my plane crashes? | What if my children grow up to be criminals? | What if my health deteriorates? |
|---|---|---|
| Supposing that were true, what would happen next? | Supposing that were true, what would be so bad about that? | Supposing that were true, what would happen next? |
| ↓ | ↓ | ↓ |
| *I would be dead.* | *I would struggle to feel close to them.* | *I wouldn't be able to get out and do the things I love to do.* |
| ↓ | ↓ | ↓ |
| Supposing that were true, what would be so bad about that? | Supposing that were true, what would be so bad about that? | Supposing that were true, what would be so bad about that? |
| ↓ | ↓ | ↓ |
| *My family wouldn't cope.* | *I might reject them.* | *I would lose contact with my friends.* |
| ↓ | ↓ | ↓ |
| Supposing that were true, what would happen next? | Supposing that were true, what would be so bad about that? | Supposing that were true, what would happen next? |
| ↓ | ↓ | ↓ |
| *They would go off the rails and end up on the streets.* | *I would be a terrible parent.* | *I would spend more time alone.* |
| What might be the theme? What might this person value? | What might be the theme? What might this person value? | What might be the theme? What might this person value? |
| What is their goal in worrying? | What is their goal in worrying? | What is their goal in worrying? |

In the examples above, what might you think were the core values and aspirations for this person? The first two worries suggest that they valued their family above all, and that their goal might be to be a good parent. Can you see how their worry developed around this theme? For the third column, a new theme is starting to emerge related to the importance of friends. We would need to chain a few more worries down to see whether or not this emerged as a theme. With our worries, all roads lead to the core, so it doesn't really matter which *Hypothetical Event Worry* you choose. Also, we may get to the core quite quickly or it may take us some time. Do not expect them to fall out in three steps like the examples above. As a rule of thumb, when you get to the bottom of the chain you will notice that the answers you come up with start to get repetitive, and then you have probably gone far enough. If you come up with a feeling as an answer, such as *I would feel terrible* or *I would feel bad*, then try to expand this by asking, *And if I felt this, what problems might that cause me?*

## GETTING TO THE CORE OF OUR WORRY — WORRY THEMES

Choose a recent *Hypothetical Event Worry*. Use the downward arrow questions and see if you can track or chain your worry back to the core ideas. Once you have done one worry, what do you notice?

Now choose another and do the same again. How are they similar? What is different about them? What themes might be emerging? What are you learning about what you value and your goals and ambitions? Step back from the exercise, take a few minutes and come back to what you have written: do you see any patterns? Do the answers seem as if they are striking a chord? Do they seem to far fetched?

And now take a third worry: do the same and review and so on. Once you have two themes, use them as a way of thinking about other worries. Can you see how these themes help you to make sense of these other worries? Can you see how your *Hypothetical Event Worry* is revolving around these themes?

This is a first step to focusing on the fears that go to make up your *Hypothetical Event Worry*. As with the monsters under the bed scenario, we now have to help you to face the worry without suppression, distraction or mental gymnastics.

## Writing down your *Hypothetical Event Worry*

You may feel a little daunted by this, which is entirely understandable. You may say to yourself, *This will make my worry much worse!* Or you may think, *I won't be able to handle facing my worry.* But how do you know this? What evidence do you have to support this? How might thinking this keep you locked into a vicious cycle?

Remember that you probably experience these nightmarish daydreams at least every day and often for prolonged periods of time and that trying to avoid them or not thinking about them has made no difference. As one client said, 'I've tried not talking and thinking about this and that didn't work.' So you have probably been trying one strategy (avoidance) to manage your worry for a very long time. Has using avoidance helped to reduce the impact of your worry?

The bottom line is that we know that writing down things that concern us works. It is a very useful strategy for all sorts of reasons and for sorts of problems, which we will go into below.

Let's return to the monsters under the bed example. Glancing under the bed is no good because it doesn't let us get to see what is *really* under there. And because we don't ever get a good look, rather than making us feel better our efforts trigger doubt and uncertainty, leading to more worry. In order to put the fear behind you, you need to have a good look – into the corners, behind whatever is under there, shaking out hidden things, using a light to see clearly, maybe even moving the bed.

How do we have a good look at out worry? Well, we don't have to do this all at once; we can gradually build up. Actually we have to do it this way, because each time you write out an account of your *Hypothetical Event Worry* you will discover new corners that you have not looked into. So this is a series of steps, eventually ending up with all of the worry exposed.

## Why should I do this?

Writing things down is helpful for a number of reasons. First, seeing things written down helps us to stand away from our worries, rather than being in them. It might also begin to change the way you think about your worry. We might be able to see how realistic your worries really are and to find out what really bothers you about your worry, rather than guessing based on glimpses and flashes. Writing has been found by research to be a powerful therapeutic intervention. It can help us to process emotions: since we feel the experience as we write it, writing can help us to explore the themes within our words, so adding understanding and structure, which again can be very helpful. Writing also forces you to organize your thoughts; it stands in the opposite corner to avoidance. As someone said, *When I hear myself speak, I know what I think*. This is also true for writing.

As a first writing attempt, chose a *Hypothetical Event Worry*. You may want to use one of those from your chaining exercise above. Take a notebook and pen and write down your worry. Imagine that you had to help someone to make a movie of your worry – think of all the *details* they would need to know. Use the prompts below to help you add the detail.

## Tips: what to include in my writing

*Setting the scene:* Who is involved in your worry? What happens in your worry? Where and when is the worry happening? What do you see? Describe exactly what you see in detail. Is there anything that would help someone to understand the context of the worry? Again, imagine the film crew trying to capture your worry; what else do they need?

*Actions:* What do you or others do in your worry? If the answer is nothing, then what motivates you or others to do nothing?

*Your emotional reactions:* Keep asking yourself, *How am I feeling now?* Add this into the account. How do you feel?

*Body sensations:* What bodily sensations are you experiencing? How does your body feel right now? Where in your body are you feeling these sensations?

*Sensory information:* What can I smell, hear, touch, feel and see?

*The meaning:* What goes through your mind as you see your worry unfolding? What does your worry say or mean to you? What do the actions of others in your worry mean? What do the picture or images tell you? What is the worst thing about this? What does this say about you as a person?

*Time information:* Is it day or night? Is it morning, afternoon or evening, summer, winter?

*Images:* Focus on these, describe them in detail: what do you see? Draw a sketch of what you see; who is in the image, where are they, what is happening to them? What goes through your mind when you see this picture?

*Hypothetical Event Worry* is a stream of thoughts. These *thoughts* do not describe real events, *they are not facts*, they are *thoughts*; they are products of your imagination, spinning around things that are important to you.

## More tips: how to write

Choose a quiet moment, a time when you know you will not be disturbed – perhaps also a time when you know you are unlikely to worry. So you may want to avoid doing this late at night to start with. Remind yourself that you have control over this process; no one can force you to do this. If you need reminding about why you are doing this, then reread the sections above.

When you start to write, do so in the first person and in the present tense. That is, write as if the account is happening right now – for instance, *I am thinking that my 17-year-old son is in a car accident; I can see his face contorted in pain and crying out for me saying . . .*, rather than, *My 17-year-old son was in a car accident and he cried out for me.* Can you see how the first version brings you much closer to the experience, which reduces the avoidance?

The key message is about wholly engaging with your worry; this means we also have to keep an eye out for mental gymnastics. As you are writing you may be trying to think of nice things to neutralize the bad things that are going on the page. This is based on the assumption that there is something to fear by writing things down. But on the first few attempts it's OK to use mental gymnastics, so long as you are moving towards the goal of writing a full account of your worry, without using them.

Sometimes it might feel as if the worry has no ending: just keep writing until you have passed what might be the worst moment for you; or, if you notice that you are going around in a circle, then this might be time to stop. Remember that we are also trying to help you sit with uncertainty: the aim is not about finding a good ending – actually, it might be better if the ending were left hanging, as this will trigger more uncertainty, which you need to learn to tolerate.

It is normal to feel upset when doing this – the ideas and images may indeed be terrible. The reason why you find them upsetting is because *you really care* and it is the last thing that you want to happen. Being able to tolerate upsetting thoughts and images will not make you insensitive or uncaring. It will mean that you can in fact tell the difference between thoughts and reality, treat thoughts as thoughts that don't need to be managed or controlled or avoided, and then get on with dealing with reality, which is the pursuit of things that are important to you. So, tolerate the upset now while learning to treat upsetting thoughts as thoughts will move you towards the things that really matter. Imagine not being hijacked and terrified by your worry; imagine being able to just be, participating and enjoying in the moment – living, not worrying.

Review the above, take a notebook and pen and start to write.

## The second draft

Once you have your first draft it's time to review it to see if you have included all the details. Are there sections that you know you have skipped through? What were the worst moments? Have you written all that you could about these worries? Were you using mental gymnastics to help?

**PIT STOP**

Let's pause again and think about what you have just been reading. What new ideas or thoughts are coming into play now? Are you thinking any differently about your *Hypothetical Event Worry*? What things are sticking in your mind?

1.

2.

3.

Once you have a detailed account of your worry, then you are now ready to move into the final stage. This requires you to expose yourself in a structured way to what you have written. Before we do this, we will spend a few moments talking about how we work with fear.

The same principles underpin the approach to worry, the approach to the monsters under the bed or, say, to a phobia of dogs. To help someone overcome the latter we would enable them to spend time with dogs, so that they can *learn* to face their fear. For the exposure to be helpful, they have to stay with the dogs until their fear naturally comes down – which it will. With the monsters, it's about working out what is a discarded sock and what is one's imagination. With dogs it's also about learning how dogs behave and how to behave with dogs, and to find out the difference between real dogs and the those of our nightmares and dreams. *There is a concern that anxiety, once started, will go on and on; this just isn't the case.* Our anxiety will come down, even without our doing anything to make it come down. We have to learn to allow the wave of fear to wash over us, letting go of all our attempts to avoid or control it so that we can find out that nothing bad will happen. Indeed, on the other side of the wave of fear we find relative calm. As we mentioned above, anxiety is a very useful emotion, and in an evolutionary sense it tells us when we need to fight, run away or freeze, but in the case of phobias, worry or fears of monsters it has ceased to be of help because it is out of proportion to the real danger. The content of our *Hypothetical Event Worry* produces anxiety because it poses threats to those things we value and hold dear, and it is this threat that we need to expose ourselves to.

The possibility that things could go wrong is in an absolute sense true, since nothing is impossible. Arguing that it might be highly unlikely is not really going to wash – the worrier has to learn to live with uncertainty rather than put great efforts into managing it. With this in mind, there are a number of things that worriers need to 'expose' themselves to. The first is worry itself; the second is the absolute certainty of uncertainty; and the third, knowing that their aspirations and goals will always feel threatened and, that at some times and for some people, goals are indeed thwarted and ambitions are not realized. Life is about adjustment, adapting and coping and then finding new goals in the event that these things do happen. Our thoughts are powerful and produce strong feelings, but, as you will know, the things that we see in our *Hypothetical Event Worry* are highly unlikely to ever happen.

### Finally

So, in order to work with your *Hypothetical Event Worry*, it is important to sit with your feelings without doing anything to make them better. The initial reaction drives us away from the thing we fear, that is, facing the detail of your worry square on. Ask yourself, *What is the worst thing that could happen?* Yes, you will feel anxious, but as you learn to face you fears, your anxiety will decrease. They will, over time come down on their own, but you need to find this out for yourself.

Take the final and detailed version of your *Hypothetical Event Worry* and read and reread it for 30 minutes a day. Use the 'Facing your fear' form below to record the experience. Note that the form asks you to rate your anxiety before, during and after using the scale provided. Once you have done this with one worry, choose another. Probably you will need to do this two to three times.

It is important to record your reflections and thoughts as you are doing this. For example, has doing this exercise taught you anything new about your worry? Has your relationship with the *Hypothetical Event Worries* changed in any way and if so, how? Do you see your *Hypothetical Event Worries* any differently? Can you recognize them sooner now? Are you able to interrupt them, or have you found things that you can say to help you to 'put the brakes on'?

### EXERCISE 17.7: FACING YOUR FEAR

Aim to fill out a form each time you face your *Hypothetical Event Worry*. Use the scale below to rate your anxiety or discomfort. Remember you need to work with your worry for long enough for the feelings to reduce.

### Anxiety/Discomfort Scale

| None | | Slight | | Moderate | | High | | Extreme |
|------|---|--------|---|----------|---|------|---|---------|
| 1 | 2 | 3 | 4 | 5 | 6 | 7 | 8 | 9 |

Session No._____

Day or date _____     Start time ___:___ Finish time ___:___

Place _____     Worry _____

Anxiety/Discomfort     Before ____ During (max) ____ After ____
*(please use scale)*

Did you use mental gymnastics?     No ____ A little ____ A lot ____
How did you do this?     _____

Session No._____

Day or date _____     Start time ___:___ Finish time ___:___

Place _____     Worry _____

Anxiety/Discomfort     Before ____ During (max) ____ After ____
*(please use scale)*

Did you use mental gymnastics?     No ____ A little ____ A lot ____
How did you do this?     _____

Session No._____

Day or date _____     Start time ___:___ Finish time ___:___

Place _____     Worry _____

Anxiety/Discomfort     Before ____ During (max) ____ After ____
*(please use scale)*

Did you use mental gymnastics?     No ____ A little ____ A lot ____
How did you do this?     _____

### Breaking down avoidance

Now you have faced your fear, it's time to review the situations that you avoided because they closely matched your *Hypothetical Event Worry* in some way. It might be that you have already started to do this, but ask yourself if there is anywhere or anything that you are still avoiding because you know that it triggers worry. It might be useful to go to the list of behavioral experiments on uncertainty in Chapter 10 and see if any of these examples stand out. You may notice that you worry a little more when you face these situations; this is normal and tells us that you are approaching situations that match closely with your *Hypothetical Event Worry*. The more you engage with these situations, the more opportunity you will have to trigger your *Hypothetical Event Worry*. Without wishing to sound mean, this is actually good because it will give you more opportunity to challenge your worry. This chapter is about facing the things that frighten us; we hope it is getting clearer now that, while it's often difficult to face your fears, you can overcome them.

You have come along way and we hope you have discovered new ideas and techniques to help you overcome your worry. The next chapter brings all the ideas together, and helps you think about how to stay well.

## Where have we got to?

As you will see from the diagram below, we have now added the emotional heart of worry to the picture. We have also added cognitive avoidance and some arrows linking worry to this. We will talk through the additional parts that have been added.

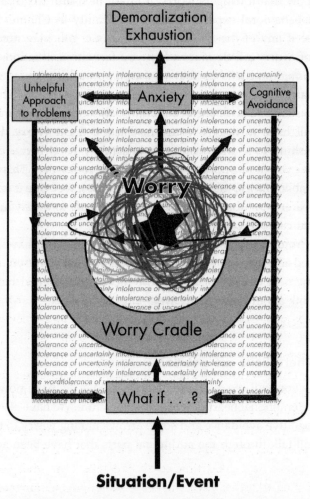

**Situation/Event**

Figure 17.2 Building the picture: the emotional heart of worry and cognitive avoidance.

At the heart of worry lie our dreams and aspirations, our ambitions and goals. All of us are afraid when the things we value are threatened. For worriers, the thing that threatens these ambitions and goals arrives in the form of worry, and usually in the form of *Hypothetical Event Worry*. The bad things in *Hypothetical Event Worry* tend to threaten all those things that are important. These bad things usually come in the form of images or flashes. Understandably, we want to avoid seeing these awful things, but the strategies we use to manage them makes us worry all the more (see the arrow heading down from cognitive avoidance to the 'What–if' box). The simple message in this chapter is about learning to face our fears, and find out that we can survive.

Cognitive avoidance is made up of avoiding mental imagery in our worry, attempts at suppression, distraction, mental gymnastics and avoidance of situations that trigger worrisome thoughts. As you now understand, the avoidance of the detail of your *Hypothetical Event Worry* means that you never fully face the fears that are bounded within them, and this means that the worry lives on. In this chapter you have learned about the importance of breaking patterns of avoidance and about the themes that lie at the core of your worry. You have learned that worry is a sign of hope.

Our journey together is nearly over: you have now reached the last big block of treatment. You have come a long way and it might be a good time to sit and reflect on what you have learned and what has happened to your understanding of worry. The diagram above might have been daunting for you to start with, but we hope that this 'central heating diagram' is now making sense to you. You may want to go back to the stories at the beginning of the book and see if you can make sense of them using the ideas you have discovered here. Or, take a piece of paper and have a go at drawing your worry patterns using the diagram.

The next chapter is about how you can stay well –there is some advice on sleep problems, for example – and there are also some loose ends that we need to tie up.

# 18

# Tying up loose ends

We are tempted to end this book in the middle of the chapter, so as to end in uncertainty, but we won't because we want to *tie up the loose ends*. You have now reached the last chapter; here we will focus on new material, namely dealing with sleep problems. Worry often happens at night, so we will give you some tips about this in the first section. We will then review the diagram of worry and remind you about what each bit of the diagram stands for. The final section will focus on staying well and planning for the future.

## The wee hours – difficulties in sleeping

To adapt a quote from the creator of Snoopy and the cartoon strip 'Peanuts', namely Charles M. Schulz: 'Sometimes I lie awake at night, and worry about where my life will go wrong. Then a voice says to me, this is going to take more than one night.'

For worriers, sleep problems are a very real issue. Here we do not have the space to go into detail about what you should do to get better sleep, but we recommend that those of you with serious sleep problems take a look at another book in this series, called *Overcoming Insomnia and Sleep Problems*. It is by Professor Colin Espie, an expert in the psychological treatment of sleep problems, and is well worth reading; you could use it as a close companion to this book.

The ideas to help you sleep better can be broken into four groups. The first are very practical things like checking that your bed is comfy. If it's not, then think about getting a better mattress or a new bed. Is your room dark enough, warm or cool enough and quiet enough? Are there practical steps you need to take to get a better sleep such as buying black-out blinds, or opening or closing windows?

The second group of things relate to forming better patterns and habits. For instance, how much caffeine do you drink during the day and before bed (including fizzy drinks, chocolate and tea)? It could be helpful to stop drinking caffeinated drinks by mid-afternoon and drinking non-caffeinated herbal or milky drinks instead. Do you have a regular sleep pattern, that is, do you go to sleep and wake at a regular time? If not, how much sleep would you like (an average is about eight hours)? Then work out how to get this (eight hours could be 11.00 p.m. to 7.00 a.m. or 10.30 p.m. to 6.30 a.m.). Go to bed when you are feeling tired and stick to a routine of getting up at the same time every day, even when you haven't slept well (don't sleep in). Do you work late using computers or games? Could you think of something else to do to help your mind wind down? Try to have your evening meal early so it is not resting on your stomach as you go to bed. Do you use alcohol or other drugs to help you sleep? Be wary of using alcohol, since while it may help to get you to sleep, alcohol also stops us from getting good restful sleep. Turn your alarm clock to the wall - you don't really need to know that it's 3.45 a.m. when you wake up. Looking at the alarm clock reminds you that you are awake and makes it harder to sleep. Your alarm clock will do its job and wake you when you need it to. What about exercise, are you taking enough – would a walk or a swim help? Avoid exercising close to bedtime, as we often feel very alert and hot after exercise making getting off to sleep difficult.

The third group of ideas are about the way you approach the bedroom. It is important to see your bedroom as a place where you sleep, not worry. So, if you are taken by worry, get up and sit somewhere until you start to feel sleepy and then return to bed. Watching TV can help, listening to relaxing music, reading a book or, as we have been suggesting, writing things down. By the way, try not to fall asleep on the sofa.

The last group are strategies to deal with your worry, such as writing your worries down on a note pad, or making a note of the problems that you are concerned about for the next day. If something is bothering you and there is nothing you can do about it right away, try writing it down before going to bed and then *tell* yourself to deal with it tomorrow. If your mind reviews the day just before you go to sleep, then do this either quietly before going to bed (see third point above), or write things down.

Poor sleep will make many of the symptoms of worry much worse, for example, it may make you feel more irritable, fatigued or mean that you suffer with concentration problems. Often people cannot escape their worries even when they are asleep because the themes of their worries, or the same daytime worries, appear in their dreams. The evidence from other emotional problems suggests that, if you are able to improve and reduce daytime worry, then worry in dreams should also improve. On a practical note, another thing to do is note down what your dreams are about. This may help you to understand more about what lies at the heart of your worry (see Chapter 17).

## Putting it all together

Over the next few pages you will find the final version of the worry diagram. In the first example we have added the final two components, which appears as an arrow pointing towards the belly of the intolerance of uncertainty. These show that life events or stressful things can influence the whole system, as can powerful emotional experiences. These events 'ratchet up' the uncertainty, and, as you will understand, with more uncertainty comes more worry. It reminds us that worry is an everyday event and from time to time we all worry when faced with difficult life circumstances.

Let's remind ourselves of Tom, who is still at the train station. Track the example through on the diagram.

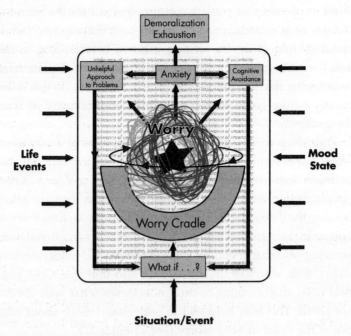

Figure 18.1. The complete picture of worry.

If you remember, Tom was waiting for a late train. He had an important meeting to attend to (situation/event). He spotted the uncertainty pretty quickly and thought to himself, *What if I am late for work?* The uncertainty he experienced fuelled his worry. He cared about his work and believed that it would show him to be uncaring if he did not worry about being late; the beliefs that made up his worry cradle 'instructed' him to worry. His worry was under way and it *telescoped* to all manner of catastrophes. His *Hypothetical Event Worry* revolved around the theme of work; it seemed that at the heart lay the aspiration of being a good and worthwhile person. He 'saw' flashes of his fall from grace, which threatened the idea of his being a worthwhile person. He started to feel more uncertain than ever about his life and his job, which triggered even more worry. He tried desperately to push his worry to the back of his mind. Yet, try as he might, he couldn't seem to shake the worry, which felt very intense. He noticed strong bodily sensations, he felt tense and edgy. As his worry whirled around, he started to believe that he was losing his mind and the turbo-charger kicked in, making his worry worse and led him to feel panicky. He felt he couldn't trust himself to make a good decision about how best to get to work and he just avoided solving the problem. He sat down and waited for his worry to subside. He was exhausted and felt down on himself for allowing his worry to get the better of him.

## What happened to Tom

Tom learned to recognize the triggers for his worry. He discovered that he worried mostly about work and his social relationships, particularly his girlfriend. He began to understand that he was intolerant of uncertainty and started to take small risks to begin to learn to tolerate uncertainty. He even tried being late for work on purpose just to see what would really happen. He learned that worrying was not the best way to show that he cared about work, and he found out that there were many other ways he could show this. Before he started to work on his worry he believed that problems only ever happened to him, and that if he tried to solve them they would go wrong. He started to recognize that he was solving problems all the time and that actually he was quite good at it. He solved a few major problems at work, which really helped his confidence. He saw that he valued his work and relationships and understood more about why he had awful images that came with his *Hypothetical Event Worry*. He learned to spot when he was climbing into the worry elevator, and that his worries were just thoughts and were not real. Rather than trying to push his worry out, he turned to face it and his worry became less problematic. As his worry receded, his anxiety lessened and he felt less tense and irritable. He started to sleep better and to enjoy work more. He continued to take risks and went on a last-minute holiday, without any planning. His relationship improved; as his worry lessened he started to feel closer to his girlfriend as they were able to do more things together. He felt more confident to move on and meet new people. He still worries from time to time, but he can manage that.

Now let's look at other versions of the worry diagram. In the next two examples we have added some annotations. The first reminds you of what the different elements are. The second reminds you what you need to do with each part of the picture of worry to get better.

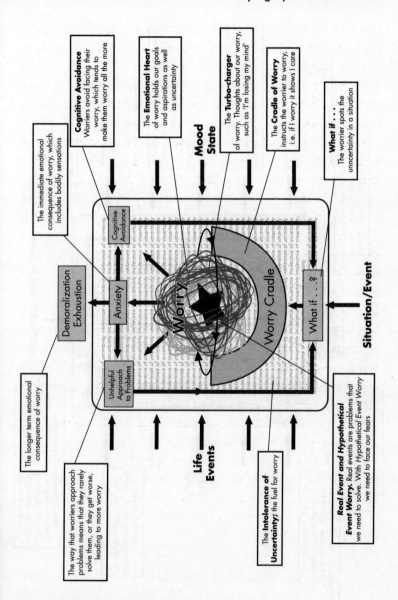

Figure 18.2. Pulling it all together – a reminder.

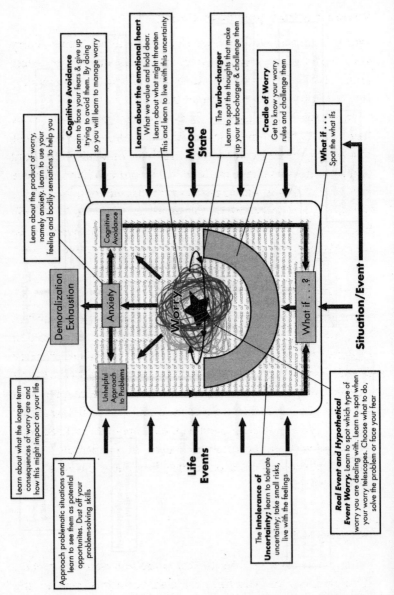

**Cognitive Avoidance**
Learn to face your fears & give up trying to avoid them. By doing so you will learn to manage worry

Learn about the product of worry, namely anxiety. Learn to use your feeling and bodily sensations to help you

**Learn about the emotional heart**
What we value and hold dear. Learn about what might threaten this and learn to live with this uncertainty

The **Turbo-charger**
Learn to spot the thoughts that make up your turbo-charger & challenge them

**Cradle of Worry**
Get to know your worry rules and challenge them

**What if . . .**
Spot the what ifs

Learn about what the longer term consequences of worry are and how this might impact on your life

Approach problematic situations and learn to see them as potential opportunites. Dust off your problem-solving skills

The **Intolerance of Uncertainty:** learn to tolerate uncertainty; take small risks, live with the feelings

**Real Event and Hypothetical Event Worry.** Learn to spot which type of worry you are dealing with. Learn to spot when your worry telescopes. Choose what to do, solve the problem or face your fear

**Mood State**

**Situation/Event**

**Life Events**

Demoralization Exhaustion

Anxiety

Cognitive Avoidance

Worry

Unhelpful Approach to Problems

What if . . ?

Figure 18.3. **Pulling it all together – what I need to do to feel better.**

## Reviewing how you have done

Worry is normal; we all worry. This book will not banish worry since worry is an everyday thing, and we all suffer from severe bouts of worry from time to time. Do not expect to be worry-free – if you are then you might be dead!

In Chapter 6 we asked you to draw up some goals. How have you done? Is there still work left to do, or are you close to reaching them? Do you need to review you goals in the light of the progress you have made? What would you like to achieve now? Next review the questionnaires. If you complete all the questionnaires and compare the scores to those you had at the beginning, what does this tell you? Is there still work to be done? Which part of the program do you need to return to?

## What have you learned?

Throughout the book we have asked you to pause and reflect on your learning. Can you now collect all this information together? What have you taken from the book? What has stuck in your mind? What has helped you to feel better? What hasn't worked so well? It may be helpful to review the chapters and see what you have taken from each, jotting down all the specific rules, actions and strategies that you have spotted that keep your worry going. Can you draw your own worry diagram? There are several versions of vicious cycles throughout the book – use whatever helps.

## Keeping well

For any new skill, in order to stay sharp you need to practise. The new ideas that you have come across in this book are the same in this respect, and so it would be useful if they were built into your routine. You need to keep mentally fit by 'working out' using the worry exercises, in particular, keep pushing yourself into uncertainty. In the annotated diagrams above we have added the main treatment targets. When you review your worry, what areas of the diagram do you need to work on? What are your Achilles' heels?

## Lapse and relapse

With any emotional problem we will all have moments when the problem gets a little worse. Just because you have a bad week doesn't mean that the worry is back. In fact, you could have two bad weeks and still this would not mean that your worry was back in the way that it was before. It could be that what you have been experiencing is big event worry and in fact your worry is in proportion to the event. So ask yourself about what has been happening in your life. Also remind yourself of how you used to worry; think about how bad your worry was before you started to do something about it. How does this compare with your worry at the moment? Is this a lapse, an everyday lull, or is this a relapse, that is, back to square one? Have you really gone back to square one, or are you having one of those weeks? Another thing that happens when people start to feel better is that they forget how bad they actually were. We talked about change in therapy being like hair growing – sometimes it's almost impossible to notice. Use the questionnaires to help you gauge where your worry is at the moment and decide whether you have suffered a lapse or a relapse.

## What might lead to a set back for me?

What life events are coming your way that you know will trigger more worry? Sometimes these revolve around life transitions such as children starting school and walking home alone, retirement, promotions or starting work. Or a setback can appear before or during predictable events such as exams or family get-togethers. How can you prepare for them? What might help in these circumstances?

Remember that worry is normal and that many of us would worry about these things. Think about how the *worrisome you* might handle these situations, and then think about how you have learned to handle them differently. Become aware of your worry and focus on the stream and the factors that influence this. Notice the uncertainty and sit with it rather than worrying. Recognize the rules that instruct you to worry and challenge them, challenge the turbo-charger, recognize when you are climbing into the express worry elevator. Approach problems rather than avoid them, see problems as opportunities to use your problem-solving skills. Your *Hypothetical Event Worry* will remind you of what you value and also what might threaten this, so face the fear. Rather than sitting on the fence, engage with problems, with worries, with people, with life.

## What if I still need help?

If you have found the ideas in this book useful but have struggled to apply them to yourself, then maybe drop in to see your family doctor and discuss the options for therapy in your local area. If you want to stick with a CBT approach, then you can ask if there are people trained in CBT locally. CBT is the treatment of choice for worry so we would advise you to see a CBT therapist if at all possible. If you want to find a therapist without going to your GP, you will find more information on how to do so at the back of this book. Tell your doctor or therapist that you have been using this book. Talk to them about what helps and what doesn't.

It takes courage to admit to and work on emotional problems. Therapy is about finding new ways of doing things. This feels risky, but the benefit usually far outweighs the costs.

## Worry feedback

We would be very interested to know what you make of *Overcoming Worry*. If you would like to let us know about your experience of using this book, please send us an email at worryfeedback@mac.com (the address will remain active until February 2012). While we cannot respond to each email you will receive an automated response to confirm receipt. We will use the information you give us to improve self-help treatment.

Here are some questions we would like to ask you:

1. What was most helpful and least helpful?
2. On a scale of 0–10 with 10 equalling total improvement and 0 equalling no improvement at all, how much progress have you made using this book?
3. Which chapters worked well and which did not?
4. Which chapters were harder to understand?
5. Which part was the most important in your progress?
6. Would you recommend this book to a friend?
7. What else would you like to see included?
8. What would you have changed?
9. Any other general comments.
10. Could you let us know if you are a worrier, the partner of a worrier or a health professional.

# Appendix 1:

# Mindfulness-based CBT

In recent approaches and ideas in CBT, there is an emerging trend towards the acceptance of emotional suffering rather than trying to control such feelings. The amount of research in these new areas is growing, but at the time of writing it unfortunately remains thin: there is very little research focused on worry. However, for many years therapists have been trying to help worriers by using similar ideas. For example, imagine your worries are clouds floating across your mind. Do not engage with them, do not judge them, just let them be, let them pass without comment. The implication of this idea is very clear for worry. If we could sit with uncertainty and the whirlwind of worry it triggers, and just let the worry be without judging it or even thinking about it, then we may be able to worry less. In mindfulness-based CBT, individuals learn to remain connected with the present moment, with the here and now, rather than with their worry. They are instructed to focus on their breathing and use it as an 'anchor' or companion to help them remain in the here and now. In mindfulness, if you stray into engaging with your worry, then the instruction is to compassionately bring your mind back to the breath, without judgement or criticism, without expectation or desire. The value of these ideas is clear: if we were less engaged with worry and were able to stand back and observe the flow without it taking us away emotionally, then worry would not be such a problem – it would become something we observe rather than something we experience.

Our current understanding is that mindfulness might be best used towards the middle to end of a program of treatment, once the person has started to understand more about how their worry works and learned to disconnect from it. Over time we may find that mindfulness can be used earlier, but for now it would appear that it is best used as a way of making sure that we don't fall back into bad habits. Indeed, mindfulness CBT might be a very powerful way of keeping people feeling well and their minds fit. If you are interested in learning more about mindfulness, you'll find some additional information in Appendix 5.

## Appendix 2:

## Worry Diary

| Day | Time | Content<br>What was the worry about? | Distress<br>How intense was the worry?<br>How uncontrollable did it seem? Scale:<br>0 = mild<br>100 = very severe | Worry type<br>Is the worry about a real, current problem: does the problem actually exist?<br>Yes/no<br>If no, is it hypothetical?<br>Have I got ahead of myself? | | | |
|---|---|---|---|---|---|---|---|
| | | | | | | | |
| | | | | | | | |
| | | | | | | | |
| | | | | | | | |

# Appendix 3:

# Help with the Penn State Questionnaire

## Table to help you score you Penn State Worry Questionnaire

Transfer your scores from the Penn State Worry Questionnaire to the second column. Questions numbered 1, 3, 8, 10 & 11 need to be reversed before you add up your total. Use the key below to help you convert your score. A score of 1 would convert to 5, a score of 2 converts to 4, 3 stays the same, a score of 4 converts to 2 and a score of 5 converts to one. Once you have converted your answers for questions 1, 3, 8, 10 & 11, then strike out your original score so you do not confuse yourself while adding. Then add the total of all 16 questions. Your score should lie somewhere between 16-80, people who have a problem with worry tend to score 57 and above. Repeat the questionnaire once every two weeks to track progress.

**KEY**

|  | Not at all typical |  | Somewhat typical |  | Very Typical |
|---|---|---|---|---|---|
| My Score = | 1 | 2 | 3 | 4 | 5 |
| Reversed Score | 5 | 4 | 3 | 2 | 1 |

**Example**

My Score
1. _2_ Reversed = _4_
2. _3_
3. _1_ Reversed = _5_
4. _5_
5. _5_
6. _5_
7. _3_
8. _2_ Reversed = _4_
9. _5_
10. _1_ Reversed = _5_
11. _3_ Reversed = _3_
12. _2_
13. _4_
14. _4_
15. _3_
16. _3_
Total _63_

Week No. ___

My Score
1. ___ Reversed = ___
2. ___
3. ___ Reversed = ___
4. ___
5. ___
6. ___
7. ___
8. ___ Reversed = ___
9. ___
10. ___ Reversed = ___
11. ___ Reversed = ___
12. ___
13. ___
14. ___
15. ___
16. ___
My Total ___

Week No. ___

My Score
1. ___ Reversed = ___
2. ___
3. ___ Reversed = ___
4. ___
5. ___
6. ___
7. ___
8. ___ Reversed = ___
9. ___
10. ___ Reversed = ___
11. ___ Reversed = ___
12. ___
13. ___
14. ___
15. ___
16. ___
My Total ___

Week No. ___

My Score
1. ___ Reversed = ___
2. ___
3. ___ Reversed = ___
4. ___
5. ___
6. ___
7. ___
8. ___ Reversed = ___
9. ___
10. ___ Reversed = ___
11. ___ Reversed = ___
12. ___
13. ___
14. ___
15. ___
16. ___
My Total ___

## Appendix 4:

## Simple problem-solving worksheet

| Problem: |
|---|

| Solution Number_____ : |
|---|

If you answer no to any of the following, stop and pick another solution.

1.  If I use this solution will it help me to solve my problem?
    Yes ☐    No ☐

2.  Is this solution practical?
    Yes ☐    No ☐

3.  What might stop me from using this solution?  What are the roadblocks?  List them here:




4.  Can I navigate a way through, around, under or over these roadblocks?
    Yes ☐    No ☐

5.  Is this solution good enough to run with?    Yes ☐    No ☐

6.  List the advantages and disadvantages of this solution.

| Advantages | Disadvantages |
|---|---|
|  |  |
|  |  |
|  |  |
|  |  |

7.  Using the scale below, please rate the solution

| | Mostly<br>Disadvantageous | | | | | | Mostly<br>Advantageous | | | |
|---|---|---|---|---|---|---|---|---|---|---|
| 5 | -4 | -3 | -2 | -1 | 0 | +1 | +2 | +3 | +4 | +5 |

8.  Is this solution good enough to put into action?
    Yes ☐    No ☐

9.  DO IT

# Appendix 5:

# Useful contacts and information

## Internet sites

### NICE

www.nice.org.uk

This website offers information about GAD within the guidance on Anxiety number CG22. Go to the menu, select 'Our guidance', then 'Guidance by type', then 'Mental health and behavioural conditions', then select 'Anxiety'. Alternatively type CG22 into the search facility on this site.

### Professor Michel Dugas

www-psychology.concordia.ca/fac/dugas/
Templates/GAD.html

Professor Michel Dugas is an expert on Generalized Anxiety Disorder. He is currently Associate Professor and Director of the Anxiety Disorders Laboratory in the Department of Psychology at Concordia University in Montreal, Canada. You will find useful information about GAD on his web pages, including some useful downloadable materials.

## The International Association for Cognitive Psychotherapy (IACP)

www.cognitivetherapyassociation.org

IACP is a professional, scientific, interdisciplinary organization whose mission is to facilitate the utilization and growth of cognitive psychotherapy as a professional activity and scientific discipline.

# UK

### British Association of Behavioural and Cognitive Psychotherapies (BABCP)
Victoria Buildings
9–13 Silver Street
Bury BL9 0EU
Tel: 0161 797 4484
Fax: 0161 797 2670
Email: babcp@babcp.com
Website: www.babcp.com

The website has a list of cognitive behavioural therapists accredited by the organization.

### British Psychological Society
Division of Clinical Psychology
St Andrews House
48 Princess Road East
Leicester LE1 7DR
Tel: +44 (0)116 254 9568
Fax: +44 (0)116 227 1314
Email: enquiry@bps.org.uk
Website: www.bps.org.uk

## MIND
15–19 Broadway
London E15 4BQ
Tel: 020 8519 2122
Fax: 020 8522 1725
Email: contact@mind.org.uk
Website: www.mind.org.uk

Mind is a leading mental health charity in England and
Wales. They provide information about Mental Health
Problems

## MIND Cymru
3rd Floor, Quebec House
Castlebridge
5-19 Cowbridge Road
East Cardiff CF11 9AB
Tel: 029 2039 5123
Fax: 029 2034 6585
Website: www.mind.org.uk

## NHS Direct
NHS Direct provides information and advice about health,
illness and health services, to enable patients to make deci-
sions about their healthcare and that of their families.
Website:  www.nhsdirect.nhs.uk
Tel: 0845 4647

**National Phobics Society**
Zion Community Resource Centre
339 Stretford Road
Hulme
Manchester M15 4ZY

Website: www.phobics-society.org.uk

The National Phobics Society is a charity that aims to provide support those living with anxiety disorders by providing information, support and understanding.

## EUROPE

The European Association for Behavioural and Cognitive Therapy (EABCT) has 41 individual associations from 29 different countries, all committed to the development and promotion of cognitive behavioral therapies.
Website:  www.EABCT.com

## USA

**Beck Institute for Cognitive Therapy and Research**
1 Belmont Avenue, Suite 700
Bala Cynwyd
PA 19004 1610
Tel: (610) 664 3020
Fax: (610) 664 4437
Email: beckinst@gim.net
Website: *www.beckinstitute.org*

**Center for Cognitive Therapy**
PO Box 5308
Huntington Beach
CA 92615 5308
Website: www.padesky.com
Website: www.MindOverMood.com

The Association of Behavioral and Cognitive Therapies is a not-for-profit organization. It serves as a centralized resource and network, enhancing public awareness of cognitive behavior, therapy, disseminating knowledge, and promoting research.
Website: www.aabt.org

## AUSTRALIA

Australian Association for Cognitive Behavior Therapy
Website:  www.aacbt.org

## INTERNATIONAL

The Academy of Cognitive Therapy is a non-for-profit organization founded by experts in the field of cognitive therapy, dedicated to providing referrals and educational resources about cognitive therapy to the general public.
Website: www.academyofcognitivetherapy.org

**The International Association for
Cognitive Psychotherapy (IACP)**
IACP is a professional, scientific, interdisciplinary organization whose mission is to facilitate the utilization and growth of cognitive psychotherapy as a professional activity and scientific discipline.
Website: www.cognitivetherapyassociation.org

# Further reading

## Close companion books in the series

Butler, G., *Overcoming Shyness and Social Anxiety* (London: Robinson, 1999).

Espie, C. A., *Overcoming Insomnia and Sleep Problems* (London: Robinson, 2006).

Gilbert, P., *Overcoming Depression* (London: Robinson, 1997).

Fennel, M., *Overcoming Low Self-esteem* (London: Robinson, 1999).

## Further self-help reading on worry

Lampe, L., *Take Control of Your Worry: Managing Generalised Anxiety Disorder* (Sydney: Simon & Schuster, 2004).

Leahy, R. L., *The Worry Cure: Stop Worrying and Start Living* (London: Piatkus Books, 2006).

Tallis, F., *How to Stop Worrying* (London: Sheldon Press, 1990).

## Mindfulness

Zinn-Kabat, J., *Full Catastrophe Living* (London: Piatkus Books, Ltd, 2004).

## Problem-Solving

Nezu, A. M., Nezu, C. M. and D'Zurilla, T. J., *Solving Life's Problems* (New York: Springer, 2007).

## Self-help books written from a CBT perspective

Butler, G. and Hope, T., *Manage Your Mind: The Mental Fitness Guide* (Oxford: Oxford University Press, 1995).

Greenberger, D. and Padesky, C. A., *Mind over Mood: A Cognitive Therapy Treatment Manual for Clients* (New York: Guilford, 1995).

## Scholarly and other texts for therapists and health professionals

A central source and influence for this book was Michel Dugas and Melisa Robichaud, *Cognitive Behavioural Treatment for Generalised Anxiety Disorder* (New York: Routledge, 2006). We would recommend this to therapists and other health professionals. Please also see Michel Dugas's website, listed above.

Bennett-Levy, J., Butler, G., Fennell, M., Hackmann, A., Mueller, M., and Westbrook, D., *Oxford Guide to Behavioural Experiments in Cognitive Therapy* (New York: Oxford University Press, 2004).

Davey, G. C. L and Wells, A., *Worry and its Psychological Disorders* (West Sussex: John Wiley & Sons, 2006).

D'Zurilla, T. J. and Nezu, A. M., *Problem-Solving Therapy: A Positive Approach to Clinical Intervention* (New York: Springer, 2007).

Westbrook, D., Kennerley, H., and Kirk, J., *An Introduction to CBT: Skills and Applications* (London: Sage, 2007).

Wilkinson, D. J., *The Ambiguity Advantage: What Great Leaders Are Great At* (New York: Palgrave Macmillan, 2006).

# Index

# Order further books in the *Overcoming* series

| Qnty | Title | RRP | Offer price | Total |
|---|---|---|---|---|
| | Bulimia Nervosa and Binge-Eating | £9.99 | £7.99 | |
| | Overcoming Anger and Irritability | £9.99 | £7.99 | |
| | Overcoming Anorexia Nervosa | £9.99 | £7.99 | |
| | Overcoming Anxiety | £9.99 | £7.99 | |
| | Overcoming Anxiety Self-Help Course (3 parts) | £21.00 | £15.00 | |
| | Overcoming Bulimia Nervosa and Binge-Eating Self-Help Course (3 parts) | £21.00 | £15.00 | |
| | Overcoming Childhood Trauma | £9.99 | £7.99 | |
| | Overcoming Chronic Fatigue | £9.99 | £7.99 | |
| | Overcoming Chronic Pain | £9.99 | £7.99 | |
| | Overcoming Compulsive Gambling | £9.99 | £7.99 | |
| | Overcoming Depersonalizaton and Feelings of Unreality | £9.99 | £9.99 | |
| | Overcoming Depression | £9.99 | £7.99 | |
| | Overcoming Grief | £9.99 | £7.99 | |
| | Overcoming Insomnia and Sleep Problems | £9.99 | £7.99 | |
| | Overcoming Low Self-Esteem | £9.99 | £7.99 | |
| | Overcoming Low Self-Esteem Self-Help Course (3 parts) | £21.00 | £15.00 | |
| | Overcoming Mood Swings | £9.99 | £7.99 | |
| | Overcoming Obsessive Compulsive Disorder | £9.99 | £7.99 | |
| | Overcoming Panic | £9.99 | £7.99 | |
| | Overcoming Panic and Agoraphobia Self-Help Course (3 parts) | £21.00 | £15.00 | |
| | Overcoming Paranoid and Suspicious Thoughts | £9.99 | £7.99 | |
| | Overcoming Problem Drinking | £9.99 | £7.99 | |
| | Overcoming Relationship Problems | £9.99 | £7.99 | |
| | Overcoming Sexual Problems | £9.99 | £7.99 | |
| | Overcoming Social Anxiety and Shyness | £9.99 | £7.99 | |
| | Overcoming Social Anxiety and Shyness Self-Help Course (3 parts) | £21.00 | £15.00 | |
| | Overcoming Traumatic Stress | £9.99 | £7.99 | |
| | Overcoming Weight Problems | £9.99 | £7.99 | |
| | Overcoming Worry | £9.99 | £7.99 | |
| | Overcoming Your Child's Fears and Worries | £9.99 | £7.99 | |
| | Overcoming Your Child's Shyness and Social Anxiety | £9.99 | £7.99 | |
| | Overcoming Your Smoking Habit | £9.99 | £7.99 | |
| | Manage Your Mood | £12.99 | £10.99 | |
| | P&P | FREE | FREE | |
| | TOTAL | | | |

Name: _____

Address: _____

_____ Postcode: _____

Daytime Tel No: _____

Email: _____

<small>(in case of query)</small>

How to Pay:

1. **By telephone**: call the TBS order line on **01206 255 800** and quote **WORRY**. Phone lines are open between Monday–Friday, 8.30am–5.30pm.

2. **By post**: send a cheque for the full amount payable to TBS Ltd, or if paying by debit, credit or Switch card, fill in the details above and send the form to:
Freepost RLUL-SJGC-SGKJ. Cash Sales/Direct Mail Dept, The Book Service, Colchester Road, Frating, Colchester, CO7 7DW

Constable & Robinson Ltd (directly or via its agents) may mail or phone you about promotions or products
Tick box if you do not want these from us ☐ or our subsidiaries ☐